The Arthaśāstra

Selections from the Classic Indian Work on Statecraft

The Arthaśāstra

Selections from the Classic Indian Work on Statecraft

Edited and Translated,
with an Introduction, by
Mark McClish and Patrick Olivelle

Hackett Publishing Company, Inc.
Indianapolis/Cambridge

Printed in the United States of America

16 15 14 13 12 1 2 3 4 5 6 7

For further information, please address
Hackett Publishing Company, Inc.
P.O. Box 44937
Indianapolis, Indiana 46244-0937

www.hackettpublishing.com

Interior design by Mary Vasquez
Composition by Innodata-Isogen, Inc.
Printed at Data Reproductions Corporation

Library of Congress Cataloging-in-Publication Data

Kautalya.

[Arthasastra. English. Selections]

The Arthasastra : selections from the classic Indian work on statecraft/ edited and translated, with an introduction, by Mark McClish and Patrick Olivelle.

p. cm.

Includes bibliographical references and index.

ISBN 978-1-60384-849-7 (cloth)—ISBN 978-1-60384-848-0 (pbk.)

1. Political science—India—History—Early works to 1800. 2. State, The—Early works to 1800. 3. India—Politics and government–To 997–Early works to 1800. 4. India—Social conditions—Early works to 1800. I. McClish, Mark. II. Olivelle, Patrick. III. Title.

JA84.I4K3813 2012

320.0934–dc23

2012014017

The paper used in this publication meets the minimum requirements of American National Standard for Information Sciences—Permanence of Paper for Printed Library Materials, ANSI Z39.48–1984.

∞

Contents

Selections from the *Arthaśāstra*

INTRODUCTION[1]

Like East Asia and the Mediterranean world, South Asia, in the first millennium before the Common Era, gave birth to a "classical" civilization. During this period, South Asia saw the integration of its political landscape, the advent of writing, the systematization of critical inquiry, the establishment of distinctive and long-lasting intellectual traditions, the rise of Jainism, Buddhism, and Classical Hinduism, and the evolution and maturation of formal disciplines of architecture, visual arts, dance, poetry, drama, and literature. In brief, this is the period during which a transregional South Asian culture took on its distinctive forms: mature, cosmopolitan, and self-reflective traditions that provided the subcontinent, as also regions of southeast and central Asia, with a shared cultural orientation and a common political, intellectual, ethical, philosophical, and aesthetic heritage. There is no consensus on the periodization of

1. We are indebted to the research of the following scholars in this Introduction: On the Cāṇakya legend, T. Trautmann, 1971, *Kauṭilya and the Arthaśāstra*, Leiden: Brill; and T. Burrow, 1968, "Cāṇakya and Kauṭalya," *Annals of the Bhandarkar Oriental Research Institute* 48–49: 17–31. On trade in the classical period, Federico De Romanis, 2000, "Esportazioni di corallo mediterraneo in India nell'età ellenistico-romana," in *Corallo di ieri corallo di oggi,* ed. Jean-Paul Morel, Cecilia Rondi-Costanzo, and Danela Ugolini, pp. 211–16, Centro Universitario Europeo Per i Beni Culturali, Scienze e materiali del patrimonio culturale, 5, Bari: Edipuglia. On the archaeology of classical urban centers, D. Schlingloff, 1969, *Die altindsche Stadt: Eine vergleichende Untersuchung,* Wiesbaden: Steiner. On the geography of the text, M. Willis, 2009, *The Archaeology of Hindu Ritual: Temples and the Establishment of the Gods,* Cambridge: Cambridge University Press. On many important issues pertaining to the content and structure of the *Arthaśāstra*, see the works of Kangle, Scharfe, and Trautmann in the Select Bibliography.

South Asian history, but for the purposes of this Introduction we consider the classical period to have lasted from approximately 600 BCE to 600 CE.

Of great importance to the evolution of a shared South Asian culture in the classical period was the development of elite intellectual traditions of inquiry into various topics and their systematization into a complete taxonomy of human knowledge. These traditions included grammar, mathematics, geometry, lexicography, poetics, astronomy, mathematics, architecture, ritual, dance, erotics, aesthetics, drama, law, philosophy, medicine, and, most pertinent to the present text, political science or "statecraft." Each of these subjects and more became discrete intellectual traditions unto themselves, evolving sophisticated theories, developing technical vocabularies, and sustaining vibrant debate among diverse scholarly perspectives. Within each of these "expert traditions" emerged distinctive schools of thought, each with their characteristic dispositions and viewpoints, that passed on the teachings of their most revered masters through the generations.

The text presented to you in this reader is the most illustrious and important treatise (*śāstra*) from the classical expert tradition on statecraft (*artha*), composed by a man named Kauṭilya and passed down by his followers, who called themselves and their school the "Kauṭilīyas" or "the followers of Kauṭilya." Hence, this treatise on statecraft is called the *Kauṭilīya Arthaśāstra*, "The Manual of Statecraft of Kauṭilya" or "of the Followers of Kauṭilya."

Part of the importance of the *Kauṭilīya Arthaśāstra* (hereafter simply referred to as the *Arthaśāstra*) derives from the fact that it is the only treatise devoted entirely to statecraft to have survived from the classical period. As such, it is an invaluable resource for understanding how intellectuals and rulers of that time understood and explained the project of running a kingdom. Given the vastness of such an undertaking, Kauṭilya's treatise provides a comprehensive look at classical society unparalleled by other sources from the period. In keeping with the enormous complexity of administering a kingdom, the *Arthaśāstra* deals with an incredible variety of topics, from the education of the king to the capturing of wild elephants, from the seasons for sowing crops to pulling down the walls of an enemy's citadel, from metallurgy to divorce. Amidst such discussions, the *Arthaśāstra* grants us panoramic views of issues such as the relationship between the monarchy and religious institutions as well as ordinary glimpses of everyday life. Furnished with a pragmatic attitude about society and culture that is unclouded by the strong religious and ideological biases that pervade contemporary texts, the *Arthaśāstra* is the foremost textual source from the classical period for the study of South Asian politics and society.

This reader consists of English translations of excerpts from the *Arthaśāstra* selected and arranged by topic so as to present the teachings of the text in a manner congenial to the interests of modern readers and students. Each excerpt is introduced by an explanatory passage intended to provide the interpretive background necessary to understand it. Technical terms and concepts benefitting from further explication are discussed in footnotes. Special care is taken throughout to distinguish between what is normative in the text (how things ought to be) from what is descriptive (how things are). Despite these aids, however, the remoteness of the *Arthaśāstra* from the assumptions and priorities of today's world requires that readers familiarize themselves with the classical South Asian intellectual, cultural, and political milieu. To that end, this Introduction provides critical background on the composition of the *Arthaśāstra*, its historical context, and its perspective on statecraft and governance.

Authorship and Date

The Cāṇakya Legend

According to a long-standing South Asian tradition that is still widely accepted today, the *Arthaśāstra* was written toward the end of the fourth century BCE by a cunning and ruthless statesman named Cāṇakya, who earned the nickname Kauṭilya, "the crooked one," because of his reputation for using unethical means to achieve political goals. According to this tradition, Cāṇakya was the chief minister of the emperor Candragupta Maurya (reigned 320–298 BCE) and a Brāhmaṇa, a member of South Asia's hereditary priestly class.

As the story goes, Cāṇakya's political career began when he was publicly insulted by a king of the Nanda Dynasty (reigned 424–321 BCE). Deeply humiliated by his mistreatment (Brāhmaṇas were traditionally due great respect), an infuriated Cāṇakya vowed to destroy the Nanda Dynasty utterly and completely. It was to be the Nanda king's great misfortune to have crossed Cāṇakya, who, the legend tells us, was possessed of a special genius for politics and born with a remarkably vindictive character. Cāṇakya recruited a young man named Candragupta Maurya to his cause, and with Cāṇakya's guidance, Candragupta eventually overthrew the Nanda king, eradicated the Nanda Dynasty, and established ancient South Asia's greatest political formation: the Maurya Dynasty (reigned 320–185 BCE). His mission accomplished, it seems that Cāṇakya retired from political life and composed his masterwork, the *Arthaśāstra*.

How much of this compelling story can actually be verified by contemporary sources? Alexander the Great invaded northwest South Asia in 327 BCE. Although he remained in South Asia for only a short time and never conquered into modern-day India, one of his successors, Seleukos Nikator, sent an ambassador named Megasthenes to the court of Candragupta. Megasthenes composed reports for his master, fragments of which have survived in the works of later writers. These and other Greek sources allow us to confirm that Candragupta did take the throne around 320 BCE and shortly thereafter had expanded his empire into the political vacuum left in northwest South Asia by Alexander the Great's withdrawal. Candragupta's accession marked the beginning of the Maurya Dynasty. His grandson, the famous Buddhist emperor Aśoka (reigned 268–233 BCE), expanded the Maurya Dynasty to its greatest extent, ruling nearly all of South Asia, and left a large number of inscriptions carved into rocks and pillars.

Regarding the existence of Cāṇakya or the *Arthaśāstra*, however, all of these sources are silent.

What is more, the composer of the *Arthaśāstra* is referred to therein only by the name "Kauṭilya" (spelled by some as "Kauṭalya") and never as "Cāṇakya." Only a single verse at the end of the *Arthaśāstra* directly links its composer to the legend of Cāṇakya, stating that

> The man who out of indignation quickly rescued the treatise (*śāstra*) and the weapon (*śastra*), as also the land that had fallen into the hands of the Nandas, it is he who composed this treatise. (15.1.73)

Many scholars, however, believe that this verse was not written by the original composer of the *Arthaśāstra*, but was actually added to the text at a later time. Thus, not only do we fail to find any evidence of Cāṇakya or the *Arthaśāstra* from the Mauryan period, but the *Arthaśāstra* itself originally made no connection between its author, Kauṭilya, and the legendary Cāṇakya.

The identification of Cāṇakya with Kauṭilya appears to have occurred only after the *Arthaśāstra* had become famous as a treatise on statecraft, some 400–600 years after the time in which Cāṇakya is said to have lived. The association between Cāṇakya and Kauṭilya in historical memory becomes relatively widespread at this point and finds its fullest articulation in the Sanskrit drama *Mudrārākṣasa*, "The Signet Ring of [Minister] Rākṣasa" (fourth or fifth century CE). The *Mudrārākṣasa*, which tells the story of the founding of the Maurya Dynasty, takes Cāṇakya as its main character, identifies him as "Kauṭilya," and displays a thorough knowledge of the *Arthaśāstra* throughout.

Cāṇakya's authorship of the *Arthaśāstra* is, based on this long-standing and firmly established historical memory, almost universally accepted in South Asia. Prominent scholars have taken the position that the existing tradition should be accepted as historically accurate until it is conclusively disproven. Nevertheless, the extant historical sources that link the *Arthaśāstra* with Cāṇakya inform us not so much about the period they purport to describe, as about the society many centuries later that produced them, in which two originally independent elements—the legend of Cāṇakya and the *Arthaśāstra* of Kauṭilya—appear to have become intertwined. Evidence from within the *Arthaśāstra*, as we will later argue, supports a dating for the text of some 200–400 years after the events recounted in the Cāṇakya legend.

The tradition that links the *Arthaśāstra* to the Maurya Dynasty via the legendary Cāṇakya is, nevertheless, significant in its own right. Although such a connection may have seemed quite natural to people living in later times—that such an erudite text on statecraft can only have come from an exemplary statesman like Cāṇakya—it is also possible that the anachronistic identification of Kauṭilya with Cāṇakya was intentional and that texts like the *Mudrārākṣasa* were written with such a purpose in mind. For imbuing the teachings of the *Arthaśāstra* with the glory of the Maurya Empire can only have enhanced the reputation of the text. Anyone associated with the text—its use or transmission—would have shared in this greatness. A later empire, such as that of the Gupta Dynasty (fourth to sixth century CE), may have actively sought to enhance its prestige by exhibiting a very public relationship with the *Arthaśāstra* as a relic of Mauryan power.

Putting aside questions of its origin and veracity, the legend of Cāṇakya makes its point clearly: the greatest empire of South Asian antiquity owed its worldly success (*artha*) to the cunning of one Brāhmaṇa, Cāṇakya—also known as Kauṭilya—whose teachings we have in the form of the *Arthaśāstra*. This convention influenced the reception of the *Arthaśāstra* from the late classical period until medieval times and continues to exert itself in modern historical memory. Rather than treat the legend as history, however, we do well to keep in mind that it is only part of the ongoing social life of the *Arthaśāstra* in South Asia and beyond.

So, if Candragupta's minister, Cāṇakya, did not write the text, who did? As with most texts of the period, which purposely avoid any reference to contemporary events or persons, the *Arthaśāstra* provides little in the way of evidence about its actual origin.

The Composer of the Arthaśāstra*: The Historical Kauṭilya*

The composer of the *Arthaśāstra* did not create the text *ex novo*, but brought together a number of preexisting sources dealing with a variety of topics pertaining to statecraft and worked them into a single, cohesive composition, just as stated in the first line of the extant work:

> This singular Treatise on Success (*Arthaśāstra*) has been composed for the most part by drawing together the Treatises on Success instituted by former teachers for gaining and administering the earth. (1.1.1)

Close examinations by several scholars confirm that the *Arthaśāstra* is a composite work and that whoever compiled these sources is responsible for the present structure of the text. This compiler also added some of his own material to bring a coherence to the text as a whole. This individual is identified as "Kauṭilya":

> The treatise composed by Kauṭilya is easy to learn and comprehend, precise in doctrine, meaning, and wording, and free of prolixity. (1.1.19)

Unfortunately, his association with the *Arthaśāstra* is all we know of Kauṭilya (aside from the later tradition identifying him with Cāṇakya). This presents significant difficulties in confirming his identity as the original composer of the treatise. In the absence of any evidence to the contrary, however, it is easiest to assume that the tradition records the composer's identity correctly: we would need *some* reason to suspect otherwise. At any rate, we know so little about the composer of the text that we lose nothing in terms of historical accuracy by referring to him as "Kauṭilya." Thus, we have a name, but little more, for the composer of the *Arthaśāstra*.

The name Kauṭilya has sometimes been understood to mean "the crooked one," and may well have been a kind of nickname given to the author because his advice so frequently promotes unethical schemes. For some, the *Arthaśāstra* had the reputation of being a "false" teaching in that it endorsed breaking any rule—even up to killing members of one's own family—if politically expedient. Even though Kauṭilya does not go out of his way to endorse immoral courses of action, he does not hesitate to advise underhanded and malevolent tactics if they promote the king's interests. In a society steeped in the ethical visions of Hinduism, Buddhism, and Jainism, the amoral pragmatism of the *Arthaśāstra* could seem shocking and degenerate. The name Kauṭilya, thus, might seem to give us some insight into the man himself. There is, however, the strong possibility his name has nothing to do with crookedness, but was simply a patronymic derived from the name of an eponymous family patriarch (Kuṭila or Kuṭala).

Kauṭilya's original composition, which closely resembled the version of the *Arthaśāstra* that has survived to modern times, underwent revision at the hands of at least one editor or redactor. This redactor did not extensively alter the structure or content of the text, although he did add certain sections and passages found in the extant treatise. The motive for redacting the *Arthaśāstra* arose from its use within some kind of academic curriculum: the various "topics" of the original text were redivided into "chapters" of a minimum length and each chapter was given a memorable verse at the end to make them more teachable sections. Most likely, we owe the preservation of the *Arthaśāstra* to its inclusion in educational curricula. It survived the centuries by being transmitted from teacher to student as part of an elite education. Thus, while Kauṭilya's original work is still strongly present in the surviving version of the *Arthaśāstra*, the text as we have it was also shaped by its subsequent social life.

To return to the identity of Kauṭilya, we must rely on circumstantial evidence provided by the *Arthaśāstra* itself to speculate about who he was. The *Arthaśāstra* was composed in Sanskrit, which might suggest that Kauṭilya was a member of the elite, hereditary class of Brāhmaṇa priests. Sanskrit was regarded as a sacred language in ancient South Asia and was primarily used by and taught to Brāhmaṇa men for ritual purposes. During the classical period, Sanskrit developed into the general language of learning. But, even though some non-Brāhmaṇas knew and composed in Sanskrit in the classical period (certain kings of the period boasted of their own expertise), the bulk of Sanskrit literature was still almost certainly composed by Brāhmaṇas. The uncertainty pertaining to the origin of the name "Kauṭilya" (discussed earlier) means that we cannot identify him as a Brāhmaṇa based simply on his membership in a lineage identified by this name.

If Kauṭilya was a Brāhmaṇa, which seems more likely than not, he was nevertheless not much influenced by orthodox Brāhmaṇical ideology, for the original *Arthaśāstra* lacks the distinctive pro-Brāhmaṇical bias or program that characterizes most Sanskrit texts of the period. The normative legal treatises known as the Dharmaśāstras ("Treatises on Law"), for example, are filled with praise for Brāhmaṇas and promote a theological vision of human society organized around the privileged status of Brāhmaṇas. Such sentiment is comparatively rare in the *Arthaśāstra*, and mostly finds its way into the text in the later passages added by its redactor(s). In fact, Kauṭilya's original treatise is remarkable insofar as its perspective on society deviates from the pro-Brāhmaṇical political theology that is nearly ubiquitous in contemporary Sanskrit texts. Instead, Kauṭilya's reputation derives from his dedication to political success (*artha*) over Brāhmaṇical law (*dharma*) or sensual pleasure (*kāma*):

> "Success alone is paramount," says Kauṭilya, "for Success is the foundation of Law and Pleasure." (1.7.6–7)

Kauṭilya's writing suggests that he may have come from a relatively cosmopolitan background. Rather than supporting the ideological bias of a theologically inclined Brāhmaṇical elite that cleaved to conservative traditions, emphasized the religious duties of the class, and often prohibited Brāhmaṇas from working for kings, Kauṭilya demonstrates an urbane and pragmatic disposition redolent of aristocratic political culture. We might, then, think of Kauṭilya as rather more "culturally Brāhmaṇical" than "ideologically Brāhmaṇical"—the kind of Brāhmaṇa scorned in many orthodox texts as not being a "true Brāhmaṇa" because he does not put the observance of orthodox Brāhmaṇical customs and values above other priorities. The role of religion in the text is discussed later in more detail.

His knowledge of Sanskrit, at any rate, implies that Kauṭilya came from an elite background and had an elite education, which probably included the study of a variety of different disciplines. His use of different sources in the compilation of the *Arthaśāstra* indicates that he was intimately familiar with the expert tradition on statecraft. Indeed, the way in which he organized such disparate texts into a grand vision of statecraft in the *Arthaśāstra* suggests that his education and intellectual prowess were formidable and that he was himself responsible for the cultivation of statecraft into a mature intellectual tradition. Beyond these scholastic horizons, however, it is also clear Kauṭilya possessed a good deal of practical knowledge. We read as much at the conclusion of his teaching on royal decrees:

> Having gone through all the treatises and observed actual usage, Kauṭilya has given the rules for composing a decree for the benefit of kings. (2.10.63)

Almost certainly, Kauṭilya lived a life in and around royal courts and inside and outside administrative offices. He displays such broad knowledge of the particular duties of individual officials that we can only assume him to have been familiar with the actual practice of governance at many levels.

If Kauṭilya is to be found anywhere in his own text, it is probably in the role he prescribes counselors (*mantrins*) (§1.2), top advisors to the king who discuss with him the most sensitive matters of the state and help him to administer and empower the kingdom. The most powerful of these, the counselor-chaplain (*mantripurohita*) (§3.1), was a Brāhmaṇa who combined political acumen with magical and divine powers and operated as the king's right-hand man or, in some cases, as the true power behind the throne:

> [The King] should appoint as Counselor-Chaplain a man who comes from a very distinguished family and has an equally distinguished character, who is thoroughly trained in the Veda [i.e., the central Brāhmaṇical scriptures] together with

> the limbs [i.e., ancillary Vedic texts], in divine omens, an(Government, and who could counteract divine and human adversities through Atharvan [i.e., magico-ritual] means. He should follow him as a pupil his teacher, a son his father, and a servant his master. (1.9.9–10)

The magisterial perspective and erudition of the *Arthaśāstra*, taken in concert with its composer's likely Brāhmaṇical background, most closely match the profile of a counselor-chaplain. For example, the text demonstrates an intimate familiarity with the royal palace and court and even provides glimpses of the king's secret consultation with his ministers. In many ways, in fact, the *Arthaśāstra* is written more for counselors and ministers who advise kings than for kings themselves. This provides us our best sense of who Kauṭilya was: an esteemed royal counselor and teacher who spent his life among other politically minded individuals in royal courts and councils debating and expounding on issues pertinent to statecraft.

Date and Location of the Arthaśāstra

As to the time and place in which Kauṭilya lived and wrote the *Arthaśāstra*, we have no definite information. The *Arthaśāstra* does not tell us where or when it was composed, and the geographic and cultural information in the text have proven inconclusive in determining a precise locus for its origin. The geographical horizons of the text cover nearly all of South Asia. One ancient theory holds that Kauṭilya was a resident of the city of Taxila, which was located in modern-day Pakistan, although there is no actual proof of this.

Three pieces of information in the text might serve as circumstantial evidence by which to locate it geographically. First, in its discussion of timekeeping, the *Arthaśāstra* (2.20.37–41) records that the gnomon of a sundial casts no shadow during the lunar month of Āṣāḍha, which falls during the summer solstice. It is only along the Tropic of Cancer that the sun is directly overhead at this time. If Kauṭilya's information was based on local conditions (which is not necessarily the case), this would place him somewhere in north-central India. Second, Kauṭilya discusses the administration of seaports within a kingdom (2.28), which gives us the impression that he was familiar with coastal areas. Given that the *Arthaśāstra* envisions a small, regional kingdom, this might indicate that Kauṭilya spent his career near to one of South Asia's coastlines. Finally, when giving information on rainfall in South Asia (2.24.5), the text only gives specific amounts for three regions: Aśmaka (Maharashtra/Andhra Pradesh), Avanti (Madhya Pradesh), and Aparānta (Konkan/coastal Maharashtra/Gujarat). These pieces of admittedly circumstantial evidence converge on what is now the state of Maharashtra on India's west coast. That Kauṭilya hailed from this region has been argued by several scholars, who also cite the presence to this day of Brāhmaṇas in the region with the lineage name "Kauṭilya."

The *Arthaśāstra* does bear witness to historical events in an incidental way. Two features of the text allow us to narrow down the period of its composition. The first of these comes from the fact that the *Arthaśāstra*, despite a detailed discussion on minting (2.12.24) and many references to silver and copper coins, never refers to coins made of gold. As the first gold coins were minted in South Asia by the Kuśāna King Kadphises at the end of the first century CE and continued to be minted by his successors, we can estimate that the *Arthaśāstra* must have been compiled sometime before this period. Certainly, texts of the second century CE and later do refer to the circulation of gold coins. This yields us an upper limit for the composition of the *Arthaśāstra* sometime around 100 CE.

A second feature of the text allows us to establish the lower limit of its original composition: its references to Alexandrian coral from the Near East (2.11.42). The *Arthaśāstra* records that this coral was highly valued (5.2.17, 7.12.14, etc.). Archaeological evidence of extensive trade with the Mediterranean world, from which red coral came, now dates as early as the second century BCE. So, allowing some time for coral trade to have become widespread, we can estimate a lower limit for the text of around 100 BCE. This gives us a rough two hundred-year period in which the original *Arthaśāstra* was probably composed: 100 BCE–100

CE. This dating conforms well with what we understand about the evolution of Sanskrit literature as well as the influence of the *Arthaśāstra* on later writers.

Historical Context

The *Arthaśāstra* is a rich and valuable source of historical information about the classical period in South Asia. In the introduction to each chapter and the preamble to each passage translated in this reader, we expound on what the text tells us about life in classical South Asia. Students and nonspecialist readers, however, will benefit at the outset from a brief sketch of South Asian history so as to better understand the social and cultural context within which the *Arthaśāstra* was composed.

In what kind of political and cultural climate did Kauṭilya write the *Arthaśāstra*? Answering this question requires that we look briefly at the history of the South Asian subcontinent. The history of civilization in South Asia begins sometime in the fourth millennium BCE, when the first towns emerged in the Indus River Valley (modern-day Pakistan). By about 2600 BCE, major urban centers had arisen across a broad swath of northwest South Asia. Scholars refer to this society as the Indus Valley Civilization. But by 1700 BCE, this highly developed society had collapsed almost completely. Its decline was followed by the emigration into South Asia of the Indo-Aryans, a predominantly pastoral people whom we know through the writings of their descendants, texts called the Vedas. Then, around 600 BCE, South Asia experienced a second wave of urbanization. This inaugurated the classical period, which ended sometime after 600 CE following the invasion of the Huns. Thus, for the purposes of this Introduction, we will divide ancient Indian history into three periods: the Indus Valley period (2600–1700 BCE), the Vedic period (1700–600 BCE), and the classical period (600 BCE–600 CE). The *Arthaśāstra*, then, was composed in the middle of the classical period, although we must look closer to determine the significance of that fact.

The Indus Valley Period

Following two or three millennia of agricultural development in northwest South Asia, towns began to emerge in the Indus River Valley sometime in the fourth millennium BCE. By about 2600 BCE, major cities had emerged throughout the Indus River Valley and neighboring Baluchistan to the west, as well as into the Ganges River Valley to the east and what is now coastal western India to the southwest.

Mature Indus Valley cities show a remarkably high degree of urban planning, including uniform construction standards, comprehensive sewage systems, and a relatively homogeneous material culture. The replication of the same model of urban planning across many of its large cities indicates that the Indus Valley Civilization was ruled by a powerful, centralized authority, perhaps emanating from the great cities of Harappa and Mohenjo-Daro. In addition to a highly developed and shared cosmopolitan culture within South Asia, archaeologists have also found evidence of intensive mercantile exchange with central and west Asia. All of these factors indicate a highly evolved and urbane culture. Climatic change in the early second millennium seems to have dealt a major blow to these cities and their agricultural hinterlands, and the Indus Valley Civilization had almost entirely collapsed by 1700 BCE.

Unfortunately, scholars have been unable to decipher the symbols inscribed on their seals and ceramics, and we, therefore, know almost nothing about their political or cultural history. Despite the collapse of their cosmopolitan civilization, certain dimensions of Indus Valley culture persisted within South Asia, some of it perhaps to modern times. Historical sources from subsequent periods, however, fail to demonstrate any knowledge or memory of Indus Valley Civilization. It was not until the twentieth century that scholars rediscovered the great urban centers of the Indus Valley and began to relate their place in the story of humanity.

The Vedic Period

The decline of the Indus Valley Civilization left a social, cultural, and political vacuum in northern South Asia into which migrated seminomadic peoples from central Asia. They arrived in waves over a long period of time as part of much larger migrations occurring throughout Europe and Asia in the period. We call them the "Indo-Aryans" because they represent the "Indic" (we might say "South Asian") branch of a broader set of Eurasian cultures and identified themselves with the word *ārya*, meaning "noble one." The Indo-Aryans brought their own culture, language, and religion into the same region where the Indus Valley Civilization had once thrived and where its social and cultural remnants endured. There they settled, forgetting they had migrated from elsewhere, and began to evolve a distinctive culture and religion that blended imported and local elements.

The Āryan identity and way of life that evolved in South Asia provided a common cultural heritage for most thinkers in the classical period, including the composer of the *Arthaśāstra*, who saw themselves as the inheritors and defenders of Āryan tradition and customs. From the time of the arrival of the Indo-Aryans, the term *Āryan* in South Asia became a cultural identity marker used to distinguish those who upheld what was conceived as the Āryan way of life against those who, either because they were from different cultures or because they simply failed to follow proper tradition, were considered "non-Āryan." What it exactly meant to be Āryan, however, was much contested, with orthodox Brāhmaṇas, Buddhists, and others seeking to appropriate and define Āryan identity in particular ways.

Our first historical sources depicting life in South Asia are the sacred texts of the Āryans called the Vedas. These texts were composed orally in an early form of Sanskrit, the sacred language that the Indo-Aryans had brought with them on their migration. The Vedas are comprised of hymns to their gods—both gods that had come with the migrations as well as what appear to have been indigenous deities—and discussion of the rituals through which these gods were worshipped. Although the Vedas are essentially liturgical documents and increasingly mystical reflections on Vedic ritual, they are sufficiently rich and extensive to give us some understanding of what life was like at the time. The earliest of the Vedas, the *Ṛgveda Saṃhitā*, contains 1,028 hymns, some of which may be as old as 1500 BCE. Because the Vedic texts are the primary way in which we can understand the period between the fall of the Indus Valley Civilization (1700 BCE) and the second wave of urbanization (600 BCE), we call the intervening era of South Asian history the "Vedic period."

During the early Vedic period (1500–1000 BCE), Āryan society was organized into seminomadic tribes and small-scale villages—the Vedas say nothing about cities or urban life. The early Vedic literature depicts society as divided into three groups: the priests (Brāhmaṇas), the warriors and nobility (Kṣatriyas), and the people of the tribe (Viś). Brāhmaṇas carried out the critical rituals that fed the gods and brought to humans such divine gifts as offspring, wealth, and long life. Kṣatriyas fought and protected society. And the Viś labored and provided society with material sustenance. These groups do not originally appear to have been strictly hereditary groups (as they become later in the period). There seems to have been a good deal of variety in the political organization between the various Āryan tribes, but most featured a chief, either Viś or Kṣatriya, who ruled in consultation with some kind of tribal council.

The Āryans themselves were cattle herders, and their culture centered very much around one of the things their ancestors had brought with them into South Asia: horses. The Indo-Aryans had introduced horse culture and chariots to South Asia, which imparted significant military advantage. The primary military activity of the Āryans was raiding cattle from other tribes (both Āryan and non-Āryan), defending their own cattle from the raids of others, and appropriating the choicest lands. Over the course of the Vedic period, they expanded their area of settlement eastward, following the line of the Himālayas and the Ganges River. This movement was not a sweeping invasion, but a gradual movement characterized largely by piecemeal expansion and appropriation. The composers of the Vedas saw their own Āryan society as being in a state of constant conflict with the Dāsas (a word that also means "slave" in Sanskrit), who represent other, possibly indigenous, inhabitants of the region. While Āryan/Dāsa conflict is a hallmark of Vedic literature, we should be aware also that a great degree of cultural integration between the two occurred in this period. This contact promoted the increasing articulation of who was an Āryan and what comprised the Āryan way of life.

The Vedas themselves were composed by the priestly Brāhmaṇa class, and it represents their perspective on Āryan society. As composers of the sacred hymns, masters of the sacred language of Sanskrit, and performers of the powerful ritual, the Brāhmaṇas positioned themselves as the keepers and defenders of Āryan culture. Control of access to these cherished institutions helped the Brāhmaṇas evolve into a powerful intelligentsia. This brought, of course, a measure of political power that required special consideration from chiefs and other rulers. The establishment of a Brāhmaṇical intellectual elite in the Vedic period would be one of the most important cultural developments in South Asian history, as Brāhmaṇical thought would go on to dominate South Asian high culture and exert enormous influence over South Asian society and self-understanding well into the modern period.

By around 1000 BCE, Vedic society was transitioning to a settled agricultural way of life. The advent of iron technology may have helped in this period to clear the dense forests of northern South Asia and expand access to arable land. This would have allowed for greater concentrations of wealth, which, in turn, would have promoted political centralization. Evidence suggests that Vedic society at this time was coming increasingly under the control of the warrior class. Later parts of the *Ṛgveda Saṃhitā* refer to a major conflict in this period known as "The Battle of Ten Kings," in which a leader named Sudās was able to unite or subdue many of the nomadic tribes of northern South Asia and exert some kind of hegemony over the region. Our knowledge of political history in this period is extremely spotty, but it is clear that during the late Vedic period, a new model of political leadership emerged. If early Vedic tribes were characterized by the rule of prominent individuals drawn from the community and endorsed by some kind of tribal council, then late Vedic polities were ruled by kings as the triumphant representatives of a distinct class of nobles.

Our understanding of the social order that emerged in the late Vedic period is strongly colored by the Brāhmaṇical view of society. By this time, a fourth group had been added to the three mentioned above: the servants (Śūdras), who were ascribed the position of serving the other three classes. Śūdras, generally speaking, would forever be considered non-Āryans, indicating that they may have originally been drawn from culturally distinct, indigenous people. (The *Arthaśāstra* is an interesting exception to this assessment, considering Śūdras to be Āryans.) This fourfold division of society is known as the *varṇa* ("color"; "category") system: Brāhmaṇas, Kṣatriyas, Vaiśyas (previously the Viś), and Śūdras.

For themselves, the Brāhmaṇa priests reserved the highest position, arguing that they outranked even the kings and nobles who ruled society. They based their claim to such exalted status on their exclusive right to perform the Vedic ritual and teach the Vedas to other Āryans. This positioned the Brāhmaṇas as the gatekeepers of the Āryan way of life, for, it is implied, no one could consider themselves an Āryan who did not partake of these central institutions. It also meant that the Brāhmaṇas were the only ones who could perform the elaborate rituals to supplicate the gods or install kings on the throne. As exemplars and repositories of Āryan culture, Brāhmaṇas thus positioned themselves as integral, even primary, within the political order—even though their texts eschew the direct involvement of Brāhmaṇas in ruling. Partaking of the Brāhmaṇically controlled social institutions so critical to Āryan identity meant, above all, endorsing the Brāhmaṇical view of society and the roles it ascribed to the different classes. Hence, we see unfolding in the Vedic period an increasingly rigid social order organized around access to Āryan cultural institutions and enforced by

Brāhmaṇically mediated rules restricting interactions and, above all, intermarriage between *varṇas*.

The Classical Period

Over the course of the Vedic period, Āryan culture gradually spread eastward through what is now North India along the courses of the Ganges and Yamuna Rivers. By about 600 BCE, the implementation of iron technology had allowed for the transformation of the North Indian jungle into farmland sufficient to support a new wave of urban civilization. Cities began to arise predominantly along the middle and lower stretches of the Gangetic plains (in the modern Indian states of Uttar Pradesh and Bihar). The emergence of these cities indicate the culmination in many regions of the transition in South Asian political organization from tribal chiefdoms and integral, small-scale communities to kingdoms—regional and transregional polities comprehending heterogeneous populations. The shift in political organization occurred in part through the increasing segmentation of society into a distinct ruling class and a distinct ruled class.

If the development of intensive agriculture and widespread urbanization were characterized by changes in political organization, so too were they accompanied by transformations in intellectual and cultural life. Urban life brought with it a degree of cultural diversity and dynamism unknown within the bounded and homogeneous life of small, rural communities. Above all, cities created new social and cultural spaces, comparatively free from much of the conservatism of village life and within which individuals and groups were able to develop in novel ways. Such conditions allowed for the interaction of distinct worldviews, perspectives, and customs.

This new interconnectivity propelled South Asian culture through an era of dramatic transformation that saw the rise of renunciate traditions and new religions (such as Buddhism and Jainism); the emergence of new religious ideologies centered around the concepts of rebirth, the ethical law of *karma*, and liberation; the development of the classical intellectual disciplines (such as grammar, law, history, and medicine); the establishment of regional kingdoms; momentous contact with foreign cultures, such as those of the Persians and Greeks; the advent of writing; the use of coins; the expansion of trade; the rise of the great theistic systems focused on cosmic deities like Śiva and Viṣṇu; and the systematic articulation of the Brāhmaṇical view of life, the universe, and everything. Not all of these occurred at once, but all happened with marked rapidity and collectively ushered in a shared culture that defines what we now think of as the classical period in South Asia.

For lack of a better term, we can think of all of this broadly as "Āryan culture," as long as we recognize that it does not denote a single homogeneous cultural or racial unit, it was not evenly distributed or accepted across South Asia (particularly in the south), and no single group controlled exactly what this identity meant to different constituencies. This common culture does, however, provide the context within which the *Arthaśāstra* was composed sometime between 100 BCE and 100 CE.

The social conditions of the classical period spawned new kinds of literature, which allow us to take a more nuanced view of South Asian culture than provided by the sources from the Vedic period. We know, on one hand, that the Brāhmaṇical vision of Āryan culture, expressed through the hierarchical social system of the four social classes, is evermore strenuously promoted in Brāhmaṇical literature as the classical period unfolds. Yet, we also know that many groups (including Buddhists and others) successfully challenged this Brāhmaṇical view and attracted a great deal of material and spiritual support. Megasthenes, the culturally Greek ambassador to the court of the Candragupta mentioned before, noted that Brāhmaṇas received high respect within society, but that Buddhists and other religious figures did as well. The most powerful ruler of the classical period, Aśoka Maurya, widely promulgated a social ethic strongly colored by his own Buddhist faith and in some respects antagonistic to Brāhmaṇical interests. Beyond even this, the classical period saw the emergence of individuals and groups who perceived the world in more or less nonreligious terms. We might think of them as materialists or atheists, but what they have in common is an orientation toward the world that does not necessarily subscribe to the perspective of religious Brāhmaṇism, Buddhism, or any other religion of the period.

What all of this indicates is a rich diversity of worldviews and interests within the shared, but contested cosmopolitan culture of classical South Asia. Even as Brāhmaṇical and Buddhist culture asserted themselves and indelibly impacted classical South Asian culture, no single philosophy or institution governed the minds and hearts of people in the period. Invasions by and contact with representatives of foreign cultures further enriched the milieu of the classical period, prompting various responses, from appropriation to rejection, to a wealth of new perspectives.

The earliest political formations in the classical period conformed to what we might think of as city-states, wherein a politically, militarily, and materially dominant and fortified city exercised control over the neighboring geographical region and the smaller settlements within it. Typically, these cities were situated on the plains along major river courses. The tradition refers to these small, regional kingdoms as *janapada*s, a term we might translate as "the territory inhabited by a people." Each *janapada* would have a capital city as well as a second tier of smaller market towns or military fortresses and a large number of agricultural villages. When cities arose at the beginning of the classical period, the political landscape was transformed into a chessboard of *janapada*s.

By the fifth century, however, some of these *janapada*s had begun to grow far more powerful than their neighbors and, through a succession of wars, marriages, and treaties, consolidated larger areas into what were called *mahājanapada*s, or "great *janapada*s." The political imagination of the early classical period saw northern and central South Asia as being divided into sixteen *mahājanapada*s. This concept persisted in the literature for quite some time, indicating either the durability of the *mahājanapada*s themselves or, perhaps, simply of the idea of the *mahājanapada*s as archetypal political units.

The process of political consolidation continued, and during the fourth century BCE one of the *mahājanapada*s, the kingdom of Magadha, began to expand aggressively and dominate its neighbors politically. Its capital at Paṭaliputra (modern-day Patna, Bihar) was the largest city on Earth in this period, estimated at twice the size of imperial Rome, covering 25 square kilometers and home to a population of over one million. Even as Magadha increased in power, its rulers were overthrown by Candragupta Maurya (reigned 320–298 BCE), who established the Maurya Dynasty. Candragupta set out on a campaign conquering most of North India and eventually challenging the successors of Alexander the Great's conquest into northwest South Asia. The Maurya Empire far eclipsed the preceding *mahājanapada*s in size, power, and reach, giving rise to a new South Asian political vision of empire. Candragupta's successors increased the size of the Maurya Empire, which reached its greatest extent under Candragupta's grandson, Aśoka Maurya.

Aśoka Maurya (reigned 268–233 BCE), who called himself *devānaṃpiya* ("Beloved of the Gods") and *piyadassi* ("He Who Looks Pleasingly"), remains by far the most famous of classical South Asia's rulers. Not only did he extend the Maurya Empire to a geographical scope unmatched until the British conquest of India 2,000 years later, but he marked out his realm and publicized his power through a series of inscriptions and monumental pillars erected across the subcontinent that have survived to this day. No other classical ruler projected his presence as Aśoka did. Even more remarkably, the inscriptions that Aśoka left provide us with a very personal view of the emperor, a man remorseful over the suffering his conquest had brought and expressing an earnest desire to rule through righteousness. His projection of both military might and moral charisma came to represent the archetypal *cakravartin*, or "wheel-turner," whose chariot wheels roll everywhere without resistance because he governs righteously. Through Aśoka, the Maurya Imperium became the iconic model of rule in South Asian political imagination.

After Aśoka's death in 233 BCE, however, the Maurya Dynasty collapsed with surprising rapidity, indicating that Mauryan power may have had more to do with the personal charisma of its rulers than the robustness of its political institutions. Within a short period of time, the Mauryan state shrunk back into its regional footprint, much of its formerly conquered domain reverted to local rule (such as the regional power of the Kaliṅgas in the east), and the center of power in South Asia shifted to the northwest—what is now Afghanistan and Pakistan. This area was ruled by the Indo-Greek kings, who had inherited the South Asian lands conquered by Alexander the Great in the late fourth century BCE. By the second century BCE, some of these kings had conquered well within the old Mauryan heartland in modern-day North India. At about this time, however, a central Asian tribe known as the Śakas began migrating into and invading the northwest, and by the first century BCE, Śaka kings had conquered much of north and northwest India, displacing most of the Indo-Greeks.

The Śakas were followed out of central Asia by the Kuśānas, who, in the first century CE had conquered all of northwest and much of northern India, establishing under King Kaniṣka (reigned late first or second century CE) a massive Asian empire that stretched from the borders of China to central India. The northern Indian city of Mathura was particularly important to them. Kuśāna rule was marked by the cosmopolitan sensibilities of some of its rulers, whose territories included a remarkably diverse set of cultures. Kuśāna kings were patrons of different religious communities, and their sponsorship helped develop distinctive schools of South Asian art. Their reign also saw the beginning of gold coinage in South Asia, the establishment of a new era in South Asian chronology, and an intensification of contact with cultures outside of South Asia through trade and the relative pacification of large stretches of south and central Asia. The conditions attending to the decline of Kuśāna rule in India are not well understood, but their reign ended sometime in the second or third century CE.

It is to this rather rich and tumultuous period of South Asian history that we can assign the *Arthaśāstra*. Specifically, the text was probably composed sometime during the decline of Śaka rule or the rise of the Kuśānas. Given, however, that we know neither where the *Arthaśāstra* was composed nor how the larger empires of the period were administered, particularly with reference to conquered states, it is difficult to understand precisely the ways in which the *Arthaśāstra* is speaking to the political history of this era. What we can see about Kauṭilya's treatise is that it envisions a small, regional polity as opposed to a large imperial formation. Whether it was written in a kingdom that recognized Kuśāna suzerainty, in a small kingdom outside of the sphere of Kuśāna domination, or within one of the less extensive transregional powers of the period—the Kṣatrapas in western India and the Śātavāhanas in central India—remains to be determined. Whatever its origin, the *Arthaśāstra* approaches interstate relations from the perspective of a small state seeking to empower itself in an environment of neighboring rivals as well as more distant and powerful rulers.

The classical period culminates with the establishment in the early fourth century CE of the Gupta Empire, of which the domain grew through conquest and marriage to include all of North and much of Central India at its height in the fifth century CE. Gupta rule saw the flowering of Classical Sanskrit as a language of learning and literature and the emergence of Classical Hinduism, as a reimagining, expansion, and consolidation of South Asian religiosity within the cosmo-political vision of the elite Brāhmaṇical class. For many, this era represents the golden age of classical India, the period in which the common South Asian heritage of Sanskritic learning recorded its highest achievements. Although it was certainly written before the Gupta period, attitudes about the *Arthaśāstra* and its position within classical South Asian intellectual history were strongly determined by the cultural outlook of this time.

The Gupta Empire began suffering limited military and political setbacks beginning in the late fifth century CE, primarily at the hands of the Huns of central Asia, who were in this period in their ascendance. By the early sixth century, the Huns had conquered much of northern South Asia and appear to have dealt a blow to the high culture of the Gupta period from which it would never recover in much of northwest India. Although their rule in South Asia was brief, the conquest of the Huns signaled the beginning of the end of what we call the classical period. In the seventh century CE, King Harṣa, another great patron of classical culture, conquered much of North India, but failed to extend his power to match that of the Guptas, and his empire collapsed quickly after his death.

The collapse of the Gupta Empire and the receding of the Huns was followed by the emergence once again of a political landscape more decidedly regional in character. This time, however, this regional pattern would persist, laying the foundation for the distinctive regional cultures that emerged in the medieval period. In contrast to earlier periods, the regional kingdoms of the post-Gupta period began increasingly to orient themselves toward distinctive local traditions rather than so exclusively align themselves with a unified, cosmopolitan Sanskrit culture. Although this was a gradual process, by about 1000 CE, literary and intellectual efforts began to shift away from Sanskrit and into the various local languages of the regional polities. As the precursor of a new political order centered around regional cultures, each its own new cosmopolis, the post-Gupta period saw a decided shift in the orientation of South Asian cultural production, away from the forms that delineated a united, Sanskritic world and toward the regional traditions of the medieval kingdoms.

Arthaśāstra: Text and Tradition

Furnished with the historical context just provided, we can turn now to examining the *Arthaśāstra* within its cultural milieu.

The Concept of Artha

As noted above, the name *Arthaśāstra* can be translated as "Treatise (*śāstra*) on Success (*artha*)," although this tells us very little about the topic we are actually dealing with. The term *śāstra* comes from the Sanskrit verb root meaning "to teach" and literally means "an instrument of education." The tradition understands *śāstras* as texts that instruct students in the timeless knowledge of a given subject. Hence, the term *Arthaśāstra*, when capitalized, refers to a specific treatise on *artha*, while the term *arthaśāstra*, in lowercase, refers to the body of knowledge concerning statecraft communicated through such authoritative texts. We will examine the unique characteristics of *śāstras* as texts in a moment.

The term *artha* has many meanings, but in the *Arthaśāstra* it refers to success in worldly affairs, such as gaining wealth, land, power, or fame. Classical South Asian thought evolved the proposition that all people are oriented toward one of four life goals: law (*dharma*), pleasure (*kāma*), success (*artha*), or spiritual liberation (*mokṣa*). Calling our treatise *Arthaśāstra* indicates that it is an instrument of education (*śāstra*) on the topic of worldly success (*artha*). This is true, so long as we recognize that the success referred to here is the political and material success of a king: literally, the "gaining" and "protecting" of the world:

> . . . this treatise [*śāstra*] . . . has been proclaimed for the gain and protection of this world and the next. (15.1.71)

The concept of *artha*, however, comprehends a much broader category of human activity than simply statecraft, one that might also explain the motivations of merchants, laborers, entrepreneurs, heads of households, political officials, and whoever seeks influence and wealth. Nevertheless, in classical South Asian society, it was the king who was the paragon of worldly success, for he possessed wealth and power unrivaled in his domain. Equating the discourse on statecraft with the general life goal of *artha* enhanced the prestige of the text, as it linked the priorities of governance with such fundamental human concerns as piety, pleasure, and personal salvation:

> This treatise brings into being and protects Law (*dharma*), Success (*artha*), and Pleasure (*kāma*), and suppresses those who are unrighteous (*adharmān*) and those who hate Success (*artha*). (15.1.72)

The Genre of Śāstra

As a *śāstra*, Kauṭilya's text purports to be an authoritative and comprehensive treatment of its subject, which we are referring to as "governance" or "statecraft." Hence, we can also translate the term *Arthaśāstra* as "Treatise on Statecraft." Different thinkers and schools of thought in classical South Asia produced independent *śāstra*s on a wide variety of topics—law, drama, aesthetics, astronomy, and so forth. Collectively, the *śāstra*s of a given subject would represent an "expert tradition." Someone who sought to become educated in a given topic would be instructed by experts in one or more of its *śāstra*s, and a polymath would have studied the *śāstra*s of a wide variety of expert traditions.

*Śāstra*s, as texts, share some unique characteristics. They treat their subjects, for the most part, as though they were an eternal and unchanging body of knowledge existing outside of any specific place and time. Local conditions may vary, but the universally applicable knowledge of a *śāstra* does not. Thus, the information they record is not seen as the result of an evolving and advancing human inquiry in which ongoing investigation yields progressively deeper insights. Rather, the eternal knowledge recorded in the *śāstra*s exists above the realm of human efforts, a timeless truth in the universe given to society by wise sages and scholars who themselves penetrated deeply into the nature of things or received it from their predecessors or the gods. Faults within the text of a *śāstra* can only be explained, therefore, as human error that has crept in as they have been transmitted. The true knowledge that lies behind the *śāstra* as text—which we might think of as the real *śāstra* itself—is singular, harmonious, and perfect.

So, Kauṭilya recognizes in the first verse of the *Arthaśāstra* (1.1.1) that he has, for the most part, composed his text by bringing together the Arthaśāstras of earlier teachers, casting it as the compilation of a received tradition, albeit a particularly good one, insofar as it presents the teachings of the tradition with greater clarity (1.1.19) and corrects the erroneous opinions given by previous teachers. Kauṭilya also, however, recognizes that some of the rules of *arthaśāstra* should be learned by observing the actual practice of governance (1.5.8). For him, the procedures of proper governance are to be found not only in texts, but also in what living people actually do. The *śāstra* itself, as authoritative knowledge on statecraft, however, remains distinct from the specific practices of any given kingdom.

This appeal to timelessness and placelessness explains a curious feature about the *Arthaśāstra* that we have noted before: it reveals nothing directly about when or where it was written. It does not refer to contemporary historical events or persons that might aid us in locating the text in space or time. (The only exception to this is the spurious attribution of the *Arthaśāstra* to Cāṇakya at 15.1.73 discussed before.) Instead, the *Arthaśāstra* was purposely composed without any historical context, precisely because such references might limit its applicability to different circumstances. We can contrast this with a text frequently compared to the *Arthaśāstra*, *The Prince* by Niccolò Machiavelli, which instructs on governance by referring in very specific terms to contemporary historical rulers and polities.

In keeping with the implicit claim of *śāstra*s to present timeless, perfect knowledge, the *Arthaśāstra* does not purport to describe how things are, but instead *how things should be*. In this way, the *Arthaśāstra*, like all *śāstra*s, is a "normative" text: it speaks mostly in "shoulds" and "oughts." The following passage is indicative of this disposition:

> He should settle the countryside—whether it has been settled before or has never been settled—by forcing people out of enemy territories or by transferring people from overpopulated areas of his own territory. (2.1.1)

The normative dimension of *śāstra*s establishes standards and norms and gives advice on how to achieve optimal outcomes in the context of those norms. For example, with regard to the king's allies, Kauṭilya states,

> Bequeathed by the father and grandfather; consistent; submissive; not prone to duplicity; eminent; and able to mobilize quickly—these are the exemplary qualities of an ally. (6.1.12)

Running throughout the text, however, is an implicit (and sometimes explicit) recognition that such optimal outcomes are sometimes not achievable. Kauṭilya instructs the king on appointing an heir:

> If [a son of evil intellect] is his only son, the king should try to get him to have a son, or get a "female-son" [i.e., a daughter appointed as a son] to bear sons. If the king is suffering from an illness or is old, he should get a son fathered on his field [i.e., wife] through one of the following: mother's kinsman, member of the royal family, a virtuous neighboring lord. Never should he, however, install an only son who is undisciplined over the kingdom. (1.17.49–51)

Here Kauṭilya is trying to present a number of options for responding to complex circumstances. By speaking in such ideal terms, the text is attempting to turn general wisdom into useful advice for real-world situations, which are invariably untidy and complex.

When modern scholars first began to translate and interpret *śāstra*s, they frequently erred in reading them as purely descriptive accounts of South Asia's past, rather than recognizing the extent to which they actually instruct through normative visions of an idealized world. Because we want to use these texts to peek into the past, the inclination to read *śāstra*s purely as descriptions of historical societies is very strong. As products of their respective cultural milieus, *śāstra*s do offer us information about the past, but only if we first understand them to be intellectualized reflections on the principles believed to underlie the proper undertaking of various human activities rather than as attempts to describe historical human practices.

If we take this disposition into account, however, we can glean from *śāstra*s valid information about actual historical practices, customs, and attitudes. They draw on real-world expertise and observation to furnish their normative visions. The balance between these two can be seen in Kauṭilya's description of the daily diet of different individuals:

> A Prastha [a little more than half a kilogram] of unbroken and fully cleaned rice kernels, one-quarter that amount of stew,

> one-sixteenth of the amount of stew in salt, and one-quarter in butter or oil constitute a single daily ration for an Ārya male; one-sixth of stew and half the above quantity of fat for lower-class males; one-quarter less for women; and one-half for children. (2.15.43–46)

Here, these amounts do not actually tell us who ate what on a daily basis, as much as we'd like them to. These numbers are, in fact, a means for the king's agents to assess how much food they have stored in the royal warehouses. And yet we recognize that the passage is drawing on some kind of observation of or reflection on consumption patterns in society. It *is* telling us something about who ate what, even though it is decidedly *not* a transparent description thereof. Perhaps this is the rationing used by the king when he provided food for his subjects at different events.

Thus, when read thoughtfully, the *śāstra*s can be uniquely useful documents for reconstructing the past. The trick for the scholar is to understand how to interpret the information in the *śāstra*—how to tell when the text is recording existing practices, when it is presenting an idealized vision, and when it is doing both at the same time. We must ask: From where is this information drawn? What is being excluded and what is being foregrounded? Where are the interests of the composer influencing the text? How do we understand the complex nexus of different viewpoints, attitudes, practices, and customs within which the text was produced, about which it is attempting to speak, and on which it was seeking to exert its influence? Ultimately, we want to answer the question: What, *exactly*, is being recorded here?

This is no simple task, but through the use of different historical data, comparison of contemporary viewpoints, creative ways of reading the texts, and rigorous debate among scholars, a clearer picture emerges over time of what kind of text the *Arthaśāstra* is and what kind of culture produced it. In the prologues preceding each selection translated in this volume, special care is taken to distinguish between the normative and descriptive dimensions of the *Arthaśāstra*, all with an eye to understanding better the culture it reflects.

The Tradition of Statecraft

We have looked already at the term *arthaśāstra* and why it is used for a treatise on statecraft. The *Arthaśāstra* itself, however, uses another term to identify the expert tradition on statecraft: *daṇḍanīti*, "administration (*nīti*) of the staff (*daṇḍa*)." The term *daṇḍa* here refers to the staff or scepter wielded by the king as the symbol of his unique royal authority. As one of his royal accoutrements, the staff as a weapon represented the king's ability and willingness to use violence in ruling his kingdom. It represented his monopoly on the legitimate use of force. Thus, the concept of "administration of the staff" refers to the theoretically constructive use of violence in service of upholding justice, preserving public order, and empowering the king—in other words, "government":

> What provides enterprise and security to [the various areas of human endeavor] is punishment (*daṇḍa*); its administration (*nīti*) is Government (*daṇḍanīti*). . . . On it depends the proper operation of the world. (1.4.3–4)

The coercive authority represented by the staff was rooted in violence, but that coercion extended through other institutional mechanisms of the state such as fines, punishments, and the king's army itself; all of these represent other meanings of the term *daṇḍa*. We might, then, think of *daṇḍanīti* as the "governing through constructive coercion."

The concept of administering punishment, then, becomes the theoretical underpinning for the project of statecraft. At the center of the enterprise stood the king, holding the staff. This is expressed in a debate recorded in the *Arthaśāstra* between Kauṭilya and the teachers of old:

> "Seeking the proper operation of the world, therefore, he should always stand ready to impose punishment; for there is nothing like punishment for bringing creatures under his power"—so state the Teachers.
>
> "No," says Kauṭilya; "for, one who punishes severely terrifies the people, and one who punishes lightly is treated with

> contempt, whereas one who dispenses appropriate punishment is treated with respect. For punishment, when it is dispensed after the proper ascertainment of facts, makes his subjects embrace Law, Success, and Pleasure." (1.4.5–11)

Governance itself, for Kauṭilya, can be understood fundamentally as the various means and manners through which the king channeled his coercive authority to constructive ends. Considerations of legitimacy, understood as the attitude among his subjects of the appropriateness of a king's being invested with authority, are implicit in this passage (as in many other places in the text), although legitimacy itself is not treated as a fundamental source of political power.

The goal of government, according to the *Arthaśāstra*, is to acquire wealth, protect those acquisitions, grow them, and use that wealth to support worthy individuals and initiatives:

> Government seeks to acquire what has not been acquired, to safeguard what has been acquired, to augment what has been safeguarded, and to bestow what has been augmented on worthy recipients. (1.4.3)

The various administrative, military, and bureaucratic institutions of the state are seen ultimately as ways of using the staff in service of this fundamental project. Thus, the study of statecraft in classical South Asia is understood by the *Arthaśāstra* as the study of the complex systems through which the king exerted his coercive authority in service of security, wealth, power, and constructive enterprise.

The *Arthaśāstra*, as noted before, borrows from, revises, and sometimes rejects the teachings of earlier scholars on the topic of statecraft. Kauṭilya refers to some of these scholars by name or simply calls them "the teachers." In this way, we recognize that the *Arthaśāstra* was part of a greater tradition on statecraft from the classical period. Regarding this tradition itself, however, we can say little: whatever treatises these other teachers may have written are lost, and Kauṭilya's citation of earlier authorities gives us only a very piecemeal picture. Some modern scholars even believe that Kauṭilya has invented this tradition by fabricating a debate among earlier teachers who never existed. Other sources, such as the great Sanskrit epic the *Mahābhārata*, discuss Arthaśāstras other than Kauṭilya's, but none of these has survived, if they ever existed. Analysis of the *Arthaśāstra* suggests that certain parts of Kauṭilya's work probably existed as independent texts or were drawn from other treatises on statecraft before he compiled them into a single work, but none of these has survived independently either. Thus, while we know that the *Arthaśāstra* relied on preexisting texts and that these texts represented some kind of "expert tradition" on statecraft, we can say little with any certainty about the individual texts, the general tradition itself, or the relationship the *Arthaśāstra* had with that tradition.

Given all of these considerations, it is most likely that the *Arthaśāstra* is the culmination of a preceding tradition on statecraft, just as the passage quoted above claims (1.1.1). The absence of any earlier comprehensive manuals on statecraft suggests that the *Arthaśāstra* might be the first fully developed treatise on statecraft, a text that organized a preexisting but scattered tradition into a proper discipline based on an integral and coherent paradigm. Certainly, the vast influence that the *Arthaśāstra* exerted over later Sanskrit literature and South Asian thought suggest that it was held in special regard as the authoritative work on statecraft.

Structure and Style of the Text

The *Arthaśāstra*, as it has come down to us, is divided into fifteen "books," each dealing with a major theme in statecraft, such as "On the Activity of Superintendents" or "On War." These fifteen books are further divided into 180 "topics," which are short, integral discussions of more limited subjects such as the "Superintendent of Elephants" and "Marching into Battle from the Military Camp." Thus, the text proceeds by presenting a series of topics organized by book.

As noted above, the *Arthaśāstra* underwent editing at the hands of a later redactor. We are not sure whether the text was originally divided into books or exactly how many topics it possessed. We do know that after it had been redacted, it possessed fifteen books divided into 180 topics and that these topics had been redivided into 150 new segments called "chapters." The reason for this redaction, as already noted, was to apportion the *Arthaśāstra* into segments more uniform in length than the topics so that the text might be better suited to standardized instruction periods. This has, however, produced a somewhat confusing situation in the extant versions of the text: the same material is redundantly divided into both 180 topics *and* 150 chapters: frequently in the extant text there are many topics within a single chapter, and sometimes one topic is spread out over several chapters. Scholars typically cite the text according to chapter rather than topic, and passages in the *Arthaśāstra* are referred to with three numbers, representing the book, chapter, and sentence, respectively (e.g., 2.35.1).

Thus, we can speak of at least three layers in the composition of the *Arthaśāstra*. The first of these would be the various sources that Kauṭilya drew upon, which existed as independent texts or parts of independent texts. The second layer is the original text of the *Arthaśāstra*, which Kauṭilya composed by bringing the earlier sources together and adding some of his own material to fuse them into a coherent and comprehensive *śāstra*. This is the version of the text composed in topics. The third layer of the text is represented by the work of a later redactor, who edited the text by adding some new material and redividing the entire treatise into 150 chapters. What we call the extant version of the *Arthaśāstra* refers to the text as it has come down to us in modern times. It contains all three of these layers. This reader takes its excerpts from the extant *Arthaśāstra*.

The fifteen books of the extant *Arthaśāstra* informally divide the text into two halves and an appendix. The first half of the text (Books One through Five) discusses domestic administration, while the second half (Books Six through Fourteen) discusses interactions with outside kingdoms and military strategy. The final book (Book Fifteen) is a formal list of the kinds of organizational elements from which the text is constructed, such as declarative statements and citations of earlier authorities. A full table of contents of the extant *Arthaśāstra* is given at the end of this Introduction.

Generally speaking, the subjects of the *Arthaśāstra* are arranged in a clear manner. Kauṭilya organizes his advice as though he were instructing a king and his ministers in the creation of an entirely new kingdom. Thus, the *Arthaśāstra* begins by discussing the training of a young prince and moves on to advise a new king on how to assemble his high council, vet and appoint new officials, settle his kingdom, construct his capital city, staff his bureaucracy, preserve public safety, resolve public disputes, pursue criminals, engage in foreign policy, and, finally, defeat his enemies on the battlefield and conquer their cities. Speaking as though the kingdom was being created *ex novo*, however, is only a pedagogical convention. For the most part the text implies that the king it is instructing has, in fact, inherited an existing kingdom of which he is a native. Most likely, Kauṭilya chooses to use this *creatio ex nihilo* for purely scholastic reasons: it allows him to discuss each aspect of statecraft comprehensively, beginning with the king and moving outward from there.

The *Arthaśāstra* is written mostly in a very straightforward prose style. It lacks any special ornamental quality that might qualify as literary merit. The 150 chapters of the text are written almost entirely in prose and conclude with one or more short verses written in the most common Sanskrit meter, the *śloka*. Because traditional wisdom was usually passed down in the form of such verses, these concluding *śloka*s provide the echo of an authoritative voice from South Asia's collective cultural wisdom, but do little to ornament the *Arthaśāstra* as a work of literature. Because of these characteristics, the *Arthaśāstra* reads very much like a textbook or instruction manual.

The World of the *Arthaśāstra*

When we read the *Arthaśāstra*, we enter a world of political institutions and political contest. Kauṭilya was, above all, concerned with articulating the structures and policies through which political power could be wielded to maximum effect. What makes Kauṭilya's text challenging for modern readers is interpreting the advice of the *Arthaśāstra* without the benefit of its historical and cultural contexts. How are we to know what the composer is assuming or what is left unsaid? These questions become particularly pertinent as we seek to understand classical South Asian society through the lens of the *Arthaśāstra*.

We begin, therefore, by exploring the world of the *Arthaśāstra*. This is, most fundamentally, an imagined world centered on the idealized representation of a generic kingdom—the "ideal-typical kingdom," in other words. The norms of statecraft exist for the *Arthaśāstra* independent of any given material context. Particular details about classical South Asia monarchies—precisely the kind of information we might like to have—are, for Kauṭilya, trivial permutations of the ideal-typical kingdom. They are of interest only as evidence of the efficacy of the *śāstra* and the danger of ignoring its teachings: after instructing the king-in-training on how to control his afflictive emotions ("the six enemies"), Kauṭilya tells of kings who failed to follow such advice:

> These and many other kings, addicted to the set of six enemies, came to ruin along with their kinsmen and kingdoms, not having mastered their senses.
>
> Having abandoned the set of six enemies, Jāmadagnya, who had mastered his senses, as well as Ambarīṣa, the son of Nabhāga, enjoyed the earth for a long time. (1.6.11–12)

In addition to being abstract, the ideal-typical kingdom of the *Arthaśāstra* is also normative, an illustration of how things should be, as opposed to how they are. Kauṭilya's primary purpose is to tell us how kingdoms can be governed most effectively, not to provide a snapshot of classical society.

We might conclude, then, that the *Arthaśāstra* is of little value in understanding classical South Asian society. But, Kauṭilya clearly drew upon the traditions in which he was educated and practices he personally observed to furnish his ideal-typical kingdom. As a master within the tradition of statecraft, Kauṭilya's genius resides not only in his command of this material, but specifically in how he distilled the various resources at his disposal into a compelling and coherent vision of proper political practice. Hence, the teachings of the *Arthaśāstra*, as decontextualized and idealized as they may be, also serve as an important record of practices and customs current in Kauṭilya's time.

The trick, undoubtedly, to retrieving useful historical information from the *Arthaśāstra* lies in understanding how to read a normative text such as this. First and foremost, the *Arthaśāstra* gives us historical information by relating Kauṭilya's own perspective on statecraft and society. If we are more interested, however, in the society refracted through the teachings of the text, we must find ways to use Kauṭilya's own perspective to illuminate the context within which he wrote. For example, requiring washermen to wear specially marked clothing bespeaks anxiety that they would wear clothes they had been hired to clean:

> [Washermen] who wear garments other than ones marked with a club-sign [denoting their ownership] should pay a fine of three Paṇas [silver coin]. (4.1.14)

Why was such a rule recorded? Certainly, such things must have happened—or been suspected to happen. Similarly, when Kauṭilya records that the positive influence of sacred texts depends on the successful practice of statecraft (1.4.3), is he making an argument against a religious authority that contested the king's authority in the period? Conversely, we might ask about things that seem to be missing in the text. Why does Kauṭilya fail to provide detailed instructions on consolidating conquered territories into a centrally administered empire? Much of the work of scholars comes out of developing useful and incisive ways of querying the text, ways similar to but more sophisticated and detailed than the examples given here.

Ultimately, then, when we read the *Arthaśāstra* we must remain aware that we are entering its timeless world. Our initial efforts are spent orienting ourselves to this vision of the abstract, idealized state, but we do not persist long in this condition.

As soon as we have found our footing, we begin to articulate increasingly useful questions meant to give us insight into the culture that gave birth to the *Arthaśāstra*. The remainder of this Introduction is taken up with exploring several major themes in the text and their cultural context.

Kingship and Royal Authority

Although some states in classical South Asia were confederations of local and regional polities, the archetypal government of the period was the monarchy (see §2.1). Kauṭilya does recognize the existence of other political formations, such as confederacies and tribes, but his text is addressed almost exclusively to kings and their ministers and considers other types of governance only insofar as the king must contend with polities so configured.

In the monarchy described in the *Arthaśāstra*, all political power is theoretically vested in the person of the king, as symbolized by his sole possession of the royal staff or scepter: Kauṭilya's monarchy accommodates no formal or regular mechanism by which other members of the nobility or society at large might withdraw their consent of the king's rule (as we would expect in confederacies or tribes). In fact, the king's theoretical monopoly on power is belied in the text by the repeated recognition that kings were not all-powerful despots, but had to negotiate with a variety of other individuals and institutions possessed of political power within a framework of traditional relationships and authoritative social customs. Given the complexity of power distribution and the unique cultural context within which it is embedded in the *Arthaśāstra*, it is best for us to dispense altogether with freighted theoretical constructs such as "absolute monarchy" or "Oriental despotism" and to examine the theory and practice of kingship as presented by the text itself.

We are best served, therefore, by thinking of kingship as a complex traditional relationship between ruler and ruled within South Asian culture. Some of the breadth and complexity of this relationship, as well as the multiple and contested interpretations of it, will emerge as we examine through this reader the different ways in which the king relates to and interacts with his subjects in the *Arthaśāstra*. Kauṭilya, however, is not (as we might be) concerned with an abstract understanding of kingship meant to satisfy intellectual or historical curiosity. Instead, Kauṭilya wants to focus attention on what he considers the sources and effective uses of royal political power, and the perspective of the *Arthaśāstra* reflects this fundamentally pragmatic intent.

Previously, we looked at the notion of *daṇḍanīti*, "administration of the staff." Recall that the staff (*daṇḍa*) symbolizes the king's monopoly on the use of coercion and violence. Kauṭilya conceives of the entirety of his governance (*daṇḍanīti*), with all of its officials, decrees, and institutions, as an extension of his administration (*nīti*) of the staff (*daṇḍa*).

Many thinkers of the period argued that monarchy was a divine institution or arose out of a primordial social contract. We hear these arguments in the *Arthaśāstra* itself, put into the mouth of a secret agent who is trying to test the loyalty of the king's subjects:

> Secret agents wrangling with each other should engage in debates at sacred fords, assemblies, congregations, and gatherings of people. [One of them should say,] "We hear that this king is endowed with all virtues. But we don't see any virtue in this man who oppresses the inhabitants of the cities and the countryside with fines and taxes." The other [secret agent] should rebut him, as also the people there who would applaud it: "Oppressed by the law of the fish, people made Manu, the son of Vivasvat, king. They allocated to him as his share one-sixth of the grain and one-tenth of the merchandise, as also money. Subsisting on that, kings provide security to the subjects. Those who do not pay fines and taxes take on the sins of kings, while kings who do not provide security take on the sins of their subjects. . . . The position of Indra and Yama—it is this that is occupied by kings, but with their wrath and grace visibly manifest. Divine punishment itself strikes those who treat them with disrespect. Therefore, kings should not be treated with disrespect." (1.13.5–12)

The second agent argues that in the beginning people made Manu, the mythical first human and lawgiver, their king to avoid a society governed by "the law of the fish," wherein the stronger prey on the weaker. This social contract required the people to pay taxes and the king to protect them (particularly from thieves, although that is not made explicit here). This agreement, according to the secret agent, is underwritten by a kind of divine reciprocity, whereby whoever fails to uphold their part of the contract takes on the sins of the other. Kings are not divine themselves, but kingship is. It is the divine institution of the god-kings Indra and Yama. Mortal kings, as upholders of order in society, receive divine protection as they carry out this duty.

Although Kauṭilya instructs the king's agents to promote such ideologies, he does not subscribe to them himself. For Kauṭilya, the origin or basis of kingship is not to be found in external cosmological or sociological conditions. Kingship is not a divine institution passed to men, nor does it emerge from an implicit social contract. Kauṭilya's search for the origin of kingship, its source and basis, leads him to only one thing: the staff—coercive political power. And it is this stark and pragmatic interpretation of royal authority that defines kingship in the *Arthaśāstra*.

This is not to imply that the *Arthaśāstra* does not adhere to a traditional notion of kingship that ascribes specific duties to a king. For example, it goes unquestioned that the king will fulfill his customary obligations to protect his subjects' lives and property, provide for the adjudication of their disputes and uphold justice, and observe cultural traditions—many of the same activities that the king is obliged to perform according to the social contract theory. Moreover, the fulfillment of these duties is not simply pro forma. The king is motivated at times by paternalistic values of justice, protection, and nurturance. Kauṭilya's focus on the staff, however, provides an underlying political explanation of the purpose and value of these traditional duties in terms of the king's practical interests: what will enrich him, what will neutralize his enemies, and what will pacify his subjects.

The *Arthaśāstra* is not a treatise on the theory of governance, however, and Kauṭilya's stark perspective on royal authority is an extension of his unrelenting pragmatism. It is not, one suspects, that Kauṭilya would find other theories of kingship entirely without merit, but simply that the symbol of the staff is most appropriate to an unwavering focus on the material sources of the king's power and effective measures for enhancing and using that power. Certainly, kingship, as a traditional institution in classical South Asia, was understood and explained differently by various constituencies, and the king of the *Arthaśāstra* rules within this complex web of expectations. For Kauṭilya, however, monarchy as a form of government does not take its shape as a response to the needs of the people, but is a traditional institution of which the inner logic is explained by the ambitions of the king and which is animated by the king's unique capacity to coerce and compel others.

Kauṭilya does, in keeping with tradition, see the righteous king as protector of social harmony, but this is more of a justification of the institution than an explanation of its origin. Without a king, he argues, the weak will be preyed upon by the strong, a terrifying state of anarchy and unmitigated predation referred to above as the "law of the fish":

> When [a king] fails to dispense [punishment] . . . it gives rise to the law of the fish—for in the absence of the dispenser of punishment a weak man is devoured by a stronger man, and, protected by him, he prevails. (1.4.13–15)

Royal authority is, however, not believed to be the origin of social order. Rather, society is seen as possessing an innate order—often referred to as *dharma* (law)—that the king must protect and promote:

> People belonging to the four social classes [*varṇas*] and orders of life [i.e., religious modalities], when they are governed by the king through punishment, become devoted to the Law and activities specific to them and follow their respective paths. (1.4.16)

In less ideological terms, this means that social order was based on tradition and that prosperity and peace resulted when different groups followed their traditional occupations and customs (or those traditionally ascribed to them).

Much of governing society, then, meant protecting and promoting the traditional activities of various groups—at least insofar as they did not conflict with royal interests. We see this attitude expressed in many places in the *Arthaśāstra*, such as when the king's top revenue agent and public safety officer, the collector, is instructed to record as part of his bookkeeping the "conventions, customs, and canons" of "regions, villages, castes, families, and associations" (2.7.2), or when laws restricting who may accompany a married woman while walking on the road are suspended in the case of certain groups:

> Accompaniment on the road is not a fault for wives of dancers, minstrels, fishermen, hunters, cowherds, and tavern-keepers, and of other men who give free rein to their wives." (3.4.22)

In the first example, the collector is expected to carry out his duties taking into account local traditions and customs, while in the second, the authority of a rule is seen to emerge out of the practices of a given community.

This does not mean, however, that the king did not still "rule" these communities. Rather, it reflects the extent to which many dimensions of what we think of today as governance were left to local communities such as castes, guilds, and villages. Moreover, it confirms that many of the norms undergirding law and order were felt to arise out of custom rather than from the king. The king was, in theory, absolutely sovereign, and kings certainly exercised that sovereignty liberally when expedient. But, in terms of regular practice, royal administration tended to leave to different communities any activities that the king, for whatever reason, did not or could not regulate. An example of this is seen in the rules on interest rates:

> One and a quarter Paṇas per month on one hundred Paṇas is the righteous rate of interest; five Paṇas, the commercial rate; ten Paṇas for travelers through wild tracts; and twenty Paṇas for seafarers. For anyone charging or making someone charge more than that, the punishment is the lowest seizure-fine. . . . When,

> however, the king is not providing security, [the Justice] should take into account the customs among lenders and borrowers. (3.11.1–3)

Royal administration is discussed in more detail later.

Much of the effort put into exerting political influence in society, then, focused on who was authorized to delineate and police the traditional activities ascribed to different communities. This is precisely the political purpose of Brāhmaṇical ideology as previously discussed. In a passage that is probably a later addition to the *Arthaśāstra* showing the increasing influence of Brāhmaṇical political ideology on the text we read that:

> When among a people the bounds of the Ārya way of life are firmly fixed and the social classes [*varṇa*s] and orders of life are firmly established, and when they are protected by the triple Veda, they prosper and do not perish. (1.3.17)

This expresses the same ideology as passage 1.4.16 cited above. The "Ārya way of life" is linked with the division of society into the four social classes or *varṇa*s, all of which are "protected by the triple Veda." This refers to the hierarchical arrangement of society that grants Brāhmaṇas exalted status and emphasizes the Vedas as authorities on the conduct of all groups in society, making it central to what it means to be Āryan. Reading between the lines, this passage assigns immense political power to the Brāhmaṇas as the preservers and interpreters of Vedic knowledge, which becomes the ultimate authority on how a prosperous society should be organized. What is not made explicit here, but can be found elsewhere, particularly in a genre of texts known as the Dharmaśāstras ("Treatises on Law"), is the argument that the king should rule society according to the instruction of Brāhmaṇas: Brāhmaṇical authority trumps royal authority.

This Brāhmaṇical political ideology is widely accepted in texts from the classical period. It has been taken by many modern scholars as generally representative of political thought in much of the classical period. Critically, however, passages expressing this ideology in the *Arthaśāstra* are, for the most part, interpolations—later additions to the text. If we look back to the older parts of the text—those that can be ascribed to the original composer of the text—we find a far different view of political power expressed:

> What provides enterprise and security to critical inquiry, the Triple [Veda], and Economics is punishment (*daṇḍa*); its administration (*nīti*) is Government (*daṇḍanīti*). Government seeks to acquire what has not been acquired, to safeguard what has been acquired, to augment what has been safeguarded, and to bestow what has been augmented on worthy recipients. On it depends the proper operation of the world. (1.4.3–4)

Kauṭilya here has, without openly opposing them, cleverly asserted the political primacy of the king over the Brāhmaṇas. While recognizing the good of the triple Veda (and, by extension, the Brāhmaṇical community), he asserts that it only has value when government is able to provide security. Political considerations are primary to everything else. In brief, royal authority trumps Brāhmaṇical authority. This is very similar to the opinion of another school on statecraft cited earlier in the text:

> "Government is the only knowledge system [i.e., fundamental area of human activity]," the Auśanasas contend, "for the pursuit of all the knowledge systems is dependent on it."

Kauṭilya, thereby, is able to support fully Brāhmaṇical religiosity, while allowing for the liberal abrogation of its customs and ethical boundaries whenever necessary. This did not escape the notice of many in the classical period and later, who considered Kauṭilya's teachings to be irredeemably wicked.

This debate highlights the extent to which kings were not the only power-holders or social authorities. Other individuals and institutions also commanded the loyalty of the population. These included the orthodox Brāhmaṇical priesthood, other religious institutions (Buddhist, Jain, etc.), families, guilds, teachers, castes, villages, regions, powerful ministers, rival nobility, wealthy individuals, and religious leaders. The actions of kings were constrained by other influential power-holders.

The *Arthaśāstra* recognizes this when it advises the king on how to punish a miserly superintendent within his administration:

> A man who accumulates wealth at the cost of causing deprivation to his dependents and himself is a miser. If he has a retinue [i.e., a large following], he should not be subjected to expropriation; in the opposite case [i.e., if he has no such support], all his property should be confiscated. (2.9.23–24)

Typically, the *Arthaśāstra* advises that the king use his vast network of secret agents, spies, and assassins to accomplish potentially unpopular goals without arousing the ire of the populous. For even though Kauṭilya does not argue that power rests on the consent of the ruled, he does recognize that disaffected subjects dramatically, and sometimes fatally, harm the king's rule (see, e.g., 1.19.27–28 and 7.5.9ff.).

Ultimately, Kauṭilya's focus on *daṇḍa* does not reduce the king to a naked tyrant. Kauṭilya does not jettison tradition, whether it concerns royal or religious practice. It is simply that he measures all things in the end according to how well they support the material power of the king. Ordinarily, the king is quite happy to conform to the traditions of kingship and Brāhmaṇism. At heart, however, Kauṭilya's true faith lies in power, and he does not hesitate to subvert these traditions if it will further the king's interests. It is perhaps best not to interpret this as cynicism, but to take Kauṭilya at his word: the fruitfulness of all human activities—many of which are quite worthwhile—relies ultimately on effective governance.

Given the various attitudes about kingship expressed in classical texts, it is easiest to think of classical South Asian kingship first as a cultural institution, a traditional relationship existing in the minds of ruler and ruled comprised of mutual expectations that transcended a given monarch and penetrated deeply into the psychology of a society. Unlike a despot who continually seeks to dismantle and undermine private groups not directly under his control, the king played his part within a society governed largely by the traditions of its constituent communities. Primary in power, kingship was nevertheless constrained in practice. Woe betide the king who consistently failed his subjects. A loss of legitimacy could quickly dry up the sources upon which his coercive authority depended: "The countryside is the source of all undertakings, and from it is derived might" (7.14.18).

Conceptualizing kingship as a cultural institution and traditional relationship is not to ignore its fundamentally inegalitarian and exploitative dimensions. Instead, it is meant to provide us the opportunity to think of kingship as more than a system of governance. Not only was it a state of affairs that could seem natural and appropriate, but it also allowed for the possibility of feeling affection for, pride in, and loyalty to a king. Kauṭilya's recommendations to the king reflect the various dimensions of kingship as a relationship: he is to variously intimidate, stupefy, overawe, and ingratiate himself to his subjects. Ideally, for Kauṭilya, the people of the kingdom will see the king as immensely powerful, watchful, benevolent, pious, wise, terrifying, dangerous, and fatherly—all at the same time.

Ruling a Kingdom

To orient ourselves properly to the topic of "ruling a kingdom" as discussed in the *Arthaśāstra*, we must expunge two assumptions. First, the government, and its wealth, was not owned by the people: it belonged solely to the king. Second, this government did not have as its primary purpose safeguarding the interests of the populous: it served first to increase the power and might of the king. What we think of as government—domestic administration and foreign policy—were merely instrumental to the primary goals of kingly rule. Hence, when the *Arthaśāstra* reduces the state to "the king and his rule" (8.2.1), we should understand by that the king and his pursuit of power.

Such a political philosophy, however, should not obscure the fact that all of this was to be accomplished through the successful administration of a prosperous kingdom and the prosecution of a successful foreign policy. Understandings of political power frame the concept of success, but mastering the minutiae of practical governance is what actually brings it about. And this is Kauṭilya's strength: he is a master of the dizzying array of complex practices required to govern a kingdom successfully.

We can break down governance as presented in the *Arthaśāstra* into a few major areas of concern: maintaining the loyalty of one's subjects, cultivating prosperity and extracting wealth, dispensing justice and preserving public safety, and outwitting one's foreign rivals. A successful king accomplished all of these either through the effective operation of governmental bodies and regulated social institutions (such as courts and markets; see Chapters 3–5) or through specific initiatives or "undertakings" meant to address acute or irregular needs (such as assassinating a political rival, building an irrigation network, or invading an enemy's kingdom; see §1.2 and Chapters 6–7).

According to the *Arthaśāstra*, the king projected power and addressed acute threats to his rule partly by means of an extensive network of spies and informants (see §5.1). They were the king's eyes and ears, and his subjects would have constantly been aware that the king's agents might be listening in on their conversations. This network was flexible enough to promote propaganda on the king's behalf, as well as to carry out extrajudicial executions and abductions. As such, it was a primary tool in grooming public sentiment and disrupting efforts opposed to the interests of the king. A king could also undertake actions or issue public decrees pleasing the population (such as granting amnesty) or intimidating them (such as imposing curfews). As a last resort, of course, the king's troops could be brought to bear on communities or regions in revolt.

The cultivation of prosperity and extraction of wealth was accomplished by institutions and policies meant to support a maximally productive society and efficient taxation thereof. Investment in agricultural infrastructure, grants of land, loans of seed, cultivation of trade, establishment of extractive enterprises (such as mines), operation of state manufacturies, monopolies on certain goods, regulation of markets, and effective collection of fees and taxes worked together to promote abundance in the countryside and city, all of which meant greater revenue for the state and happiness for the subjects.

The preservation of social order rested, in no small part, on the king's ability to provide a minimal level of material abundance to his subjects. Beyond this, public order was maintained through access to courts for dispute resolution, proactive efforts to root out criminal enterprise, and the investigation and prosecution of criminal offenses such as theft and murder. The king also materially supported and regulated temples and took efforts to prevent or counteract calamities such as famine, fire, and disease. Finally, kings had to address the possibility of attacks by forest tribes, bandits, and, above all, foreign armies.

A king's success hinged to a great extent on his ability to "outwit" his foreign rivals. The *Arthaśāstra* has a technical term for this, *atisaṃdhā-*. The "outwitting" or "overreaching" of rivals was the goal of all deliberations on foreign policy. Whether through diplomacy, intimidation, supplication, or open hostility, a king always sought some kind of advantage against ally and enemy alike. The king had at his disposal, to this end, a body of counselors who reflected deeply on strategy and tactics; envoys able to carry through his stratagems in the courts of other kings; secret agents capable of inciting revolt, recruiting double agents, and assassinations; and, not least of all, his army, which he could use to intimidate or vanquish his adversaries. Kings who could outwit their opponents might find success even in the face of a stronger enemy. Conquest, thus, did not necessarily mean occupying and integrating rival kingdoms, but rather expanding one's influence to the greatest extent possible through the most effective means.

The King's Administration

While the king attended personally to some aspects of governance, most he left to his appointed officials. For, as the *Arthaśāstra* tells us:

> Because tasks are numerous and have to be carried out at the same time and in different places, he should employ Ministers to carry out what he cannot directly observe for fear that the proper time and place may pass by. (1.9.8)

The structure and officials of the royal administration are discussed in detail in Chapters 3–5. Only a brief sketch is offered here.

The king, of course, is the chief executive and ultimate authority in all matters. He is directly assisted by an elite leadership team. His main advisor, confidant, and operative is a powerful and learned Brāhmaṇa called the counselor-chaplain (§3.1). A number of other powerful counselors also advise the king on a daily basis (§1.2) as well as the crown prince and army commander (§7.1). Between them, these elite officials conferred with the king on the most sensitive matters of state.

Reporting directly and only to the king and the counselor-chaplain is the king's extensive intelligence network (§5.1). These agents not only gathered intelligence on officials as well as subjects, but also carried out whatever the king needed done secretly. Some of the ministers, such as the collector and the magistrates, also maintained extensive spy networks.

Assisted by his counselors and agents, the king vetted and appointed a number high-ranking ministers, such as the treasurer (§3.1), collector (§3.1), city manager (§2.4), justice (§4.1), magistrate (§5.2), head of the palace guard (§2.3), and envoy (§6.3). Each of these ministers is ascribed specific rights and duties, such as managing the treasury (treasurer), collecting revenue from the countryside (collector), adjudicating disputes (justice), and investigating murders (magistrate). From among these ministers the king convened a council that

> . . . ponder[s] over the king's own party and that of his enemy. With regard to activities, they should initiate what has been left undone, complete what has been initiated, enhance what has been completed, and bring the commission to a successful conclusion. (1.15.51–52)

Day-to-day operation of state functions were largely carried out by a lower class of official called superintendents (§3.2). Each superintendent oversaw a specific area of state activity, such as the regulation of markets, mining, shipping, or alcohol. Although appointed by the king and theoretically answerable to him, it appears that the collector managed the activities of the superintendents. All superintendents were provided with a budget at the beginning of the fiscal year and were expected to return a profit to the treasury. As the chief revenue officer, it was the collector who oversaw their accounts.

Other dimensions of daily administration were carried out by ministers such as the city manager (§2.4), justices (§4.1), and magistrates (§5.2) and their underlings. These offices were focused primarily on public safety and order, but also had the capacity to generate revenue through the assessment of fines, the seizure of property, and, in the case of the city manager, tax collection.

Much of royal administration focused on diplomatic and military operations. Frequently, the most consequential (and also invigorating) decisions made by kings involved matters of peace and war with other kingdoms (§6.1–2). Kings relied heavily on envoys (§6.3) and secret agents (§6.4) to outwit foreign rulers. Diplomatic forays were potentially momentous affairs, with envoys sometimes authorized to negotiate on behalf of the king.

The *Arthaśāstra* favors treaties to open hostilities, but once diplomacy had ended and conflict had become inevitable, the king took his army into the field under the coordination of the army commander. The army (§7.1) was comprised of many kinds of troops, from permanent, hereditary warriors to military guilds, tribal warriors, soldiers provided by allies, and captured troops. Rank was assigned based on the number of troops under one's command. A full army consisted of an elephant corps, chariot corps, cavalry, and infantry. Military expeditions were extensive and required the construction of a city-size military encampment (§7.2). Along with opportunistic guerrilla tactics, combat was generally carried out in pitched battles (§7.3), and the battlefield conduct of honorable warriors was highly scrutinized. Victory in a pitched battle often meant the elimination of a foe's offensive fighting force; conquest of his kingdom frequently required, in addition, laying siege to and assaulting the fortified defenses of the capital city (§7.4). The king is advised to be magnanimous in victory and to try to win the people of the conquered kingdom to his side through various generous and pious displays (§7.5).

The Layout of the Kingdom

Kauṭilya has in mind in the *Arthaśāstra* a small, regional kingdom. He discusses a settlement hierarchy that begins, at the lowest level, with the countless agricultural villages that dot the countryside (§2.6). These villages are to be populated mostly by lower-class agriculturalists, people with the knowledge and work ethic to produce abundance from the backbreaking work of farming. Each of these villages has a headman, probably one of the larger landholders, who acts as a representative to the king's officials. It is easy to imagine that, aside from the visits from an agent of the collector (come to take the king's share of the harvest), villages saw very little of the king and his rule. Indeed, life at the village level, where the vast majority of the population lived, occurred within a very small, local horizon. Most were self-sufficient in terms of food, governance, and education, and most villagers would never have need or occasion to travel far from the village of their birth.

To visit markets, to see a justice, or to meet with a revenue officer, however, a villager would have to travel to the next largest settlement, the collection center. Kauṭilya says that there should be a collection center for every ten villages. These market towns would have been the smallest settlements to house even the most humble agents of the king and his officials. Above the collection center are successively larger cities, such as the county seat and district municipality, where higher-ranking state officials and judicial services could be found.

The chief authority in the countryside was the collector. His responsibilities gave him control over not only the various superintendents and their activities, but over a vast network of revenue agents and spies. He needed the latter to determine the actual tax burden of the countryside through a detailed census of households, fields, and economic activities. Undoubtedly, they also made much other valuable information available to him.

Moreover, the collector guided the activities of the magistrates, who investigated crimes and those suspected of criminal behavior. The residents of the countryside, from the villages to the larger cities, probably had far more awareness of and contact with the collector than the king himself.

In the middle of these villages and progressively larger cities lies the capital (§2.2). It is a massive city surrounded by imposing fortified walls and a series of crocodile-filled moats. Within its ramparts the city is laid out, we are told, according to a neat, geometric plan. The general plan calls for three north/south highways and three east/west highways to divide the city space into sixteen sectors. The king's palace and the main temples lie at the center of the city, and the different social groups and hereditary vocations are assigned to different sectors. Each of the six highways terminates at a gate set in the city walls.

The capital is governed by the city manager (§2.4), who commands the city guard and has the power to enforce public safety ordinances, building codes, fire bans, curfews, and entry and exit from the city. The city manager is also responsible for collecting income tax from the city's inhabitants, a massive undertaking that endowed him with a great deal of power and knowledge over who dwelt in the city, the nature of their business, their finances, and their movement. The king's palace is overseen by the head of the palace guard, who tightly controls all persons and materials moving into or out of the palace (§2.3).

Arable land in the kingdom is given over to agriculture, and the king actively promotes the development of farmland. He also, however, exploits the timber, mineral, and forest resources of the countryside. Forests were classified as producing elephants, game, or produce such as timber, and the king appoints officials to protect forests, cultivate elephant herds, start mining operations, and operate factories. Marginally productive enterprises could be leased out to private groups, yielding a "mixed economy." Finally, the king maintained the major trade routes—waterways as well as roads—and ensured the safety of merchants traveling the land.

The borders of the countryside abutting neighboring kingdoms are defended by fortresses controlled by frontier commanders. Such fortresses served not only to regulate traffic into and out of the kingdom, but also as retreats for the king during invasion or revolt. Frontiers bordering wild regions are defended through alliances with the various tribes that dwell there. Along with the frontier commanders, they discourage banditry and guard the countryside against dangerous elements.

The coasts of the kingdom, particularly at the mouths of rivers, supported port cities overseen by the superintendent of shipping. He maintained the king's fleet of ships, from river ferries and fishing boats to oceangoing vessels. The *Arthaśāstra* emphasizes overseas trade with distant lands, and lists of trade goods in the text include items imported from the eastern Mediterranean as well as East Asia. The superintendent of shipping was responsible for collecting revenue from private fishermen and merchants as well as maintaining the health of their enterprises through tax remediation, provision of equipment, and disaster aid. Just as with the countryside, the kingdom's rivers and seas supported a mixed economy of both royal and private enterprises.

Society

The world of the *Arthaśāstra* is a world seen from the throne, or, at least, from right behind it. It provides, in other words, a top-down view of the kingdom. What is more, the *Arthaśāstra* is really only concerned with society inasmuch as it intersects with state activities. Thus, the text is not particularly well suited to providing a sense of the composition of society or what everyday life might have been like for the king's subjects. Nevertheless, we can glean a good deal of useful information about how people lived from incidental references in the text.

To begin with, people did not think of themselves as "citizens" of "nations," but as subjects of a king—among other things. Being the subject of a king in classical South Asia was understood within the roles ascribed by the traditional relationship of kingship as noted before. But, it did not invoke a positive legal framework strongly defining the individual in relation to the state after the manner of citizenship. Most individuals would have defined themselves through a series of traditional relationships: child of a certain family; member of a certain clan, guild, or ethnos; practitioner of a certain vocation; inhabitant of a certain region; student of a certain teacher; employee of a certain master; and so forth. For many, their relationships with other institutions were far more formative of personal identity than being the subject of a certain king. Certainly, as we have seen, the lives of most people were ruled as much or more by the traditions of the various communities to which they belonged than by the king's edicts and rules.

The picture of society that emerges through the *Arthaśāstra* is at the same time both thoroughly patriarchal and hierarchical. To begin with, the *Arthaśāstra*, like all Sanskrit treatises of the period, was written by men for men and primarily about men. The archetypal social agent in the treatise is the independent man, who, by definition, is permitted to engage in valid public transactions such as contracting labor or lending money. He has reached the age of maturity (16 years old) and is the head of his own family, whether as father or elder brother in a joint family. The opportunity to carry out valid public transactions was disallowed for most others:

> Transactions . . . shall not be valid . . . [that are] executed by dependents, by a son living with his father, by a father living with his son, by a brother excluded from the family, by a younger son who is a coparcener [of an undivided family estate], by a woman living with her husband or son, by a slave or a person given as a pledge, by one who is below or beyond the legal age, and by a notorious criminal, renouncer, cripple, or someone who has fallen on hard times—except when they have been appointed to execute the transaction. (3.1.12)

Such a list paints a stark picture of how power was distributed within society, and how most were kept in a state of dependence by virtue of sex or family status. Nevertheless, we must keep in mind here the strongly normative dimension of the text: mitigating circumstances might grant individuals other than independent males access to certain public institutions.

Women appear in the text in a number of subsidiary roles, such as queens, courtesans, wives, daughters, but also as nuns or palace guards and secret agents (here, again, Kauṭilya demonstrates his willingness to disregard customary boundaries when politically expedient). Outside of renunciation and royal service, however, women are assigned to traditional roles of dependence, from birth through death, where they could expect much of their lives, including their movement and communication, to be controlled to a greater or lesser extent. Kauṭilya conforms to these customs, but does not display the strident misogyny found in many contemporary treatises: he generally defends women's control of their own marital property, the right to divorce with cause, and the choice to remarry as widows, although doing so (particularly against the wishes of their in-laws) will cost them their marital property. More detail can be found in the discussion of family law at §4.4. While certain women experienced greater measures of freedom, most would have suffered the many injustices to be expected in a society in which access to public institutions was limited for the most part to men.

As previously mentioned, this *Arthaśāstra* represents one expression of classical Āryan culture. For the *Arthaśāstra*, the term "Āryan" refers to the indigenous, "civilized" inhabitants of South Asia. Excluded groups include *mleccha*s (foreigners), *aṭavī*s (tribal inhabitants who lived on the periphery of Āryan society), and Caṇḍālas (the lowest of all classes), all of whom were thought to deviate in some manner from the Āryan way of life. For the most part, we can presume that the text is addressed primarily to Āryan society, however construed.

There is some ambiguity in the text as to the composition of Āryan society. The orthodox Brāhmaṇical view of society held that only the three upper *varṇas*—Brāhmaṇa, Kṣatriya, and Vaiśya—were Āryans. Members of the fourth *varṇa*, Śūdras, were non-Āryan, as were a whole range of outcaste and foreign groups "beneath" the Śūdras, who were considered *avarṇa*, "without *varṇa*." The concept of *varṇa* plays a limited role in the *Arthaśāstra*, and passages in which it does appear frequently bear marks of having been added to the text after its original composition. Even where we do read of *varṇa* in the extant treatise, we note that the *Arthaśāstra* considers almost all indigenous communities to be Āryan, including Śūdras and most lower-class communities (Caṇḍālas, who may originally have been a tribal group, are the exception).

From the perspective of governance, the *Arthaśāstra* identifies individuals based on the following parameters, here as recorded by a court clerk prior to a lawsuit:

> [The court clerk] should first write down . . . the region, village, caste, lineage, name, and occupation of the plaintiff and the defendant. (3.1.17)

A similar list is found among the information the city manager's agents are to record in their census:

> [The revenue officer] should find out the number of individual men and women within each [group of households] in terms of their castes, lineages, names, and occupations, as well as their incomes and expenditures. (2.36.3)

The information pertinent to identifying an individual are his or her place, caste (*jāti*), lineage (*gotra*), name, and occupation. Caste (*jāti*) refers to the "clan" or "birth group" within which the individual was born. Each *jāti* had its own "law," or specific customs, that would have been enforced on its members by some kind of leadership. The functioning of *jāti*s is not described in the *Arthaśāstra*, but based on later information, we can assume that membership in a *jāti* governed whom one could marry or consort with. These *jāti*s comprise the basic units of the hierarchical "caste system," but are different from *varṇa*s, which are theoretical groupings of actual *jāti*s. Lineage (*gotra*) refers to a family's identity based on the husband's descent through father and grandfather back to the patriarch of the line. Occupation is self-evident. These were the formative elements of an individual's identity inasmuch as the state was concerned. Other information was either generally irrelevant to the state or easily implied from the information given.

For the most part, however, the *Arthaśāstra* takes hierarchy for granted. Several passages allude to encounters among "superiors," "equals," and "inferiors"—a key indication of pervasive hierarchical awareness. This hierarchy depended on many factors, such as ranking between *jātis*, biological sex, seniority within a family or *jāti*, seniority within unions or corporations, and administrative rank. The Brāhmaṇical system of *varṇa* attempts to provide one interpretation of hierarchy, but actual conditions were much more complex and not so baldly linear nor necessarily favorable to Brāhmaṇas.

Caste and lineage designations, however, do not figure strongly into governance itself. Perhaps Kauṭilya avoids discussing specific castes so as not to link his text too closely with any given social context (see above). For this purpose, instead, the *Arthaśāstra* focuses on basic vocational groups. We find no master list of these groups in the text, but the recurrence of certain phrases allows us to identify the major categories. We read, for example, that the collector's revenue agents, as part of their census, were to record, among other things:

> . . . [how] many . . . are farmers, cowherds, traders, artisans, laborers, and slaves. (2.35.4)

Clearly, these are the productive groups and represent the bulk of society. Other major groups discussed include renouncers, magicians and other arcane specialists, various performers, brothel-keepers, tavern-keepers, food venders, householders, village officials, royal agents, soldiers, physicians, and attendants. Although the class identities reflected in the concept of *varṇa* played a role in private disputes, the state, as reflected in the *Arthaśāstra*, tends to govern the king's subjects based on vocation, age, sex, etc., rather than class. Of course, we must assume that in classical South Asia, as in other times and places, vocation was strongly related to class and status, which must in fact have dramatically influenced how states actually governed.

As an all-powerful ruler drawn from an aristocratic family, the king existed far away from and above the daily experience of nearly all his subjects. There could be reverence, fear, respect, awe, and even love or hatred, but there could be no sense of camaraderie or bonhomie. The king's authority required that he be treated publicly with the greatest formality and the highest level of respect. The model used in the *Arthaśāstra* is generally paternal: the king stands in relation to his subjects like a good father to his children. And, just as between a parent and child, there is never equality, nor could the king be treated generally as another member of society.

All dimensions of the king's authority were highly personalized and perceived to reflect directly his character. His agents, both secret and public, extended this sensibility broadly into society. And, while his singular authority made him the ultimate judge and defender of justice, most of his subjects tried simply to keep to themselves and stay away from the unsolicited notice of his servants. The *Arthaśāstra* likens a king to fire, emphasizing his capacity to scorch anyone who might have dealings with him:

> For a wise man must always protect himself first; for the conduct of those who serve the king is said to be like (that of those who work with) fire. (5.4.16)

The personalized quality of a king's rule also meant that popular disaffection among his subjects did not discriminate between the king as a ruler and the state as a political entity. Kauṭilya notes that a king with disaffected subjects might easily welcome a conquering king to institute an entirely new rule. Perhaps because of this, the *Arthaśāstra* encourages the king to be approachable, lest injustice persist in his kingdom because his subjects are too fearful to seek justice from him.

Religion and Ethics

The ideology of the *Arthaśāstra* is thoroughly pragmatic. Political power, one might argue, is Kauṭilya's religion. Nevertheless, the extant text advises the king to observe traditional ritual practices, employ Brāhmaṇas priests, render gifts and exemptions to Brāhmaṇas (particularly the learned), enshrine deities in government buildings, situate temples at the center of the capital, and carry out other "religious" activities. While many of these instructions were undoubtedly added to the text after Kauṭilya composed it, the *Arthaśāstra* nevertheless takes what we might think of as Brāhmaṇical or Hindu religiosity as its norm—including the honoring of Brāhmaṇas and use of Brāhmaṇical religious concepts—as opposed to the contemporary Buddhist or Jain practices. How are we to reconcile this apparent adherence to Brāhmaṇism with Kauṭilya's commitment to political expedience?

An excellent example of Kauṭilya's attitude toward religion is provided in the first test the king administers to determine the integrity of a candidate for an office within his administration:

> The Counselor-Chaplain becomes indignant at being appointed to officiate at a sacrifice of a person at whose sacrifice one is forbidden to officiate or to teach such a person. The king should then dismiss him. He should send secret agents to instigate each Minister individually under oath: This king is unrighteous. Come on! Let us install in his place some other righteous person—a pretender from his family, a prince in disfavor, a member of the royal household, the man who is the sole support of the kingdom, a neighboring lord, a forest chieftain, or a man who has risen to power. Everyone likes this idea. What about you? If he rebuffs it, he is a man of integrity. That is the secret test relating to righteousness [*dharma*]. (1.10.2–4)

This ruse has the king publicly asking his counselor-chaplain, a learned Brāhmaṇa, to break Brāhmaṇical law. To pass this test, an official must demonstrate that his loyalty to the king is greater than his religious convictions. The so-called test relating to righteousness encapsulates Kauṭilya's treatment of religion. On the one hand, it is assumed that the king publicly supports Brāhmaṇical religion: he has a Brāhmaṇa as his counselor-chaplain and sends him to perform religious tasks within a Brāhmaṇical ritual framework. On the other hand, the king not only asks him to break Brāhmaṇical custom, but actually uses his Brāhmaṇa counselor to ensure that his officials are not overly pious! Hence, we see an adherence to Brāhmaṇical religion that belies a radical and amoral pragmatism.

Kauṭilya exploits the religious faith of others in the text repeatedly, but this, by itself, does not indicate a fundamental atheism. In a few places, it appears that Kauṭilya might be expressing some kind of personal faith. For example, he instructs the king to maintain private religious practice as part of a daily routine (§1.3). Similarly, the *Arthaśāstra* advises the king to have rituals performed to counteract calamities assailing the kingdom alongside practical remediation efforts (§2.7). Other such examples can be cited, and yet we can never be certain that Kauṭilya isn't promoting such religious activities for purely pragmatic reasons.

Perhaps his attitude about religion is best expressed in a discussion of what makes for good and bad policy:

> Good and bad policy pertain to the human realm, while good and bad fortune pertain to the divine realm. Divine and human activity, indeed, makes the world run. The divine consists of what is caused by an invisible agent. Of this, attaining a desirable result is good fortune, while attaining an undesirable result is bad fortune. The human consists of what is caused by a visible agent. Of this, the success of enterprise and security is good policy, while their failure is bad policy. This is within the range of thought, whereas the divine is beyond the range of thought. (6.2.6)

In other words, there are forces that we can control and those that we can't. What we can't control affects us as good or bad luck. The work of politics—of enacting effective policy—is working with what we can control. The question, then, is to what extent Kauṭilya believed humans could effectively petition divine powers. This, unfortunately, is not clear in the text. But, we can observe that Kauṭilya works almost exclusively within a materialist paradigm, relying on effective human actions to bring about desired results. All of this while maintaining the trappings of Brāhmaṇical religiosity.

One exception to Kauṭilya's materialism is his faith in the arcane arts, particularly magic and divination. Along with certain practical measures, magical concoctions help to protect the royal residence (§2.3) and gems reputed to have special powers safeguard the king from poisoning (§1.4). In addition to his personal priests, chef, and physician, the king is advised daily by his astrologer (§1.3), and the counselor-chaplain is himself a master of not only statecraft, but also several arcane arts including divination and magico-ritual practices of the *Atharva Veda* (§3.1). Moreover, Book Fourteen deals extensively with magical and nonmagical recipes for use against enemy troops. Generally, Kauṭilya gives more credence to what we might think of as magic—supernaturally effective practices—than to the supplication of independent divine powers.

Kauṭilya's public promotion of Brāhmaṇical religiosity is also belied by the extreme amorality of many of his instructions. The text repeatedly advises the king to carry out murders, frame innocent people, and do generally whatever is necessary to enhance the king's political power. It isn't that Kauṭilya revels in the immorality of these acts. One is struck, rather, by the matter-of-fact manner in which such advice is rendered. Nowhere does the text recognize any misgivings about the appropriateness of its nefarious plots, nor does Kauṭilya ever raise the question of ethics or the spiritual consequences of committing such heinous deeds. Kauṭilya tells us without irony that the ideal king is, among other things, "righteous, truthful . . . providing the prescribed retribution for benefits provided and wrongs done . . . [and] free of . . . brutality" (6.1.6). We might, then, think of such "dirty work" as a necessary evil of governing, precisely the reality prompting some orthodox Brāhmaṇas to forbid their kind from serving kings at all.

Yet the traditional bond between king and Brāhmaṇa is evident in the text, even if not in the precise form promoted within orthodox Brāhmaṇical ideology. Rather than as the servant of the Brāhmaṇa, it is the Brāhmaṇa—in the form of the counselor-chaplain—who serves the king and his interests. The mutual benefit of this relationship is evident: the king gains from the prestige of the Brāhmaṇical elite by observing Brāhmaṇical custom (at least publicly), and Brāhmaṇas and

Brāhmaṇical ideology gain from his royal patronage. This model holds good, as long as we realize that, from the perspective of the *Arthaśāstra*, what happens within the king's administration has everything to do with the king's interests and only marginally to do with Brāhmaṇical interests (if at all).

The religiosity of the king's subjects is minimally discussed in the *Arthaśāstra*, although we read that it included domestic rituals, public rituals, festivals, pilgrimage, and worship at the temples of Hindu deities. In addition, we read of belief in ghosts and spirits, consultation with various kinds of diviners, devotion to holy men, and renunciation. Kauṭilya makes mention of these temples to various deities, sects, hermitages, monasteries, Brāhmaṇical villages, and other religious institutions without shedding much light on them. Several kinds of renunciates are mentioned, including what we would now identify as different kinds of Hindu renouncers as well as Buddhists and Ājīvakas, toward whom the extant text has a somewhat ambivalent attitude.

The baseline religiosity of the treatise conforms generally to what we think of as "Hinduism" in the classical period, although we have very little sense of how the various elements came together to represent a coherent "religion" or "religions." While there are some interesting facts to be gleaned incidentally in the text, it would be more accurate to say that Kauṭilya actually pays religion little mind, as though it were a given in society, but only related to issues of governance in limited ways. The major presence of religious institutions in the text comes in the form of religious professionals—whether Brāhmaṇa priests, magicians, astrologers, or, especially, ascetics—as servants and agents of the king. It is ascetics, in particular, whom Kauṭilya discusses most, as they seem to have been very useful as informants, spies, and secret agents for the king, given their ability to wander across political boundaries without arousing suspicion.

Conquest and Success

As mentioned at the beginning of this Introduction, the *Arthaśāstra* has in mind a small, regional polity. Nevertheless, the text conceives of the king as "one desiring conquest" (*vijigīṣu*) (§6.1). The second half of the *Arthaśāstra*, covering foreign policy, gains its shape by following a king through the process of contemplating foreign policy, negotiating pacts, preparing his army, marching, engaging in battle, and besieging an enemy's fortress. This is the focus of ambitious kings. The ultimate goal is the conquest of the world "to its four directions."

Despite this outlook, however, the *Arthaśāstra* is not an explicitly imperial text, for it contains no instructions on how to deal with the political and administrative challenges of ruling a large, transregional polity. All of the administrative detail in the text occurs at the level of the capital city or the local region. We read nothing of how a network of such polities might be fitted into larger political frameworks, although it is possible that the model presented in the *Arthaśāstra* is meant to be scalable to larger political formations by establishing a generic template for regional administration across a large empire.

But, if conquest provides one logic for kingship in the *Arthaśāstra*, another is provided by the general purpose of statecraft: acquiring greater wealth, protecting that wealth, growing that wealth, and spending it on worthy people and projects. This model emphasizes the enrichment of one's inherited kingdom and bequeathing it to one's heirs in a better condition than received. If kings find their calling in glory and conquest, they find it also in stability and survival. We might be best served to think of the first half of the *Arthaśāstra* as emphasizing the king's role as wise administrator and the second half emphasizing his role as conquering hero. Somewhere within this polarity, kings established their identities and found either success or failure in the pursuit of statecraft.

Contents of the Complete *Arthaśāstra*

(Selections presented in this volume are taken from Topics appearing in bold.)

BOOK ONE
On the Subject of Training

BOOK TWO

On the Activities of Superintendents

BOOK SIX
Basis of the Circle

BOOK SEVEN
On the Sixfold Strategy

BOOK EIGHT
On the Subject of Calamities

BOOK NINE

Activity of a King Preparing to March into Battle

BOOK TEN

On War

BOOK ELEVEN

Conduct Toward Confederacies

BOOK TWELVE

On the Weaker King

BOOK THIRTEEN
Means of Capturing a Fort

BOOK FOURTEEN
On Esoteric Practices

BOOK FIFTEEN
Organization of a Scientific Treatise

Select Bibliography

Drekmeier, Charles. 1962. *Kingship and Community in Early India*. Stanford: Stanford University Press.

Kangle, R. P. 1972. *The Kauṭilīya Arthaśāstra.* Part II: An English Translation with Critical and Explanatory Notes. 2nd ed. (1st ed., 1963). Bombay: University of Bombay.

———. 1965. *The Kauṭilīya Arthaśāstra.* Part III: A Study. Bombay: University of Bombay.

McClish, Mark. 2009. *Political Brahmanism and the State: A Compositional History of the* Arthaśāstra. Ph.D. Dissertation, University of Texas, Austin.

Olivelle, Patrick (Tr.). 2013. *King, Governance, and Law: Kauṭilya's* Arthaśāstra. New York: Oxford University Press.

Scharfe, Hartmut. 1989. *The State in Indian Tradition.* Leiden: Brill.

———. 1993. *Investigations in Kauṭalya's Manual of Political Science.* Wiesbaden: Harrassowitz.

Spellman, John W. 1964. *Political Theory of Ancient India. A Study of Kingship from the Earliest Times to Circa A.D. 300.* Oxford: Oxford University Press.

Trautmann, Thomas. 2012. Arthaśāstra: *The Science of Wealth.* New Delhi: Allen Lane/Penguin.

———. 1971. *Kauṭilya and the* Arthaśāstra: *A Statistical Investigation of the Authorship and Evolution of the Text.* Leiden: Brill.

Selections from the *Arthaśāstra*

Chapter One

How to be a Good King

The *Arthaśāstra* gives advice on rulership to kings. The kingdom envisioned by the text is a small, regional polity. As we read the *Arthaśāstra*, we must keep in mind the intimate relationship between a king and his kingdom. More so than other kinds of rulers, a monarch is uniquely identified with the state itself. The *Arthaśāstra* does not distinguish between the king's rule and the kingdom itself, often referring to both with the same Sanskrit term, *rājya*. The king's rule constitutes the state, and his personal character equates to the quality of his governance.

Although carried out within a framework of customary relationships and durable governmental institutions, the *Arthaśāstra* nevertheless conceives the king's rule as a necessarily proactive and ongoing project. Successful governance did not result simply from the regular functioning of state institutions, but was felt to depend to a great extent on the specific initiatives undertaken by the king, on his ability to see these initiatives successfully completed, and on his success in effectively policing his officials and subjects. If his kingdom were to enjoy stability, abundance, and safety, it was because of his ability to conceive and carry out shrewd initiatives.

As such, the *Arthaśāstra*'s advice to the king goes beyond policy and political strategy to include the care of the king as a physical, emotional, spiritual, and ethical being. All of these aspects of the king's person were felt to have a direct impact on his governance and the lives of his subjects. Thus, while the *Arthaśāstra* never departs from its instinctive focus on realpolitik, it also demonstrates in its teachings a concern for the well-being and personal development of the king himself.

The importance of the person of the king is also evident in the *Arthaśāstra*'s concern for his physical safety. Assassination was an ever-present threat, and monarchies, where the solvency of the government and the maintenance of social order relied so greatly on the personal authority of the king, particularly feared the political and social disorder unleashed by a power vacuum. The institutions of the state were neither designed nor empowered to ensure a smooth transition of power, and the sudden demise of the ruler was an invitation to chaos as competing interests looked to improve their lot.

The following selections illustrate how the successful practice of kingship is rooted in an attentiveness to a king's inner development and outer safety, embracing such far-flung concerns as a firm grounding in the different areas of intellectual inquiry, the cultivation of moral character, learning how to navigate the tricky matter of seeking counsel, the organization of daily activities, and the protection of the king's person. Ultimately, a successful king is marked by the cultivation of self-control through training in intellectual and physical pursuits. In the hands of knowledgeable elders, wise counselors, and reliable guardians, the king is meant to evolve into a shrewd and disciplined leader capable of protecting himself from the lure of destructive vices, skillfully administering his kingdom and outmaneuvering his enemies.

1.1 Training of a King

Education

The *Arthaśāstra* begins by listing the four sciences or "knowledge systems." Each knowledge system represents a fundamental sphere of human understanding and activity: reasoned inquiry, religious authority, economics, and government. Collectively, the knowledge systems provide a taxonomy that organizes human activity into its most basic categories. Among the different intellectual circles in classical South Asia, there were significant disagreements over the nature, number, and relative importance of the knowledge systems, a debate ultimately about which kinds of human activities were the most fundamental or important. The reader gains insight into the intellectual, social, and political attitudes of the *Arthaśāstra*'s composer by analyzing his presentation of the knowledge systems.

Among the four, Kauṭilya holds the science of government (*daṇḍanīti*) in special regard. This is only to be expected, perhaps, as the *Arthaśāstra* is itself a treatise (*śāstra*) on government. Even though he recognizes the benefits of the three other knowledge systems, Kauṭilya considers them all to depend on meeting the political requirements of the science of governance. His bias is, however, more than parochial: by claiming special status for the science of government, Kauṭilya has implied that political interests must be satisfied before intellectual, spiritual, ethical, or economic concerns can be addressed. Without directly or wholly rejecting the other three, Kauṭilya uses his presentation of the knowledge systems to argue that political necessity always trumps philosophical, economic, or religious objections. This puts him at odds with the orthodox worldview of South Asia's elite religious community, the priestly Brāhmaṇa class, according to whom governance was meant to be carried out according to the scriptural injunctions of the triple Veda (i.e., "the Triple"). Thus, in the opening to his text, Kauṭilya has made his first crafty move: he has endorsed the authority of the triple Veda while actually asserting the prerogative of politics over religion, of the royalty over the Brāhmaṇical elite.

Literally, *daṇḍanīti* means "administration of the staff." The staff (*daṇḍa*) is a royal implement symbolizing the king's coercive authority. It signifies that its bearer possesses a unique right (and responsibility) to use violence and an ever-present willingness to do so. Hence, *daṇḍa* is most frequently translated as "punishment." That the threat of violence was recognized as the source of the king's coercive power is evident in the various ways the term *daṇḍa* was used in political discourse, where it might refer to a monetary fine, corporal punishment, or the king's army. Backed up by the threat of force, these various kinds of *daṇḍa* were understood as the chief means by which the king exerted his will and ruled his kingdom.

The term *daṇḍanīti*, however, does not refer only to the use of coercion in the *Arthaśāstra*, but acts as a synecdoche for the practice of governance in general. Even though successful governance was felt to be rooted in the king's monopoly on violence, the project of governing was considered a much larger and more complex undertaking. Although the office of the king was to a great extent defined by unchallenged possession of the *daṇḍa*, the successful use of that staff nevertheless sometimes required strategies other than coercion.

> Critical Inquiry, the Triple, Economics, and Government—these are the knowledge systems. [1.2.1]
>
> Sāṃkhya, Yoga, Lokāyata[1]—these constitute Critical Inquiry. It benefits the people by critically inquiring through logical reasoning into the Triple to determine what is Law (*dharma*) and what is contrary to Law, into Economics to determine what is Success (*artha*) and what is contrary to Success, into Government to determine what is good policy and what is bad policy, and about the relative strength and weakness of these knowledge systems. It keeps their mind steadfast in times of adversity and prosperity. And it makes them skillful in thinking, speaking, and acting. [1.2.10–11]
>
> The three Vedas—Sāma, Ṛg, and Yajur—constitute the Triple; and the Atharva Veda and Itihāsa Veda[2] are the Vedas. This Law laid down in the triple Veda is of benefit because it enunciates

1. Sāṃkhya is one of the oldest philosophical systems. It is especially important because it provided many of the cosmological categories that became commonplace in later Indian thought. Yoga in this context probably refers to the system of logic, later known as Nyāya, rather than to the well-known system of mental training. Lokāyata (also called Cārvāka) was an old system of materialistic or natural philosophy that rejected the existence of a spiritual realm and the belief in rebirth.

2. *Atharva Veda* is traditionally counted as the fourth Veda. However, in the earlier enumeration expressed in the terse Triple only three are recognized as authoritative. *Itihāsa Veda*: the category *itihāsa* (narratives that are viewed within the tradition as historical) generally applies to the two major Sanskrit epics, the *Mahābhārata* and the *Rāmāyaṇa*. Whether that is the meaning here is unclear, even though the *Mahābhārata* itself claims to be the fifth Veda. However, later the *Arthaśāstra* (1.5.14) gives a longer list of texts comprehended by this term, where *Itihāsa* appears to have the broader meaning of traditionally authoritative texts.

> the Laws specific to the four social classes and the four orders of life.[3] [1.3.1–2, 4]
>
> Agriculture and animal husbandry, along with trade, constitute Economics. It is of benefit because it provides grain, livestock, money, forest produce, and labor. By means of that he brings under his power his own circle (see §6.1) and his enemy's circle using the treasury and the army. [1.4.1–2]
>
> What provides enterprise and security to critical inquiry, the Triple, and Economics is punishment (*daṇḍa*); its administration (*nīti*) is Government (*daṇḍanīti*). Government seeks to acquire what has not been acquired, to safeguard what has been acquired, to augment what has been safeguarded, and to bestow what has been augmented on worthy recipients. On it depends the proper operation of the world. [1.4.3–4]
>
> Punishment, therefore, is the foundation of the three knowledge systems. [1.5.1]

Kauṭilya opens the *Arthaśāstra* with a discussion of the knowledge systems not only to make an ideological argument, but also to introduce the subjects in which a future king was to develop expertise. In a sense, then, the *Arthaśāstra* opens with a comprehensive taxonomy of human activity to provide an outline of its curriculum for the intellectual and practical education of the young prince as king-in-training.

Not all princes, however, made equally promising students. The success of the kingdom might rely on the cultivation of the prince's virtues through education, but the success of that education was felt to rely on the quality of each prince as a student. Thus, Kauṭilya begins his discussion of the future king's training by describing the ideal qualities of a student. Undoubtedly, a list such as this served both to encourage the cultivation of these characteristics in the young prince, as well as to identify those potential heirs who best exemplified them.

3. The four social classes (*varṇa*) are Brāhmaṇa, Kṣatriya, Vaiśya, and Śūdra. The four orders (*āśrama*) are those of the Vedic student, householder, forest hermit, and world renouncer.

A prince began his formal education as a young boy. His daily regimen was rigorous and included both martial and intellectual training. For a student with the right qualities, education, according to the *Arthaśāstra*, leads to the development of valuable personal qualities, culminating in the ability to control one's unprofitable or destructive emotions.

> Punishment, when it has training as its foundation, provides enterprise and security to living beings. Training is both acquired and innate, for an activity can train only a suitable subject, not an unsuitable one. A knowledge system can train only someone whose intellect is endowed with these qualities: desire to learn, attentive listening, grasping, retention, comprehension, reasoning, rejection, and devotion to truth; and not anyone else. Training and drilling in the knowledge systems, however, depend on the authority of the teachers of each respective knowledge system. [1.5.2–6]

> During the first part of the day he should undergo training in the knowledge systems pertaining to elephants, horses, chariots, and weapons, and during the later part in studying Lore (*itihāsa*). Lore consists of Purāṇas, Reports (*itivṛtta*), Narratives (*ākhyāyikā*), Illustrations (*udāharaṇa*), Treatises on Law (*dharmaśāstra*), and Treatises on Success (*arthaśāstra*).[4] During the rest of the day and night he should learn new materials and commit to memory what he has already learnt, as well as study repeatedly materials he has not learnt. For studying produces a keen intellect, a keen intellect produces disciplined performance, and disciplined performance produces the exemplary

4. *Purāṇas*, at least in later times, are texts dealing with a variety of topics, including creation and dissolution of the universe, genealogies of gods and dynasties, as well as other didactic and sectarian teachings. They are grouped into eighteen major and eighteen minor Purāṇas. The meaning of Reports (*itivṛtta*) is unclear, although a commentary identifies the epics *Mahābhārata* and *Rāmāyaṇa*. Probably this category includes reports of incidents and events that were thought to have happened in the past, what could be called history. It is also unclear what narratives (*ākhyāyikā*) and illustrations (*udāharaṇa*) refer to, although some think that they may refer to fables and stories, such as the *Pañcatantra*, also called *Tantrākhyāyikā*.

> qualities of the self:[5] such is the capacity of the knowledge systems. [1.5.12–16]

Training of Character

A rigorous training in the four knowledge systems provided the king with an incisive understanding of himself and the world. A king equipped with such insight would be able to recognize the dangers to himself and his kingdom posed by the inability to control his negative emotions—passion, anger, greed, pride, conceit, and boisterousness—the so-called set of six enemies. Referring to these emotions as "enemies," a term most often used to discuss hostile kings, indicates how serious of a threat to the kingdom political thinkers considered them.

Classical South Asian thought held that negative emotions such as passion resided within an individual's various senses and could be eliminated by developing the ability to control the inputs from one's sensory organs. Hence, self-control is discussed in the *Arthaśāstra* under the rubric of *indriyajaya*, "mastery (*jaya*) over the senses (*indriya*)."

In addition to the cultivation of sense control through intellectual, practical, and moral education, the king's behavior was guided from moment to moment by an array of teachers and advisors who organized his daily activities and consulted with him privately. They were to keep his less noble urges in check by observantly shepherding him through his daily routine of prescribed duties. This is another illustration in the *Arthaśāstra* of how the personal virtues of the king were felt to affect the ultimate success of the state.

> Mastery over the senses results from the training in the knowledge systems and is to be accomplished by giving up passion, anger, greed, pride, conceit, and boisterousness. Mastery over the senses consists of the senses—ear, skin, eye, tongue, and nose—not wandering inappropriately among sounds, touches,

5. At 6.1.5 numerous such qualities are enumerated, including being articulate and bold and being endowed with memory, intellect, and strength.

> visible forms, tastes, and smells; or rather, putting into practice what the treatise prescribes. For this entire treatise boils down to the mastery over the senses. A king who behaves contrary to it and has no control over his senses will perish immediately, even though he may rule the four ends of the earth. [1.6.1–4]

> Therefore, he should gain mastery over the senses by abandoning the set of six enemies. . . . Having thus brought his senses under control, he should shun the wives and property of others and refrain from causing injury, as also sloth, frivolity, falsehood, wearing lavish clothes, associating with pernicious individuals, and transactions that go against Law or Success. [1.7.1–2]

> He should designate teachers or Ministers to set the proper bounds, individuals who would keep him away from harmful situations or, when he wastes his time away in private, prod him using the goad of the sundial and the water clock.[6] [1.7.8]

1.2 Taking Counsel

After he entrusts the various bureaucratic functions of his government to a variety of ministers and superintendents (see §3.1 and 3.2), the king governs his state personally through a series of "undertakings." Such undertakings could include any non-routine activity that would require the approval or guidance of the king, such as the commencement of public works, the issuance of royal decrees, the dispatching of envoys to neighboring kings, or the remediation of disasters and calamities. It was through such undertakings that the king guided the state. The archetypal undertaking in the *Arthaśāstra* is that pertaining to decisions regarding whether to pursue peace or war with neighboring rulers.

---

6. The reference is to measures of time. The implication is that these individuals would tell the king when it is time for him to perform particular functions or reproach him for being negligent when he has failed to perform his duties at the proper time. The sundial is described at 1.19.6–8 and 2.20.39, and the water clock at 2.20.34–36.

The *Arthaśāstra* emphasizes the importance of seeking counsel before any such undertaking is initiated. Because he could not be expected to be an expert in all of the matters pertinent to his rule or to see deeply into all aspects of every situation, a king relied heavily on the advice of his counselors for making decisions. In the spy-ridden world of the *Arthaśāstra*, keeping his deliberations with these counselors private was a chief concern of the king. The text goes into some detail on measures for keeping counsel secret, from controlling one's nonverbal communication to expunging birds able to mimic human speech from the place of deliberation.

Ultimately, however, the decision on a given undertaking lay with the king, and he needed to take care not to fall prey to the machinations of scheming counselors. Hence, the king is not only taught the proper method for taking counsel, but is also instructed on how to keep himself from being manipulated by his advisers.

> The initiation of all undertakings presupposes counsel. The place where it is conducted should be enclosed, a place from which it is impossible to overhear conversations and into which even birds cannot peek; for we hear of counsel being divulged by parrots and myna birds, as also by dogs and other animals. Therefore, no unauthorized person should go near the place of counsel. [1.15.2–5]

> He should exterminate anyone who divulges counsel. Now, counsel is divulged by the gestures and bearing of envoys, ministers, and the king. Gesture is acting in a non-normal way. Bearing is putting on an expression. All that should be kept concealed and the officers appointed should be kept under surveillance until the time when the undertaking is completed. For, their blathering through carelessness or when they are drunk or asleep, or their indiscretions such as a love affair, or else someone who has remained hidden or who has been treated with disrespect, may divulge counsel. Therefore, he should safeguard counsel. [1.15.6–12]

> Counsel has five components: strategy for initiating the undertakings, men and material of exemplary quality, allocation of place and time, precautions against failure, and bringing the undertaking to a successful conclusion. [1.15.42–44]

1.3 Daily Routine

Nowhere is the epistemological habit of Sanskrit theoretical treatises more evident in the *Arthaśāstra* than in Kauṭilya's prescriptions for the king's daily routine. Composers of theoretical treatises demonstrated their authority in part by exhibiting comprehensive knowledge of a given subject. Because the appearance of comprehensiveness is so important to the authority of these texts, prescriptions given in them are frequently shaped by the theoretical framework used by the composer to conceptualize the subject in toto. The result is often a rigidly formal and highly intellectualized set of prescriptions for practice.

In this case, Kauṭilya, who demonstrates a comprehensive understanding of governance as well as of the king's personal needs, presents a strict and organized schedule for the king's daily routine that is too regular and formalized to be taken as a transparent description of practice. The challenge for scholars is to understand precisely how these kinds of models were understood by readers in the classical period and how they related to the actual practice of kingship. At the least, we can say that political theorists in the classical period used models like this to think about and assess a king's actual schedule.

Despite the uncertainty regarding the relationship between theory and practice, Kauṭilya's schedule of the king's daily routine gives us good insight into how the institution of kingship was conceived in the classical period. In particular, this schedule represents a convergence between the duties of the king as chief executive and the needs of the king as a living person. The different tasks distributed over the sixteen watches of the day and night encompass the king's manifold duties as chief security officer, chief financial officer, chief judicial officer, chief executive, chief of the diplomatic corps, chief espionage officer, and head of the military. The king's routine, however, also needed to nourish him physically, intellectually, emotionally, and spiritually. Hence, the times of his meals and baths are regulated, occasion is provided for exercise and recreation, he is given time for study and intellectual pursuits, and he receives daily guidance from religious teachers, priests, astrologers, chefs, and physicians. Here we get a sense of how the institution of kingship transcends narrow political, social, and religious categorization.

Certain activities in the king's daily routine link him to the orthodox Brāhmaṇical community: Vedic recitation, his performance of the twilight worship, and his daily blessing by his two chief priests, who carry out his sacrificial obligations as prescribed in the Sanskrit ritual literature. The observation of these practices meant that the king would be considered to have fulfilled his obligations under sacred Brāhmaṇical law. In doing so, he would have lent his political prestige to orthodox Brāhmaṇism and drawn prestige from it.

Although Kauṭilya's discussion of the king's routine offers a tantalizing glimpse of how a king may have discharged his duties on a daily basis, we are yet left in the dark as to how the performance of these specific activities at these specific times came together in such a way as to make any given king a particularly effective ruler. It is interesting to consider, therefore, what the precise arrangements of these activities can tell us about the practice of monarchy in the classical period.

> Using a water clock, he should divide the day and the night into eight parts, or using the shadow of a sundial. [1.19.6]

> Of these, during the first eighth part of the day, he should listen to reports on defensive arrangements and on income and expenditure. During the second, he should try cases brought by inhabitants of the cities and the countryside. During the third, he should bathe, take his meal, and engage in Vedic recitation. During the fourth, he should attend to monetary receipts and to the Superintendents. During the fifth, he should consult with his Council of Counselors by dispatching letters and find out the secret intelligence carried by his informants. During the sixth, he should engage in recreational activities of his choice or in taking counsel. During the seventh, he should inspect elephants, horses, chariots, and troops. During the eighth, he should ponder over military strategies together with the Army Commander. At the end of the day he should perform the twilight worship. [1.19.9–17]

> During the first part of the night, he should meet with clandestine operatives. During the second, he should bathe, take his meal, and engage in Vedic recitation. During the third, he should retire to the sound of music and sleep during the fourth and fifth. During the sixth, he should wake up to the sound of music and reflect on the Treatise [i.e., the *Arthaśāstra*] and on activities that need to be carried out. During the seventh, he should attend to counsel and dispatch clandestine operatives. During the eighth, he should receive the blessings of the officiating priest, teacher, and chaplain, and meet with his physician, chef, and astrologer. After circumambulating clockwise a cow with a calf and a bull, he should go to the assembly hall. [1.19.18–24]

> Having come to the assembly hall, he should permit free access to those who have come to plead their cases. For when people find it difficult to see the king, those surrounding him make him do what ought not to be done and not do what ought to be done. As a result, the people will revolt against him or he will fall into the clutches of his enemy. Therefore, he should try the cases—those relating to gods, hermitages, members of religious orders, Vedic scholars, farm animals, and holy places; those relating to children, the elderly, the sick, those in distress, and the helpless; and those relating to women—in that order, or according to the gravity of the case or its urgency. [1.19.26–29]

1.4 Personal Security

The critical importance of the king's person to the stability of the state is manifest in the detail and intensity with which his personal security is to be maintained. The construction and staffing of the king's palace are governed primarily by such safety concerns: his personal apartments lie at the center of a series of concentric or serial "courtyards." Within each of these courtyards are found different types of guards and attendants, many of whom strike an exotic aspect: female archers, eunuchs, and tribal warriors. It is not entirely clear why the king's personal chambers should be defended by a set of warriors so remarkably distinct from his regular troops, but they would have conferred a cosmopolitan and prestigious quality to his rule. One seeking entrance to the palace would find access increasingly limited by these guards as he or she approached the king's personal chambers. The king's movements outside the palace grounds are carefully coordinated events, with his troops in attendance and any potential danger addressed by a forward guard.

Access to the king is tightly regulated and is ideally limited to individuals of known loyalty. The chief concern in terms of the king's safety was the threat of assassination, whether through poison or by hidden weapon. As such, the *Arthaśāstra* lays out detailed protocols intended to block the admission of poison-bearers, as well as instructions on how to identify poisoned food or individuals. We see in the text's description of the latter the comprehensiveness that characterizes Sanskrit theoretical treatises.

The king is regularly attended by a sizable retinue of servants, including barbers, valets, bathing-women, masseurs, musicians, artists, and courtesans. Each of these individuals is to be vetted thoroughly, searched, and kept under constant supervision by the king's guards. Any of their implements that might touch the king's body is tested first on its bearer. When practical, the implements used by these attendants are stored and kept within the palace itself and given to the king's attendants to use only while they remain in the palace.

> When he rises from bed he should be escorted by teams of female guards armed with bows; in the second courtyard by eunuch stewards wearing robes and turbans; in the third by hunchbacks, dwarfs, and Kirātas;[7] in the fourth by Counselors and relatives and by the gate-guards armed with spears.
>
> He should place close to him individuals who have served his father and grandfather, who are bound to him by close relationships, and who are trained, loyal, and men of accomplishment, but never individuals who are from another country and have not been granted wealth and honors, and not even individuals from his own country who have been taken into

7. *Kirātas* probably referred to members of forest tribes.

service after they had been slighted. Troops of the palace guard should protect the king and the royal residence.

The chef should get all the cooking carried out in a secure location, tasting it frequently. The king should eat it in the same manner,[8] after first making an offering to fire and birds.

The signs of food mixed with poison are the blue color of the flame and smoke of the fire and its crackling sound, as also the death of birds. The signs of articles mixed with poison are the following: in the case of boiled rice—steam the color of a peacock's neck, frigidity, quick discoloration as if stale, presence of water, and not being moist; in the case of curries—becoming dry quickly, bubbling continuously, having a dirty appearance, frothing, curdling, and the destruction of smell, texture, and taste; in the case of liquids—appearance of a hue more faint or more pronounced, and appearance of upward streaks at the edges of the froth; in the case of juice—a blue streak in the middle; in the case of milk—a reddish streak in the middle; in the case of liquor and water—a black streak in the middle; in the case of curd—a dark streak in the middle; in the case of honey—a white streak in the middle; in the case of wet substances—becoming quickly withered, becoming overcooked, and a bluish dark color while boiling; in the case of dry substances—crumbling quickly and discoloration; in the case of hard and soft substances—softness in the former and hardness in the latter, as also the death of small creatures in their vicinity; in the case of bedsheets and covers—appearance of dark circles and the crumbling of the thread, wool, and hair; in the case of articles made of metal and gems—appearing soiled with muddy dirt, and the destruction of the smoothness, pigment, weight, potency, color, and texture.

The signs of a poisoner, on the other hand, are as follows: dry and dark look on the face, stuttering speech, excessive perspiration and yawning, trembling, stumbling, looking around while speaking, agitation while working, and not remaining in his place.

---

8. The meaning is that he should eat with the same kinds of precautions with which the food was cooked, that is, having it tasted repeatedly by his food tasters to make sure that the food is not poisoned.

Therefore, experts in the cure of poisons and physicians should remain close to him [the king]. The physician should take the medicine, whose purity has been tested by tasting, from the pharmacy, have it tasted by the cook, the pounder, and himself, and then present it to the king. The discussion of medicine explains also the handling of drink and water.

Barbers and valets, with clean clothes and hands after a bath, should take the implements in a sealed container from the hands of the chief of the palace guard and wait on him. Female slaves of proven integrity should perform the work of bath attendants, masseurs, preparers of beds, washermen, and garland-makers, or artisans should do so under their supervision. They should give him garments and garlands after touching their own eyes with them, and bath oils, rubbing powders, perfumes, and bathing lotions after applying them on their own chests and arms. This explains also the handling of anything that has been received from someone else.

Performers should entertain him without employing performances involving weapons, fire, or poison. Their musical instruments should remain within the palace, as also the ornaments of their horses, carriages, and elephants.

He should ride a carriage or a mount under the control of a trusted officer and a boat captained by a trusted boatman. He should not get into a boat tied to another boat or buffeted by a strong wind. Troops should stand by at the water's edge.

He should enter a body of water that has been cleared by fishermen, and visit a park that has been cleared by snake catchers. He should go to a game forest for practice on moving targets after fowlers and those who hunt with dogs have cleared it of dangers posed by thieves, vicious animals, and enemies. [1.21.1–23]

Chapter Two

The Kingdom

2.1 Constituents of a Kingdom

The *Arthaśāstra* is the first South Asian text of which we know to offer a theory of the state as being comprised of seven "constituent elements." Dividing the state into seven basic components allows not only for assessing the individual strength or weakness of each constituent, but also for strategic assessments of their relative importance, as, for example, when a king must decide between protecting his army or his treasury.

It is a matter of debate whether the polity envisioned in the *Arthaśāstra* can be properly understood as a "state" in the modern sense of the term, but the text makes clear what it has in mind: "the king and his rule, this is the epitome of the constituent elements" (8.2.1). The latter of these, the king's rule, includes elements not often conceived as constituents of the state itself, such as the ally and, as an added eighth constituent element, the enemy. We might not consider allies and enemies to be part of a given state but the strengths and weakness of a king's allies and enemies invariably bear on any strategic assessment of that king's capacities.

Each of the seven constituent elements is defined by a group of ideal qualities. As such, the constituent elements are described in the text by listing the qualities that define the best of their kind. Such an approach serves a diagnostic function by allowing the observer to judge quickly the relative strengths of a given state's constituents, either to bolster the position of one's own king or to exploit the weaknesses of an enemy.

These elements are themselves not equal: the *Arthaśāstra* lists them in descending order of importance. By far the most important, as befitting a text on monarchy, is the king himself. The text goes into great detail on the ideal qualities of a king, grouping them according to the categories of approachability, intelligence, diligence, and self-possession. As implied in the discussion of the king's education, the monarch is expected to be a man possessed of a wide range of excellent characteristics, from noble lineage and weak enemies to generosity and discrimination. The resulting illustration of the ideal king is a man of perfect character in all regards. This list is particularly interesting in its promotion of moral virtues alongside political strengths, leading one to question whether Kauṭilya considered these virtues valuable only because they contribute to political success or whether he is here expressing some measure of idealism alongside his more famous tendency for pragmatism. A third possibility is that he felt these qualities identified potentially trustworthy allies.

Also presented in this passage are the ideal qualities of the sixth constituent element, the army. Most of its desirable qualities pertain to loyalty and effectiveness. Interestingly, we read that the army should be composed mostly of Kṣatriyas, the "warriors" of the *varṇa* class system. This would seem to indicate some distinction between those who are soldiers by birth or profession and others who may have been conscripted to serve in the military.

> King, Minister, countryside, fort, treasury, army, and ally are the constituent elements.
>
> Of these, the following constitute the exemplary qualities of the king. Coming from a noble family; endowed with good fortune, intelligence, and spirit; visiting elders; righteous; truthful; not breaking his word; grateful; generous; with immense energy; not given to procrastination; with pliant neighboring rulers; with a resolute mind; with a council that is not petty; eager to be trained—these are the qualities of a man who is approachable. Desire to learn, attentive listening, grasping, retention, comprehension, reasoning, rejection, devotion to truth—these are the qualities of intelligence. Bravery, indignation, quickness, skill—these are the qualities of energy. Articulate;

bold; endowed with memory, intellect, and strength; exalted; easy to manage; trained in the crafts; free of vices; providing leadership to the army; providing the prescribed retribution for benefits provided and wrongs done; modest; taking the appropriate action in times of adversity and normalcy; judicious and farsighted; placing emphasis on tasks undertaken at the proper place and time and with the right human effort; able to discriminate between entering into a peace pact and initiating hostilities, releasing and detaining, and keeping to the agreement and seeking the enemy's vulnerable points; guarding himself well; not laughing in an undignified manner; looking without squinting or frowning; free of lust, hatred, greed, rigidity, inconstancy, brutality, and slander; affable; speaking with a smile and with dignity; and acting according to the instructions of elders—these are the exemplary qualities of the self. [6.1.2–6]

Bequeathed by the father and grandfather; consistent; submissive; one in which the sons and wives of hired soldiers are content; not prone to insubordination during long marches; without obstacles anywhere; able to bear hardships; one that has experienced many battles; expert in the science of all kinds of warfare and weaponry; not prone to duplicity, being partners in both prosperity and decline; and consisting mainly of Kṣatriyas—these are the exemplary qualities of the army. [6.1.11]

2.2 Construction of Fortified Cities

Construction of Forts

The fourth constituent element of the state is the fortress. Crucial to the defense of the realm, fortified cities protect important border regions, serve as sanctuaries during times of attack, and house the major economic and administrative centers of the state. The ideal state of the *Arthaśāstra* possesses a number of fortresses, differing in geographical setting and purpose. Collectively, they are the critical nodes in the infrastructure of the kingdom.

The kingdom is to have fortresses built on its borders and frontier zones to provide protection on all sides. These frontier fortresses are sited so as to take advantage of the local terrain, and the most steadfast and redoubtable among them serve as places of retreat for the king and the essential members of his kingdom during invasions and other calamities. These frontier fortresses were built more exclusively for defensive purposes than the large fortified population centers of the realm.

The largest of the fortresses is the capital city, which operates as an administrative, economic, and military hub for the kingdom. Kauṭilya goes into great detail about the site and construction of the capital: it must be well supplied with water and strategically located along major thoroughfares. It is to be defended by an impressive series of moats filled with crocodiles and a large earthen rampart crowned by a turreted palisade of brick and stone. The rampart itself is designed with many defensive features allowing for the effective defense of the city.

> At each of the four directions along the frontiers of the countryside he should have a fort built providing an advantage in battle and natural protection: a water fort—an island in the middle of water or a high ground encircled by water courses; a hill fort—a rocky outcrop or a cave; a desert fort—land without water and shrubbery or a salt flat; and a forest fort—a marshy swamp or a thicket of shrubs. Of these, the river and hill forts are locations for the defenders of the countryside, while the desert and forest forts are locations for forest tribals or a place of retreat in a time of adversity.
>
> In the center of the countryside, he should construct a provincial capital as a revenue collection center on land recommended as a building site at the confluence of rivers or on the bank of a lake—either a natural pond or a reservoir—that never dries up. It should be round, rectangular, or square, or as required by the lay of the land, with water flowing clockwise,[9] and function as a market town served by a land route and a water route.
>
> Around it, he should get three moats constructed at distances of one Daṇḍa [1 Daṇḍa = 1.82 m] from each other. Each should be fourteen, twelve, and ten Daṇḍas wide, respectively.

9. The water should be moving from the left to the right as one faces it from the city. This is, of course, the auspicious direction of movement in India.

The depth of each is one-quarter or one-half its width; the bottom width of each is one-third its width at the surface, or their bottoms should be square. They should be revetted with stone or their sides should be lined with stone or brick. They should be fed either by natural springs or by channeled water, and they should be provided with means of drainage and stocked with lotuses and crocodiles.

At a distance of four Daṇḍas from the moat, he should get a rampart constructed using the earth that has been dug out. It should be six Daṇḍas high, well contained, and twice as wide as that. It should be vaulted with a flat top or pot-bellied, and it should be compacted using elephants and bulls and covered with thorny shrubs and poisonous creepers. With the remainder of the dirt he should have the cavities in the building sites or the royal residence filled.

On top of the rampart he should get a wall constructed whose height is twice the width. It should be built with bricks to a height of more than twelve Hastas [1 Hasta = 47 cm]—either an odd or an even number—up to a maximum of twenty-four Hastas. It should have a passageway for chariots and a foundation reinforced with Palmyra trunks, its top being capped with [merlons called] "drums" and "monkey heads." Alternatively, he should have it built of stone, using wide stones stacked together tightly, but never of wood, for fire lurks hidden within it.

He should have towers with rectangular foundations built at a distance of thirty Daṇḍas from each other. They should be equipped with drop-down ladders of the same height. Midway between two towers he should get a postern gate[10] built, its length one and a half times its width, and having two stories equipped with a hall. Midway between each tower and postern gate he should get an embrasure built, large enough for three archers and constructed with tightly fitting planks with shuttered loopholes. In the intervening spaces he should construct a "god's path"[11] two Hastas wide and four times as long along the side. [2.3.1–13]

10. A gate for pedestrians to enter and exit the fort, distinct from the main gates.

11. Probably a path behind the embrasures for movement of soldiers and archers.

Layout of the Fort

The internal layout of the fortified city is governed by the strict design logic of the classical South Asian science of geomancy, called *vāstuśāstra*. The statutes of this tradition dictate that the residential interior of the fortified city be divided by three royal highways running north/south and three running east/west, creating sixteen major city blocks in a four-by-four grid. The six royal highways terminate at each end with a gate in the city ramparts, giving the fortified city twelve gates. The size of various roads within the city are determined according to a hierarchy of width, with royal highways about fifteen meters wide and city streets about seven meters wide.

The location of buildings within the city is based on a second division of the city, this time not into the sixteen city blocks generated by the six royal highways, but into nine sectors of nine blocks each arranged in a three-by-three grid. This division into nine sectors is superimposed over that generated by the six royal highways, and may indicate the influence of two different traditions of urban planning coming together in this chapter of the *Arthaśāstra*. Among the nine sectors, the central sector houses the king's palace. The text then goes on to distribute the location of residences and businesses within the central block and in each surrounding direction, demonstrating a clockwise hierarchy, beginning with the Brāhmaṇas in the north, Kṣatriyas (warriors) in the east, Vaiśyas (merchants and farmers) in the south, and Śūdras (farmers, laborers, and servants) in the west. The temples to the major gods occupy the central sector of the city.

Each of the twelve city gates is guarded by a specific deity, and the city is surrounded by a constellation of smaller shrines. Outside the city are the cremation grounds.

Although some cities certainly developed in a more haphazard fashion, archaeological evidence suggests that some South Asian cities in the classical period did conform to the general outline of these prescriptions, featuring a regular grid of standardized roads. Determining whether the occupation of specific city sectors by individuals of different classes and professions was as rigorous as suggested here is very difficult, but we do know that similar habitation patterns can be traced in some South Asian cities.

> Three royal highways running east and three running north constitute the division of the area for building sites. It should have twelve gates and contain suitable places for water canals, drainage ditches, and clandestine passages.
>
> Streets should be four Daṇḍas wide [1 Daṇḍa = 1.82 m]. Royal highways and roads in district municipalities, provincial capitals, provinces, and pasture land, as well as roads in port towns, military encampments, cemeteries, and villages, should be eight Daṇḍas wide. Roads on dikes and in forests should be four Daṇḍas wide; roads for elephants and in fields, two Daṇḍas; roads for carriages, five Aratnis [1 Aratni = 47 cm]; roads for farm animals, four Aratnis; and roads for small animals and humans, two Aratnis.
>
> The king's dwelling should be on an excellent building site suitable for inhabitation by the four social classes [see note 3]. In the one-ninth sector to the north of the center of the area for building sites, he should get the royal residence built according to the prescribed plan and facing either the east or the north.
>
> In its east-northeast sector is the dwelling for the teacher and chaplain and location for sacrifices and water—and the Counselors should reside there. In the east-southeast sector are the kitchen, the elephant stables, and the storehouse. Beyond that, in the eastern direction, should be the residences of traders dealing in perfumes, garlands, and juices, and manufacturers of toiletries, as well as Kṣatriyas.
>
> In the south-southeast sector are the warehouse, bureau of official records, and workshops; and in the south-southwest sector, the storage facility for forest produce and the armory. Beyond that, in the southern direction, should be the residences of the City Manager, grain dealers, director of factories, military officers, traders dealing in cooked food, liquor, and meat, prostitutes, and dancers, as well as Vaiśyas.
>
> In the west-southwest sector are the stables for donkeys and camels and the workshop, and in the west-northwest sector, the garages for carriages and chariots. Beyond that, in the western direction, should be the residences of workers in wool, yarn, bamboo, leather, armor, weapons, and shields, as well as Śūdras.

In the north-northwest sector are the stores for merchandise and medicines, and in the north-northeast sector, the treasury, as well as cattle and horses. Beyond that, in the northern direction, should be the residences of the deities of the city and deities of the king, and workers in metal and gems, as well as Brāhmaṇas.

In an area along the walls unsuitable as a building site should be the housing for guilds and foreign traders.

In the middle of the city he should have these built: shrines for Aparājita, Apratihata, Jayanta, and Vaijayanta,[12] and abodes for Śiva, Vaiśravaṇa, Aśvins, Śrī, and Madirā.[13] He should install deities of the building sites according to the location. The presiding deities of the gates are Brahmā, Indra, Yama, and Senāpati.[14] Outside at a distance of one hundred Dhanuṣes [1 Dhanuṣ = 1.82 m] from the moat should be built sanctuaries, holy places, groves, and reservoirs, as also in each quarter its respective deity,[15] or in the north-northeast.

Conveyance to the cemetery is through the southern (gate and the rest) incrementally for each social class [see note 3]. For violating this, the punishment is the lowest seizure-fine [= 48–96 Paṇas, a silver coin].

The residences of religious orders and Caṇḍālas[16] are on the outskirts of the cemetery. [2.4.1–23]

---

12. The names of all four deities signify victory and invincibility. Some scholars identity them as forms of Skanda or Kumāra, the son of Śiva.

13. Some scholars identify Madirā with the goddess Jyeṣṭhā.

14. Moving clockwise from the north, Brahmā is the presiding deity of the northern gate, Indra of the eastern, Yama of the southern, and Senāpati (Skanda) of the western.

15. The guardian deities of the quarters are from the north clockwise: Kubera, Indra, Yama, and Varuṇa. However, as the previous sentence shows, for the *Arthaśāstra* Brahmā and Senāpati may have taken the place of Kubera and Varuṇa.

16. Religious orders (*pāṣaṇḍa*) are non-Brāhmaṇical ascetic orders. The provision here is contradicted by 2.36.14, which assumes that at least some of these ascetics lived within the city. We think that the passage 2.4.21–23 is an interpolation reflecting Brāhmaṇical viewpoints, including the denigration of *pāṣaṇḍas* not found elsewhere in the *Arthaśāstra*. Caṇḍālas are the lowest class of people, later known as untouchables, with whom social interaction was forbidden.

2.3 Security of the Royal Residence

We have seen already (§1.4) the elaborate security procedures for individuals who sought access to the person of the king. Complimentary to these practices are measures recommended in the text for the protection of the king's residence itself. The head of the palace guard would presumably have been responsible for implementing them.

These protective measures show that two things were considered to pose a particular threat to the king's safety: fire and poison. It is interesting to note that the text advises the use of magical countermeasures as well as the deployment of plants and animals with protective attributes, some demonstrable, others seemingly more fanciful.

Certain individuals were considered potentially dangerous to the king, including, most remarkably, his own queen. The *Arthaśāstra* illustrates this danger by referring to legends and stories of past kings who were slain by their mates. The danger posed by other women, such as courtesans and slaves, is evident from the protective measures taken against each. The ladies of the king's harem were under constant suspicion and surveillance, with dedicated attendants continually investigating each to uncover any potential threat to the king. These attendants were also responsible for establishing among the members of the harem goodwill toward the king.

Renunciates of various types were thought to possess extraordinary powers. In the following passage, they are forbidden from even meeting with the king, although we are told elsewhere in the *Arthaśāstra* that the king could meet with ascetics possessing special powers provided he was protected by trustworthy soldiers (*Arthaśāstra* 1.24.21) or he could adjudicate the disputes of ascetics and magicians in the presence of three Brāhmaṇas who know the Veda (*Arthaśāstra* 1.19.32).

Despite the generally materialist disposition of the *Arthaśāstra*, the following passages give a sense of Kauṭilya's healthy respect for magic and unseen powers. The extreme caution of the text with regard to the safety of the king prompts it to exhaust all available protective measures and to guard against any potential threat. As the *Arthaśāstra* itself advises the use of ascetics as covert agents of the king, the text harbors a healthy suspicion of such figures, as well as queens and courtesans, as potential agents of the king's enemies and a danger to his rule.

> When a fire produced by churning human bones is taken around the royal residence three times counterclockwise, no other fire will burn it and no other fire will flare up there; this happens also when it is daubed with ash produced by lightning and with water from hail mixed with earth.
>
> Snakes or poisons are powerless in a place protected by Jīvantī, Śvetā, Muṣkaka, Puṣpa, and Vandākā[17] and by the aerial root of an Aśvattha tree growing on a drumstick tree. Releasing peacocks, mongooses, and spotted deer exterminates snakes. Parrots, myna birds, and Bhṛṅgarāja-drongo cry out when they suspect the presence of a snake or poison. In the presence of poison, a Krauñca crane becomes exhilarated, a Jīvaṃjīvaka-pheasant faints, a Mattakokila-cuckoo dies, and the eyes of Cakora-partridge turns red.[18]
>
> In this manner he should take countermeasures against fire, poison, and snakes. [1.20.4–9]
>
> Going to the inner chamber, he should meet with the queen after she has been inspected and cleared by elderly women. For Bhadrasena was killed by his brother hiding in the queen's chamber, and Kārūṣa by his son hiding under his mother's bed. The king of Kāśi was killed by his queen with puffed grain mixed with poison disguised as honey; Vairantya with an anklet smeared with poison; Sauvīra with a girdle-jewel smeared with poison; and Jālūtha with a mirror smeared with poison. And the queen killed Vidūratha by hiding a weapon in her braids.[19] Therefore, he should avoid these situations.

---

17. Names of various plants: *Jīvantī* = *Leptadenia retriculata*; *Śvetā* = *Terminalia tomentosa* or *Aconitum ferox*; *Muṣkaka* = *Schrebera swietenioides*; *Puṣpa* = unidentified; *Vandākā* = *Vanda Roxburghii.*

18. *Bhṛṅgarāja* = large racket-tailed drongo; *Krauñca* = a species of large waterbird, probably the common crane; *Jīvaṃjīvaka* = peacock pheasant; *Mattakokila* = the same as Kokila, the Asian Koel or cuckoo; *Cakora* = partridge, *Perdix rufa.*

19. These are references to well-known stories found in various texts about kings who were killed in various ways by people near to them.

> He should prohibit interaction with shaven-headed and matted-haired ascetics,[20] and charlatans, as well as with female slaves coming from outside. The members of their families should not be permitted to see them, except in the maternity room and the infirmary. Prostitutes, after they have cleansed their bodies by bathing and rubbing and changed their clothes and jewelry, may be permitted to visit them. Men at least 80 years old and women at least 50 years old, appearing as mothers and fathers, and elderly eunuch stewards should find out the honesty and dishonesty of the inmates of the harem and make them devoted to what is beneficial to the king. [1.20.14–21]

2.4 Rules for the City

The *Arthaśāstra* was composed in an urban context, and the capital (§2.2) is the backdrop for most of the text's discussions. The actual day-to-day administration of the kingdom is divided between the collector (§3.1)—a kind of regional governor—and the city manager (*nāgarika*), who is his counterpart in the city. Both are royal appointees with broad powers, overseeing public safety, law enforcement, and, perhaps most importantly, revenue from taxes and fines. The following excerpt outlines some of the duties of the city manager.

From the breadth of his duties, we can infer that the city manager was quite a powerful official within the state bureaucracy. Through his subordinates and spies, he attempted to keep track of everyone residing in the city. This information was useful both for the determination of taxes due to the royal treasury, as well as for identifying individuals potentially injurious to public safety or to the king's economic or political interests. The office of the city manager routinely engaged in aggressive activity meant to root out dangerous or seditious persons. He carried out these duties through both the city guard and a robust network of spies.

---

20. These are the two standard kinds of ascetics. Those with shaven heads are the world renouncers who lead a wandering life and beg for their food. The matted-haired ascetics generally live in hermitages located in forests.

The city manager was also responsible for dealing with civil disturbances and annoyances, such as fires and the obstruction of rights of way. The city manager's office enforced civil codes, possessed the power to levy and collect fines, and had the authority to order curfews, close the city gates, conduct searches, and make arrests. True to the fundamentally economic character of his office, the city manager also oversaw revenue agents.

> Just like the Collector, the City Manager should look after the city, while a Revenue Officer should look after a unit of ten households, twenty households, or forty households. The latter should find out the number of individual men and women within each unit in terms of their castes, lineages, names, and occupations, as well as their incomes and expenditures. [2.36.1–3]
>
> Craftsmen and artisans should provide lodgings to their colleagues in their own work places, and traders should give lodgings to each other in their own work places. They should inform on anyone who sells commodities at unauthorized places and times or without proof of ownership. [2.36.6–7]
>
> A physician who informs the Revenue Officer or the County Supervisor about a man who has made him treat a wound secretly or has done something pernicious is to be released—and so would a head of household; otherwise he becomes guilty of the same crime. [2.36.10]
>
> Secret agents deployed on roads and in roadless tracts should arrest anyone with a wound, carrying harmful tools, hiding behind a package, agitated, overcome by intense sleep, or tired from travel, or any stranger within or outside the city, in temples, holy places, woods, and cemeteries. Likewise, inside the city they should carry out searches in empty houses, workshops, taverns, places for selling boiled rice and cooked meat, gambling halls, and residences of religious orders. [2.36.13–14]
>
> In the summer, moreover, there should be safeguards against fire. During the two middle quarters[21] of the day, the fine for

21. Here the daytime appears to be divided into four equal parts of three hours each. So, if we take the day to go from 6:00 a.m. to 6:00 p.m., then the times when open fires are forbidden within the city would be 9:00 a.m. to 3:00 p.m.

lighting a fire is one-eighth (of a Paṇa). Alternatively, people should do their cooking outdoors. For not keeping ready five jars, as well as a pot, trough, ladder, ax, winnow, hook, "hair-grabber" [a hooked pole], and water-skin, the fine is a quarter (Paṇa). He should remove all coverings of grass or thatch. He should have people whose occupation involves fire live together in one area. [2.36.15–20]

For throwing dirt in a street, the fine is one-eighth; for obstructing the flow of dirty water, a quarter—if it is done on a royal highway, the fine is doubled. For voiding excrement in a holy site, a place for water, a temple, or a royal precinct, the fine is one Paṇa successively increased by one Paṇa; for voiding urine the fines are halved. If this is caused by medicine, sickness, or fear, they should not be fined. [2.36.25–29]

He should question anyone arrested in a suspicious place, with a suspicious mark, or because of a previous offense. For approaching the royal precincts and for climbing the city defenses, the punishment is the middle seizure-fine [200–500 Paṇas]. People moving about on account of childbirth, to get a physician, because of a death, with a lamp, in a carriage, when the City Manager has sounded the instrument,[22] to see a show, or because of a fire, as also those carrying a sealed pass, are not subject to arrest.

During nights of free movement, people wearing secretive or incongruous attire, renouncers, and people carrying clubs or weapons should be punished in accordance with their offense. [2.36.36–39]

2.5 Rules for Constructing Neighborhoods

The *Arthaśāstra* contains a relatively detailed housing code that governs the construction of dwellings. The code is given in the text as part of the titles of law governing disputes between private parties, but also echoes the civil statutes enforced by the office of the city manager.

22. Perhaps to alert the citizens to an imminent danger, much like a siren in modern cities, or to summon them to a gathering.

Boundary disputes must have been common among civil plaints in the period, and the code requires the public demarcation of boundaries before any development of a plot can begin. Plots can then only be developed after care has been taken that certain potentially dangerous, destructive, or noxious elements are sufficiently spaced from neighboring property. Interestingly, houses also had ingress and egress requirements as well as requirements governing the placement and size of windows. Ultimately, however, the text admits that these codes could be superseded by an agreement between neighbors, hinting at the authority of local convention in building habits.

Here we witness the extent to which the king's authority was not necessarily expressed through the proactive enforcement of codified laws and statutes. Certain guidelines were set that the king or his officers might choose to enforce, but the resolution of disputes and the determination of adherence to such codes could ultimately (and frequently did) reside with the involved parties. In such disputes, the king and his officers existed as an overarching authority, but one that did not seek to govern every aspect of daily life in the fashion of the modern developed nation state.

> Alongside the house there is a boundary line with a border marker of Karṇa-posts[23] or iron. He should get the house built in keeping with the boundary line; or, in its absence, he should have the foundation wall constructed two Aratnis [1 Aratni = 48 cm] or three Padas [1 Pada = 28 cm] away from the wall of the neighbor's house.
>
> The latrine, drain, or well should not be located in places suitable for a house, except a water ditch during childbirth until the tenth day.[24] For violating this the punishment is the lowest seizure-fine [48–96 Paṇas]. . . .

23. *Karṇa* probably refers to the golden shower tree, *Cassia fistula*.

24. Water and waste from one house should not go into or near the neighbor's house, except in such emergencies as childbirth, when a lot more water than normal would be used.

He should have the place for carts and animals, the fireplace, the place for the water tank, the grinding mill, or the pounding machine constructed one Pada [1 Pada = 28 cm] or one Aratni [1 Aratni = 48 cm] removed (from the neighbor's property). For violating this the fine is twenty-four Paṇas.

Between any two residential properties or two protruding halls there should be a passageway of one Kiṣku [1 Kiṣku = 64 cm] or three Padas. Between the eaves of their roofs there should be a gap of four Aṅgulas [1 Aṅgula = 2 cm], or they may overlap.

He should get a side door a full Kiṣku wide built in such a way that it would not collide and permit the door pane to open wide in the passageway.[25] He should get a small window built high up to let in light. When the house is occupied he should have it covered.

Alternatively, the house owners may come together and jointly get them constructed as they like and prevent what they do not like. [3.8.3–7, 11–18]

2.6 Settling the Countryside

In keeping with the normative disposition of Sanskrit theoretical literature, the *Arthaśāstra* describes how things *should be* as opposed to how they are. As such, its description of the countryside proceeds as if the ruler were building his kingdom from the ground up. Although the settlement of new territory augmenting a king's tax base was likely an ongoing concern, the *Arthaśāstra* is not only addressed to rulers founding new kingdoms. The trope of "settling the countryside" simply provides the text with the opportunity to describe the ideal settlement and development of the greater part and economic backbone of the kingdom: the agricultural hinterlands.

Ideally, the countryside should be populated by farmers from the lowest social class, individuals acculturated to and skilled

25. This must refer to a space left open between two houses, perhaps to the backyards without having to go through the house itself. From the measurements given, it is clear that the houses were built very close to each other, so much so that the eaves of the roofs could overlap.

in the rigorous requirements of the agricultural professions. These farmers are settled in villages, which are the smallest unit of group habitation mentioned in the text, ranging from 100 to 500 families. The settlement hierarchy grows from there, including larger cities scaled to the administrative, economic, and military requirements of boroughs, districts, counties, municipal districts, and, finally, the entire region.

In addition to this, the basic settlement fabric of the kingdom, the king was also to construct a number of forts on the frontiers of his territory for the purpose of defense and control of traffic into and out of the region. Nonagricultural tracts within the territory, which is to say ecological zones not conducive to farming and not populated by villages of farmers, were to be occupied by a variety of tribal groups, hunters, and other groups collected under the rubric of "outcastes."

The countryside was undoubtedly the major source of income for the kingdom, and the text demonstrates the various investment, reward, and punitive strategies used by the state to maximize its tax income based on agricultural production. This included loans, development of infrastructure (such as irrigation systems), and tax abatements. While the text indicates that the king could grant land to farmers that might then be treated as family property, we also read that he reserved the right to appropriate and reassign land not being put to productive use. The state held a monopoly on the right to extract raw materials from the countryside, and the ruler is advised to set in place an array of extractive enterprises that provided wealth and critical raw materials for both public consumption and royal use.

The final elements of the countryside are the trade routes and port cities, the inclusion of which here demonstrates the extent that economic interests dominated the king's sense of his own greater territory.

> He should settle the countryside—whether it has been settled before or has never been settled—by forcing people out of enemy territories or by transferring people from overpopulated areas of his own territory.

He should settle villages with mostly Śūdra agriculturalists, each village consisting of a minimum of 100 families and a maximum of 500 families, with boundaries extending one or two Krośas [1 Krośa = 3.6 km], and affording mutual protection. He should make the junctures of their boundaries demarcated by a river, a hill, a forest, a band of pebbles, a cave, a dike, a Śamī tree [*Bombax ceiba*], a Śālmalī tree [*Mimosa sums* or *Prosopis spicier*], or a milk-tree.

In the middle of an 800-village unit he should establish a provincial capital, in the middle of a 400-village unit a district municipality, in the middle of a 200-village unit a county seat, and a collection center for each collection of ten villages.

At the frontiers he should construct Frontier Commanders' forts as gateways into the countryside and under the control of the Frontier Commanders. Areas between them should be guarded by trappers, tribals, mountaineers, Caṇḍālas [see note 16], and forest dwellers. [2.1.1–6]

He should give cultivated land to taxpayers for as long as they live, and uncultivated lands, made exempt from taxes, to those who would cultivate them. He should seize lands from those who do not cultivate them and give them to others. Alternatively, village servants or traders should cultivate them; or else, those who have not cultivated them should compensate the losses.

He should assist them with grain, farm animals, and money. They should return those later at their convenience. He should grant them the kinds of favors and exemptions that would enhance the revenue to the treasury and avoid those that would cause a decrease in revenue to the treasury; for a king with a depleted treasury devours the very inhabitants of the cities and the countryside. At the time of settlement or when the people actually arrive, he should grant them exemptions. Like a father, he should assist those whose exemptions have come to an end.

He should set up the operations of mines, factories, produce-forests, elephant-forests, herd stations, and trade routes, as well as water routes, land routes, and ports.

He should get reservoirs constructed, reservoirs that are fed either with naturally occurring water or with water channeled from elsewhere; or he should render assistance to others

> constructing them by giving land, routes, trees, and implements, as also to those constructing holy places and parks. [2.1.8–21]

2.7 Protecting Against Calamities

The king's interest in safeguarding his kingdom is self-evident. The *Arthaśāstra* takes as its primary focus the augmentation and protection of the king's wealth and power, both of which are rooted in the kingdom itself. Certainly, kings and those loyal to their interests would have responded as robustly as possible to any calamity afflicting his kingdom that would hurt his economic or political interests.

The *Arthaśāstra* relates several standard kinds of calamities, such as fire, flood, disease, famine, and infestation. As with the protection of the king, the text advises in response to such calamities a variety of both material and supernatural preventatives and remedies. Thus, along with practical rules concerning cooking fires in the dry season, we find also the use of spells and rituals to address disease. Kauṭilya excludes no potential avenue of redress during times of great need. Undoubtedly, some of these strategies resulted from the hard lessons of calamities past.

> In the summer, villagers should do their cooking either outdoors or overseen by a group of ten households. Prevention of fires has been explained in the Regimen of the City Manager and, with reference to the royal compound, in the Regimen of the Residence. Further, he should have rites of fire worship carried out on days of the moon's change with Bali-offerings,[26] fire offerings, and the proclamation of blessings. [4.3.3–5]

> During the rainy season, villagers along river banks should live away from the flood plain. They should also keep at hand planks, bamboos, and boats. [4.3.6–7]

26. The days of the moon's change are the new moon, the eighth day after the new moon, the full moon, and the fourteenth day after the full moon. Balis are offerings of food made to various spirits.

Further, on the days of the moon's change he should have rituals of river worship carried out. Those proficient in magical practices or those knowledgeable in the Vedas should perform spells against the rain. [4.3.10–11]

They should counteract the danger of disease through occult remedial measures, physicians through medicines, and thaumaturgic ascetics through pacificatory rites and penances. [4.3.13]

During a time of famine the king should first gather a stockpile of seeds and foodstuff and then grant favors: work on forts or irrigation projects in exchange for foodstuff, or distribution of foodstuff, or handing over the region. Alternatively, he may seek refuge with allies or bring about a reduction or a transfer of population. Or else, he may migrate along with the people of the countryside to another region where crops have flourished, or repair to an area by the sea, a lake, or a reservoir. [4.3.17–19]

When there is a danger from rats, cats and mongooses should be released. [4.3.21]

He should strew grains smeared with the milk of the Snuhi-plant or mixed with secret compounds. Or he should institute a rat-tax;[27] or thaumaturgic ascetics should perform a pacificatory rite. On the days of the moon's change, moreover, he should have rites of rat worship carried out. [4.3.23–26]

When there is a danger from vicious animals, he should scatter corpses of farm animals mixed with a coma-inducing liquid or entrails filled with Madana and Kodrava-grain.[28] Fowlers or hunters should set to work with concealed cages and pits. Men with protective armor and carrying weapons should kill the vicious animals. [4.3.28–30]

When there is a danger from snakes, experts in the cure of poisons should set to work with incantations and medicines. Or else, people should get together and kill the snakes. [4.3.35–36]

27. The probable meaning is that each household is assessed a "tax" in rats, that is, each must bring so many dead rats per day or week.

28. *Madana* = Emetic nut, *Randia dumetorum*; and *Kodrava* = Kodo millet, *Paspalum scrobiculatum*.

Chapter Three

Central Administration

The state in the *Arthaśāstra* is structured so as to execute or support the various economic, administrative, and military dimensions of the king's rule. Because of the scope of these undertakings, the king employed and directed a variety of servants ranging from counselors, who advised on major decisions, to ministers and lesser officials, who carried out the king's orders and operated the kingdom's various bureaucratized functions. In addition to these appointees, the king employed a variety of specialized agents such saboteurs, informants, and envoys. Many of these officials, in turn, oversaw their own employees and agents depending on the function of their respective offices.

When trying to conceptualize the administration of the state as depicted in the *Arthaśāstra,* we must always remain aware that neither the king nor his subjects understood the kingdom in the way that modern individuals think of the nation-state. Effective governance in the *Arthaśāstra* is not the product of impersonal governmental institutions (as we might think of modern states governing through properly functioning courts, legislatures, executive offices, etc.). Instead, a monarchy governs effectively because a king is able to put his authority and resources behind beneficial undertakings and empower effective proxies to carry them out as directed. Hence, the central administration in the *Arthaśāstra* is not conceived so much as a collection of bureaucratic institutions and offices as it is a group of individuals appointed by the king to oversee the activities deemed critical to the successful operation of the state. The text provides instruction of varying specificity to each of these officials, but their success ultimately depended on their personal ability to wield power and command respect.

This perspective on governance devolves from the fundamental theory of political power in the *Arthaśāstra*: the king, one man among all others, possessed an overwhelming capacity for violence through his personal skill, his alliances, his wealth, and his army. His capacity for violence was so far in excess of what could be mustered by any other entity that the king was able to rule, to compel adherence to his will, through the threat and occasional use of violence. This coercive capacity is the foundation of the king's ruling power. The primary aim toward which this power was directed was its own increase. Other goals, such as the promotion of piety (*dharma*) and the preservation of peace, are clearly instrumental to it. Thus, the structure of the state administration as presented in the *Arthaśāstra* is best understood as an archetype of the set of functions through which kings attempted to increase their power.

This should not lead us to the conclusion that the king was merely a despot, who governed solely as prompted by his whim, nor should we be led to assume that his administration was a skeletal affair whose sole purpose was the extraction of wealth. Kingship in South Asia, as elsewhere, was itself conceived as a traditional institution and, as such, was shaped and constrained by custom. This larger tradition of kingship comprehended that the king had many important obligations that diverged from the directly extractive, such as ensuring public safety, providing for the adjudication of lawsuits, and generally promoting his subjects' well-being. Moreover, the various administrative institutions, such as courts, depositories, and the like, possessed their own traditional forms.

Thus, while Kauṭilya identifies the increase of power and influence as the chief aim of statecraft, this does not mean that kings had unlimited freedom in pursuing their interests and, concomitantly, in how they formed their governments. In fact, a king was constrained by a number of factors, including but not limited to the economic interests of his (more powerful) subjects, limits on his resources, the actions of neighboring kings, cultural notions of justice and righteousness, custom, and, ultimately, the acquiescence of the ruled. A monarchy existed within and relied upon a network of relationships that influenced and sculpted its administration and from which it derived critical forms of legitimacy.

The *Arthaśāstra* divides the activities of the state into internal affairs and foreign policy (the latter is discussed in Chapters 6 and 7). Internally, the state was focused primarily on economic activity, acting as both provider and consumer of certain types of goods and fostering an economic environment beneficial both to the king and to private parties through direct control of markets and other economic institutions. The majority of the officials in the central administration were, therefore, engaged either fully or partially in different kinds of economic activities, from overseeing commodities and setting prices to collecting taxes and running the treasury. Even the most senior security officials seem to have had important economic components to their offices.

We turn now to an examination of the officials of the state and the policies enacted by their offices.

3.1 Appointments to the Central Administration

Senior state officials are referred to in the *Arthaśāstra* by the generic title "minister" (*amātya*). A select number of these officials wielded great influence over the state's most vital functions. Some of these figures, such as the king's counselor-chaplain, apparently outranked members of the royal family. Other high-ranking appointees included the commander of armed forces, head of the palace guard, city manager, justices, and magistrates, as well as the counselor-chaplain, treasurer, and collector, who are discussed below.

General Qualifications

The king and his handlers were always keen to find capable, loyal, and compliant men to fill out the ministerial ranks. The *Arthaśāstra* gives us a very specific list of qualities to be found in the ideal minister. Certainly, any king would leap at the opportunity to employ the kind of individual described in the text. We should not, however, assume that the following was a list of requirements for state service. Instead, these are ideal qualities that serve as a diagnostic for judging the relative merits of actual candidates to the office of one or another ministership. That the text also mentions individuals who possess only one-half or one-quarter of these ideal qualities indicates a concession to the reality that not all those seeking office possessed all of the desired qualities. Interestingly, we note that the text makes no restrictions on the class (*varṇa*) of the candidate, requiring only that he be "of noble birth."

The ideal qualities in this list give us a good sense of the disposition favored in state officials by political thinkers of the classical period. That such qualities were highly valued is indicated by the lengths to which the king would go to test for their presence. The overall picture of the state administration inferred from this list is that of a meritocracy within the strictures of a traditionally hierarchical society. After having met the requirements of birth (place and status), an ideal minister was a man possessing exemplary personal traits. The demonstration of these meritorious qualities, particularly loyalty to the king, determined to which office a candidate could be appointed.

> Native of the country, of noble birth, easy to manage, trained in the crafts, insightful, intelligent, with a keen memory, skilled, articulate, bold, quick-witted, possessing energy and might, able to endure hardships, honest, friendly, firmly loyal, endowed with character, strength, health, and spirit, free of obstinacy and fickleness, amiable, and not a fomenter of enmities—these are the qualities of an exemplary Minister. Someone who lacks one-quarter of these qualities is mid-ranked, and someone who lacks one-half of them is low-ranked.
>
> Of these qualities, one should investigate the country of origin, nobility of birth, and ease of management through reliable close acquaintances of his; training in the crafts and insight into the treatises through experts in the same branches of knowledge; intellect, resolution, and skill from the way he carries out undertakings; articulateness, boldness, and presence of mind from the way he engages in conversations; energy, forcefulness, and ability to endure hardships from the way he

> handles adversity; honesty, friendliness, and firm loyalty from the way he interacts with others; character, strength, health, and spirit, as also lack of obstinacy and fickleness, from those who live with him; and amiability and the nonfomenting of enmities by direct observation. [1.9.1–3]

Counselor-Chaplain (*Mantripurohita*)

The highest-ranking minister in the central administration was the king's *mantripurohita*, or counselor-chaplain. The office of the counselor-chaplain emphasizes mastery of both supernatural and practical skills. Not only should the counselor-chaplain be thoroughly versed in all of the orthodox Sanskrit scriptures, denoting his high attainment and respectability among the Brāhmaṇical religious elite, but he is also supposed to be a master of reading omens and casting spells for the sake of protecting the kingdom. In addition to mastery of these arcane and ritual arts, the counselor-chaplain must also be a master of *arthaśāstra* itself. He is the king's right-hand man, able to protect the kingdom both by supernatural means as well as by the cunning of his political acumen.

When we consider the complete set of skills required of the counselor-chaplain, it becomes clear that he is a critical accessory to the king. Originally, a king's chaplain was assigned the responsibility of protecting his lord and supporting his conquests through magical rites. In the *Arthaśāstra*, however, the counselor-chaplain is involved with more operational dimensions of statecraft, fulfilling the role of a personal political adviser as well as carrying out specific political functions on the king's behalf. The personal chaplain of any king would have been highly educated and also had the responsibility of counseling the king on spiritual and ethical matters, a role that shaded quite easily into that of the king's primary political adviser. In the *Arthaśāstra*, the counselor-chaplain does not attend to the king's daily ritual obligations, which are assigned to another, more purely religious, priest.

Not everyone among the priestly Brāhmaṇa class from which the counselor-chaplain was drawn was comfortable with a

Brāhmaṇa serving in this role. There is a well-known prohibition from other Sanskrit texts of the period against a Brāhmaṇa taking up service with a king. This stems, undoubtedly, from the concern that such individuals (and by extension the greater Brāhmaṇical community) would be sullied by direct involvement in political affairs, which so frequently require activities anathema to their strict ritual and ethical codes of conduct. Nevertheless, there seem to have been a number of different attitudes about this office, and it is characteristic of the *Arthaśāstra*'s thoroughly pragmatic outlook and its unflinching emphasis on political necessity that it bears no indication of this controversy.

> He should appoint as Counselor-Chaplain a man who comes from a very distinguished family and has an equally distinguished character, who is thoroughly trained in the Veda together with the limbs,[29] in divine omens, and in Government, and who could counteract divine and human adversities through Atharvan[30] means. He should follow him as a pupil his teacher, a son his father, and a servant his master. [1.9.9–10]

Treasurer (*Samnidhātṛ*)

The office of the counselor-chaplain, discussed in the previous section, was very closely attached to the king. Indeed, he is frequently understood to accompany the king and to undertake actions related to the king's personal duties and safety. The next two high-ranking ministers who we will discuss were relatively less proximate to the king himself. These individuals oversaw aspects of the king's rule that required engagement with the greater society, and it is with the storehouses, factories, fields,

29. There are the six supplementary knowledge systems that helped in exploring and understanding the Vedic texts: phonetics, ritual, grammar, etymology, metrics, and astronomy. The notion of limbs evokes the image of an animal with the six extremities (head, four feet, and tail) protruding out of the main torso, which in this conception would constitute the Veda proper.

30. These are ritual means for warding off impending catastrophes given in the *Atharva Veda* or in literature and practices connected to that Vedic tradition.

markets, courts, prefectures, and forests of the kingdom that they were concerned. These ministers were endowed with a great deal of power and oversaw their areas of authority like small kings themselves.

The first of these is the treasurer (*samnidhātṛ*), who might also be called the "depositor." This official was in charge of the construction and management of the various depositories that the kingdom relied upon to act as places for the accumulation and redistribution of many different kinds of items. These included not only the treasury itself, but many other kinds of depositories, such as the armory and depots for forest produce. As such, the treasurer needed to be an expert in constructing secure facilities, as well as an expert in understanding their staffing. In short, he must have been extensively trained in both structural and human security. The text describes in detail how the various depositories should be constructed, and they would have been some of the most intensively designed and expensive buildings in the kingdom. As the repositories of wealth, securing their supplies was a matter of vital interest to the king, and the exalted position of the treasurer bears testament to this fact.

Another aspect of security within the depositories overseen by the treasurer relates to protecting the integrity of these caches. The treasurer oversaw a staff of experts (including the superintendent of the treasury; see §3.4) and their underlings who inspected all of the items and merchandise brought into the respective depositories. This is for the purpose of keeping a strict count on holdings, as well as preventing the acceptance of low-grade materials or fakes. In keeping with the expansive powers exercised by other high-ranking ministers, the treasurer could levy fines on individuals found guilty of fraud. Whether this power was checked by an independent judiciary is not stated.

> The Treasurer should have a treasury, a depot for merchandise, a storehouse, a storage facility for forest produce, an armory, and a prison constructed.
>
> He should have an underground chamber constructed by getting a square pit free from water or dampness dug and lining it with large slabs of stone both on the sides and at the bottom.

It should have joists of strong timber, be level with the ground with a triple floor of different compositions—a paved floor inlaid with pebbles, a local floor, and a standing floor—and have a single door with a staircase attached to a mechanical device and concealed by a statue of a deity.[31] Above that he should have the treasury constructed—it should be sealed off on both sides,[32] have an entry hall, and be built of brick and surrounded by trenches for the storage of equipment—or a mansion. At the border region of the countryside he should get people condemned to death to construct a place containing a permanent treasure for a time of adversity.

He should have the following constructed: on the two sides a depot for merchandise and a storehouse—built with burnt-brick pillars, containing four halls with a single door and several ground and upper floors, and equipped with escape routes through hollow pillars; in the middle a storage facility for forest produce with several long halls, and with its walls lined with courtyards; an armory constructed to the same specifications and equipped with an underground vault; and separately a lockup

---

31. The floor is made up of three separate layers. The underground pit has a framework of joists as the ceiling. These joists probably rested on the stone slabs lining the sides of the pit. On this framework was laid the lowest of the three floors; this probably consisted of wooden planks that made the floor (if viewed from the ground level) or ceiling (if viewed from within the pit) stable and able to withstand people standing and walking on it. Over these planks was laid the second floor with a layer of local soil. Over this soil was laid the third and uppermost layer of the floor. Both literature and archeology have shown a type of floor in ancient India made up of small stones or pebbles within a mixture of lime, a sort of a concrete floor. This floor is level with the ground floor of the treasury or the mansion built on top of the underground chamber. The entry to the chamber is hidden under a statue of a god, and the staircase leading down to it is controlled by a mechanical device known only to the king or treasurer. All these precautions were taken to prevent burglaries. The large slabs of stone lining the walls and bottom would prevent access through an underground tunnel. The triple floor is meant to fool would-be burglars. After digging through the first layer of the floor consisting of pebble-lime, they would encounter the local earth underneath. This would fool them into thinking that there is nothing underneath the floor.

32. We take this to mean that on the two broad sides of the building there are no entrances, or even that there were barricades on those sides. So everyone had to pass through the single entrance.

> for the office of the Justices and a jail for tribunals of high officials with separate facilities for men and women, and a prison with well-guarded courtyards to prevent escape. [2.5.1–5]
>
> Guided by a bureau of experts in each commodity, he should accept precious stones, articles of high or low value, and forest produce, both new and old. When there is fraud in these transactions, the punishment for both the man who did it and the one who put him up to it is the highest fine [500–1,000 Paṇas] in the case of precious stones, and the middle fine [200–500 Paṇas] in the case of articles of high value; in the case of articles of low value and forest produce, they should pay compensation and a fine equal to the value.
>
> He should accept money after it has been authenticated by the Examiner of Coins, and cut up any that are counterfeit. [2.5.8–11]

Collector (*Samāhartṛ*)

No minister in the *Arthaśāstra* had such broad and indistinct authority as the official known as the collector (*samāhartṛ*). His title implies that he was the chief financial officer of the kingdom, responsible for collecting the taxes, fines, tariffs, and duties that represented the bulk of the kingdom's regular income (outside of war and beneficial treaties). Authority over these areas implies a vast scope and reach to the collector's duties, which included the undertaking of detailed censuses, the overseeing of various networks of informants and spies, the establishment and oversight of scores of regional collection offices and officials, control of the movement of peoples and goods, oversight of all economically productive activities (mines, forests, irrigation, agriculture, animal husbandry, trade, etc.), and oversight of property boundaries. No other official would have been more deeply embedded in the social fabric of the kingdom, nor would any other official have possessed the commanding grasp of the state's finances, as the collector.

Given the expansive power invested in his office, it is not surprising then that the collector also had duties ranging beyond the economic sphere. His network of collection agents and spies were also responsible for the protection of public safety. His regional revenue offices also served as criminal courts, over which he would have wielded considerable influence. Moreover, the collector oversaw the activities of the most powerful public safety official, the "magistrate" (*pradeṣṭṛ*), who investigated actual and suspected crimes among the public as well as the king's other officers (§5.2).

His ability to generate revenue, collect information secretly, investigate individuals, and prosecute criminal offenses made the collector one of the most powerful individuals in the kingdom. The scope of his authority suggests a figure more like an appointed regional governor than a simple revenue officer.

> The Collector should oversee the following: fort, province, pit-mine, irrigation works, forest, herd, and trade route. [2.6.1]
>
> These constitute the corpus of revenue. [2.6.9]
>
> The Collector, after dividing the countryside into four, should make a record of the total number of villages classified into best, middling, and lowest, stating which is exempt from tax, which supplies soldiers, and which provides grain, farm animals, money, forest produce, labor, or counter-levy,[33] and how much.
>
> Under his supervision, a Revenue Officer should look after a five-village unit or a ten-village unit. He should have a written record made of the total number of villages according to their boundary limits and the total number of fields by enumerating the plowed and unplowed fields, dry and wet lands, parks, vegetable plots, flower gardens and orchards, forests, buildings, sanctuaries, temples, reservoirs, cemeteries, rest-houses, water dispensing sheds, holy places, pasture lands, and roads. In accordance with that, he should, with reference to the boundaries and the fields, have a written record made of the dimensions of the borders, wild tracts, and roads, and of grants, sales, favors, and tax exemptions, as well as of the houses, enumerating which ones pay taxes and which are tax exempt, and stating—in them, there are so many who belong to the four social classes; so many who are farmers, cowherds, traders, artisans, laborers, and slaves; there are so many who are two-footed and

33. This is probably a tax assessment paid in the form of agricultural produce (2.29.1, 5).

four-footed; and this is the money, labor, duty, and fines accruing from them. With regard to men and women of the families, furthermore, he should find out how many are children and old people, what their occupations and customs are, and the amount of their earnings and expenditures.

In the same manner, furthermore, the County Supervisor should look after one-quarter of the countryside.

In the offices of the Revenue Officers and County Supervisors, Magistrates should carry out the examination of lawsuits and the collection of tributes. [2.35.1–7]

The Collector should post in the countryside agents acting undercover as thaumaturgic ascetics, renouncers, traveling holy men, wandering troubadours, charlatans, entertainers, diviners, soothsayers, astrologers, physicians, madmen, mutes, deaf persons, idiots, blind persons, traders, artisans, craftsmen, performers, brothel-keepers, tavern-keepers, and venders of flat bread, cooked meat, and boiled rice. They should find out the honesty and dishonesty of village officials and Superintendents. And when he suspects any one of them of having a secret source of income, he should employ a secret agent to spy on him. [4.4.3–5]

3.2 Superintendents of Departments

Ministers of lower rank—not occupying an upper ministerial post such as those previously described—were called superintendents (*adhyakṣas*). Superintendents were granted authority over a specific area of the king's business, such as the control of markets, the production of yarn, or management of the elephant corps. Because the king's chief interest in many of these areas was the generation of wealth, the activity of superintendents is often oriented toward the economic dimensions of their respective spheres. Nevertheless, the complexity of their domains, as is evident, for example, in the duties of the superintendent of mines (*ākarādhyakṣa*), demonstrates that these were much more than financial officers. More than anywhere else in the text, the descriptions of these officials give us a sense of the complex systems on which the economic health of the kingdom depended.

Appointment and Conduct of Superintendents

Superintendents are vetted according to the same ideal qualities desirable in all ministers. They are, in this regard, not so much posts for lesser men (although their relatively lower position in the bureaucratic hierarchy certainly implies this) as positions requiring specific expertise.

The *Arthaśāstra* does not make this explicit, but it appears that the various superintendents reported, for the most part, to the collector, at least insofar as they are required to show profits from their enterprises on an annual basis. We get the sense from the text that a successful superintendent was a profitable superintendent. As the primary interest in their undertakings was the generation of income for the king, the superintendents were to be managed in such a way as to maximize the economic health and productivity of their enterprises.

> All Superintendents, endowed with the exemplary qualities of a Minister [see 3.1], should be employed in various tasks according to their abilities. And he should have them constantly investigated with respect to their tasks, because men's minds are fickle. For, given that their nature is like that of horses, men become corrupt when employed in tasks. Therefore, he should keep himself informed of the worker, the bureau, the place, the time, the work to be carried out, the investment, and the profit, with respect to those tasks.
>
> They should carry out their tasks according to the instructions, without conspiring or quarreling with each other. If they conspire, they will consume, and if they quarrel, they will destroy. They should not initiate any undertaking, moreover, without informing their master, except for remedial measures against disasters. [2.9.1–7]

Superintendent of Customs

The superintendent of customs (*śulkādhyakṣa*) represents well how the sphere of authority possessed by each superintendent was defined by a given administrative function. It is the responsibility of the superintendent of customs to control trade goods brought into the city and to assess and collect the custom or toll due depending on type and quantity.

He carries out his work in a small building with a tall flag erected near the main entrance to the city (see §2.2). Traffic through the gates of the city would have been watched closely, and transporting merchants would have known to report to the custom house identified by its tall flag. There, the agents of the superintendent of customs would inspect and record not only the goods being imported or exported, but also the merchants themselves, where they have come from, and under whose authority the goods were exported from their native place.

Imported commodities were sold at the custom house to local traders, meaning that long-distance merchants did not sell their wares directly in city markets. In an attempt to resist price fluctuations injurious to consumers or merchants, the king set prices for the sale of goods in local markets. As such, the margins between what local traders paid for imported goods and the price for which they could sell them were relatively set. The bidding over imported commodities by local traders mentioned in the passage cannot have become too inflated.

Likewise, long-distance merchants purchased domestic goods from local traders at the custom house, giving the superintendent of customs and his men the opportunity to control the flow of commodities out of the kingdom as well. Certain goods considered particularly important to the security of the kingdom, such as military equipment, seed, and farm animals, were forbidden to be exported. The superintendent of customs purchased any such imports before they reached the customs house, sending them directly to the storehouses and preventing them from reaching the public markets.

The superintendent of customs was part of a larger network, including agents at the points of origin for domestic goods as well as border guards for imported goods, that regulated the movement of commodities within the kingdom. Their work nurtured the economic health of the kingdom not only by regulating commodity markets but also through the direct assessment of taxes, tariffs, and duties on all imports and exports.

A second official, the frontier commander (*antaḥpāla*), had responsibilities related to those of the superintendent of customs. The frontier commander was responsible for documenting imported goods as they passed into the kingdom itself. He provided foreign caravans with documentation and seals and sent them directly to the capital city, and any imported goods that arrived not bearing his authorized seal were fined heavily. He also assessed and collected "road taxes" from all merchants traveling the trade routes maintained by the kingdom. These taxes were based on wear to the roads such that wagons paid a higher fee than men on foot. In return, the frontier commander was responsible for maintaining security on the trade routes and was liable for goods plundered by thieves. Certainly, it was in the kingdom's interest to promote long-distance imports, even as officials worked to contain the potentially pernicious results of such trade.

> The Superintendent of Customs should set up the customs house along with the flag facing the east or the north near the main gate.
>
> The customs collectors, four or five in number, should write down with regard to the traders arrived in caravans—who they are, where they are from, how much merchandise they have, and where the identity card or the seal was issued.
>
> The penalty on goods without a seal is twice the amount due. The fine on goods with forged seals is eight times the customs duty. The penalty on goods with broken seals is distraint in the Ghaṭikāsthāna.[34] When the royal seal has been altered or the name has been changed, he should be made to pay one and a quarter Paṇas for each load.
>
> The traders should announce the quantity and price of a commodity that has reached the foot of the flag: "Who will buy this commodity at this price for this quantity?" After it has been proclaimed aloud three times, he should give it to the bidders. If there is competition among buyers, the increase in price along with the customs duty goes to the treasury.
>
> When a man, fearing customs duty, declares a lower quantity or price, the king shall confiscate the amount in excess of that;

34. Normally *ghaṭikā* refers to a water jar and by extension a water clock. In later texts and inscriptions *ghaṭikāsthāna* refers to a school or college. The term here may refer to a warehouse. It is unclear for how long the distraint lasted and what the traders needed to do to get their merchandise released.

or, he should pay eight times the customs duty. He should do the same when someone decreases the value of a package containing merchandise by presenting a lower-quality sample, or when someone conceals a package with goods of high value within a package containing goods of low value. [2.21.1–12]

When a trader takes away for export goods on which customs duty has not been paid mixed with goods on which customs duty has been paid, or carries away a second item under a single seal by breaking open a package of merchandise, his punishment is its confiscation plus a fine of an equal amount. One who carries away merchandise from the customs house using cow dung and straw as the standard[35] should be assessed the highest seizure-fine [500–1,000 Paṇas].

Anyone who takes away for export any of the following items that are forbidden to be exported, namely, weapons, armor, coats of mail, metals, chariots, gems, grain, and farm animals, is assessed the promulgated fine and the merchandise is confiscated. If any of these items is brought in as an import, it is to be sold outside [the city] duty free.

The Frontier Commander should collect a road levy of one and a quarter Paṇas for a vehicle loaded with goods, one Paṇa for a one-hoofed animal, half a Paṇa each for farm animals, a quarter Paṇa each for small farm animals, and one Māṣika [copper coin] for a man carrying a load on his shoulder. He should, moreover, pay compensation for anything that is lost or stolen. He should dispatch to the Superintendent [of Customs] any foreign caravan after examining its goods of high and low value and providing an identity card and a seal. [2.21.20–26]

Superintendent of Yarn

The description of the superintendent of yarn (*sūtrādhyakṣa*) provides another good example of the range of a superintendent's

35. Some scholars think that the merchant presents cow dung and/or straw on the basis of which the customs duty is assessed, while the actual merchandise is of far greater value. But it is difficult to see how this can be done, unless the real merchandise in a cart is covered by cow dung and straw. I wonder whether this is another example of a maxim of which the true meaning may be eluding us.

duties. In this case, the superintendent oversees more than cotton yarns, but is also responsible for the production of different types of cloth and cordage, which is put to a variety of uses. Here we see an industry in which the kingdom had a vital stake: some measure of stability depended on a predictable supply of quality material. The superintendent of yarn is the officer responsible for the production of these commodities for supply to royal factories as well as for supply to public markets. He is responsible for the production of industrial-grade material from a wide variety of fibers for use in armor and industrial application, as well as for the production of fine fabrics for use in clothing and bedding.

One of the most interesting aspects of his office is the employment of disenfranchised and extremely marginalized women. It is often stated in Sanskrit legal and political literature that the king had a special responsibility to look after those who are most vulnerable, those lacking protection. The superintendent of yarn is explicitly instructed to employ women in difficult straits, such as widows and women who are poor or in dire circumstances. In an attempt to prevent the exploitation of such women, the *Arthaśāstra* requires that their personal interests be defended by the superintendent of yarn. Women not wishing to venture out to a worksite could choose to work from home, the agents dealing with the women producers were prohibited from looking them in the eye, their privacy was protected by allowing for the inspection of materials by lamplight, and malfeasance in rendering payment to them was met with special fines. Such instructions indicate some sensitivity to the plight of particularly vulnerable women, albeit within the dominant framework of patriarchy characteristic of social thought and attitudes in the period.

> The superintendent of yarn should organize trade in yarn, armor, cloth, and rope through experts in each.
>
> He should employ widows, crippled women, spinsters, female renouncers, and women paying off a fine through manual labor, as well as prostitutes and madams, old female slaves of the king, and female slaves of gods whose divine service has ended, to spin yarn from wool, bark-fiber, cotton, silk-cotton, hemp, and flax.

After determining whether the yarn is fine, coarse, or middling, as well as whether its quantity is large or small, he should set their wages. After finding out the quantity of yarn, he should regale them with unguents of oil and myrobalan. He should induce them to do the work by giving them gifts and honors on festive days. When the quantity of yarn decreases, the wages should be decreased proportionate to the value of the material.

He should have the work done by artisans after he has come to an agreement with them as to the amount of work, the time for completion, the wages, and the final product, and he should keep in close touch with them. As he sets up weaving factories for flax, Dukūla,[36] silk, Raṅku-hair,[37] and cotton, he should win their goodwill with perfumes, garlands, and gifts, as well as other kinds of favors. He should initiate the production of various kinds of clothes, spreads, and coverlets; and he should set up factories for armor using specialized artisans and craftsmen.

He should employ secluded women—women whose husbands have gone away, widows, crippled women, and spinsters—who wish to maintain themselves to carry out the work, being considerate by sending his own female slaves.[38] Or else, if they come to the yarn-workshop on their own, he should arrange for the payment of wages in exchange for the wares early in the morning. A lamp should be used only to inspect the yarn. For looking at the face of a woman or for speaking with her on other matters, the penalty is the lowest seizure-fine [48–96 Paṇas]; and for delay in paying the wages, the middle fine [200–500 Paṇas], as also for giving wages for work not completed. [2.23.1–14]

36. The meaning is unclear. The term probably refers to a plant fiber used to manufacture textiles.

37. A species of deer or antelope producing good-quality hair. Some identify this as the goat from which we get pashmina wool. Others take it to be the Himalayan ibex.

38. The meaning is that these women remain in their own homes, and raw material for their work is sent by the superintendent through his female slaves (perhaps the term *dāsī* here may simply refer to low-level indentured servants) to their homes.

Superintendent of Agriculture

The king had a vital interest in agriculture, which represented his primary source of income. No other revenue stream could rival that generated from taxation of the agricultural lands worked by the kingdom's largely agrarian population. The king's taxes were taken from these holdings in kind, meaning that the king took a share (usually one-sixth of grains and one-tenth of other produce) of the agricultural output of cultivated lands. In addition, the king also held his own agricultural lands outright; presumably his personal holdings would have been sizeable. The superintendent of agriculture (*sītādhyakṣa*) was responsible for ensuring the productivity of the king's lands. This was important not only as a source of revenue for the king, but, as the following passage shows, for the provision of specific foodstuffs.

The skill set of the superintendent of agriculture involves mastery of a number of related areas, including understanding of land, weather, cultivation, and botany. In addition to their agricultural and economic value, the king's lands employed slaves and laborers, frequently those somehow indebted to the king through the assessment of fines they were unable to pay.

The responsibilities of the superintendent of agriculture also provide an excellent illustration of the variety and relative value of agricultural products expected from fertile land.

> The Superintendent of Agriculture, who must be either proficient in agricultural science, geometry, and plant science, or assisted by experts in these, should collect in the appropriate seasons seed stock from all kinds of grains, flowers, fruits, vegetables, bulbous roots, roots, creepers, flax, and cotton.
>
> He should have them sowed by slaves, workers, and men paying off their fines through manual labor on land that is suitable for each and has been thoroughly plowed several times. He should make sure that they are not hampered on account of plowing implements, equipment, and oxen; also on account of artisans, as well as smiths, carpenters, hunters, rope-makers, snake-catchers, and the like. If there is a loss in the output of their work, the fine is equal to the loss of the output. [2.24.1–4]

> The land that is left over after sowing may be cultivated by those who sharecrop for half the harvest or by those who subsist on their labor, receiving one-fourth or one-fifth share. [2.24.16]

> He should plant a wet crop, a winter crop, or a summer crop according to the amount of irrigation water available. Śāli-rice and so forth are the best; vegetables are middling; and sugarcane is the worst, for sugarcane plants are beset with many dangers and require a lot of expenditure.[39] An area where foam strikes the banks is good for fruits growing on creepers; areas near overflows, for long pepper, grapes, and sugarcane; areas near wells, for vegetables and root vegetables; areas near canals, for green herbs; and ridges for plants reaped by cutting, such as herbs for perfume and medicine, Uśīra-grass, Hrībera, Piṇḍāluka.[40] And in fields suitable for each he should plant dry-land and wetland herbs. [2.24.19–23]

Superintendent of Liquor

The *Arthaśāstra* not only condones the consumption of alcohol within society, it charges the superintendent of liquor (*sūtrādhyakṣa*) with the control of its manufacture and distribution. He maintained quality control while ensuring the availability of liquor to the citizens of the city and countryside, as well as to the soldiers in the military. This acceptance of liquor stands in stark contrast to the ethics of the orthodox Brāhmaṇical community, which took a prohibitionist stance toward alcohol. Undoubtedly, the *Arthaśāstra* reflects the attitude of most kingdoms toward liquor, which amounts to an allowance of its production and consumption within certain boundaries.

Kauṭilya recognizes the need to control the production and movement of liquor: unchecked, liquor could create

---

39. Sugarcane cultivation was apparently expensive, requiring processing after the harvest. This passage indicates that the return on investment was less in the case of sugarcane than in the case of rice, grains, and vegetables.

40. *Uśīra* = Khus or cuscus grass, *Vetiveria zizanioides*; *Hrībera* = *Plectranthus vettiveroides, Coleus vettiveroides*; *Piṇḍāluka* = probably sweet potato, *Ipomoea batatas*.

problems for the social order. Limiting production to families who have long produced and sold liquor helped to ensure a kind of quality control, while rules against transport and hoarding meant that excessive amounts of liquor could not be accumulated. The text is well aware of the potential problems brought by alcohol, which can be summarized by its tendency to promote transgression of custom and tradition, the guardians of social order.

> The Superintendent of Liquor should organize the trade of liquor and ferment in the fort, countryside, and military camp through traders with expertise in liquor and ferment, the trade being carried out either in one place or in several locations, or else according to the demands of sale and purchase. He should impose a penalty of six hundred Paṇas on those who manufacture, buy, or sell elsewhere.
>
> Liquor may not be taken out of a village or be hoarded because of the following dangers: people commissioned may neglect their work, Āryas may transgress the proper bounds, and assassins may become emboldened. Or else, people known to be upright may take out a small quantity that is clearly marked—one-fourth or one-half of a Kuḍuba, or a full Kuḍuba [1 Kuḍuba = approximately 0.3 kg], or half a Prastha or a full Prastha [1 Prastha = approximately 0.6 kg]. Or rather, they should drink in taverns without wandering around. [2.25.1–5]

Superintendent of Shipping

The kingdom maintained a fleet of small and large sailing vessels to support maritime enterprises and allow the movement of people and goods throughout the realm and beyond. The superintendent of shipping (*nāvadhyakṣa*) was responsible for overseeing this fleet, from oceangoing ships to smaller ferries that served as the primary means of traversing the rivers and lakes of the kingdom. His duties involved not only setting and enforcing standard usage rates on rented watercraft, but also the stewardship of trade along waterways and coastal defense. Such management took the form of various enforcement duties, such as collecting tariffs, requiring documentation for cargo, fending off pirates, and enforcing the rules of ports as set by the superintendent of ports (*pattanādhyakṣa*).

In addition to these proscriptive tactics, the superintendent of shipping was also responsible for nurturing fishing and sea trade, particularly through the provision of emergency services or tax remittances to fishermen and merchants afflicted by disasters. Thus, he regulated the departure of boats to different regions based on weather and season.

> The Superintendent of Shipping should oversee within provincial capitals and the like the operations of seafaring vessels and ferries at the mouths of rivers, as also ferries across natural lakes, artificial lakes, and rivers.
>
> Villagers located along their shores and banks should pay a fixed levy. Fishermen should pay one-sixth portion [of their take] as boat-fee. Traders should pay a portion as duty prevailing at the port, and those traveling by royal boats, also the charges for the trip. Conch and pearl fishermen should pay the boat-fee or travel in their own boat. [2.28.1–5]
>
> The Superintendent of Shipping should uphold the customs of a port recorded by the Superintendent of Ports.
>
> Like a father, he should come to the aid of boats battered by gale winds, and charge no customs duty or half the customs duty on commodities damaged by water. He should dispatch these boats, moreover, at times suitable for sailing from the ports, according to their assignments.
>
> He should demand customs duty from boats traveling by sea when they sail within his territory. He should destroy pirate ships, as well as those approaching from an enemy's territory and those that violate the customs of the port. [2.28.7–12]
>
> At the frontiers, ferrymen should collect custom duties, escort charges, and road tolls; and they should confiscate the packages of anyone leaving with unstamped goods, as well as of anyone who crosses with an excessive load or at an unauthorized time or crossing point.

> When a boat without the requisite crew or equipment or in bad repair capsizes, the Superintendent of Shipping shall be liable for anything that is lost or destroyed. [2.28.25–26]

Superintendent of Horses

The importance of horses to classical South Asian kingdoms can hardly be overstated. Valued primarily for their martial capacity, horses were a top priority for kings in this and later periods. The armed forces were divided into four "limbs" (*aṅgas*): infantry, cavalry, chariot corps, and elephant corps (§7.1). Horses constituted, therefore, a crucial component of contemporary military forces and of the battle plans of military strategists.

The first responsibility of the superintendent of horses (*aśvādhyakṣa*) is to conduct a full census of the king's horse herds with the purpose of developing a herd sufficient for the king's needs. The purpose of this accounting is not only to have accurate and current records of equine assets available, but also to identify those horses lacking the capacity for the strenuous requirements of combat.

The superintendent of horses also oversees the construction of the king's sizeable stables and collects monthly the massive allocation of foodstuffs and medicine made directly by the treasurer from the king's stores. The stable is an enclosed area with room for all of the king's horses in individual stalls. It also possesses an entrance hall and seats, the latter presumably for audiences of the king and his officials. The horses are provided with a number of curious companions: monkeys, deer, mongooses, and myna birds. These creatures are desirable because they are believed to be able to warn against or ward off threats to the horses, such as fire, snakes, and noxious plants (see §2.3).

> The Superintendent of Horses should get the total number of horses recorded in writing—those received as gifts, those acquired by purchase, those gained by war, those born to the herd, those procured in return for assistance, those pledged in a treaty, and those temporarily borrowed—according to their pedigree, age, color, marks, class, and provenance. He should report those that are defective, crippled, or sick.

The horse keeper should take care of them, collecting the monthly allotment from the treasury and the storehouse.

He should have a stable constructed, a stable whose length corresponds to the number of horses, whose width is twice a horse's length, which has four doors and a central area for rolling on the ground, as well as an entrance hall, and which is equipped with planks for seating near the main door and teeming with monkeys, peacocks, spotted deer, mongooses, Cakora-partridges, parrots, and myna birds. He should have a stall facing east or north constructed for each horse, a stall that is square in shape with each side the length of a horse and with a floor made of smooth planks, that is equipped with a hamper for feed and an outlet for urine and excrement. Alternatively, he may adjust the direction in accordance with the requirements of the stable. The stalls for mares, stallions, and foals should be at separate ends. [2.30.1–7]

Superintendent of Elephants

Before the advent of canon and firearms, victory in combat for South Asian armies frequently depended on the overwhelming might of elephants. The elephant corps, when used effectively, was the dominant unit on any battlefield, able to wreak havoc on infantry lines and shatter an opponent's combat array. A line of enraged, charging elephants was particularly effective at demoralizing the enemy's troops. Unlike horses, however, elephants were not usually bred in captivity. One of the key duties of another official, the superintendent of elephant forests (*nāgavanādhyakṣa*), was the cultivation and protection of healthy wild herds from which the elephant corps was stocked.

The superintendent of elephants (*hastādhyakṣa*) oversaw all aspects of elephant acquisition and maintenance. Having constructed the stables for the king's elephant corps, he was then responsible for overseeing the collection (from the king's stores) and distribution of their rations, as well as the storage and care of the equipment used to outfit the elephants for war, work, and ceremony. Domesticated elephants require specific care, and the text indicates that they were constantly attended by veterinarians and kept to a strict daily routine.

The superintendent of elephants was the manager of the team of individuals required to keep the animals in good health. He also managed the employment of these very powerful and useful animals in various kinds of work, both commercial and military.

While one set of royal stables existed within the fortified city, in proximity to the king's quarters (§2.2), the superintendent of elephants also maintained lesser stables outside of the city for the purpose of training captured elephants and that could house those that proved less trainable or irredeemably vicious. From here, his teams organized the capture of elephants in the wild according to elaborate methods. We know that the superintendent of elephant forests kept a close census on the elephants within the realm, undoubtedly for the purpose of helping the superintendent of elephants find the best elephants.

> The Superintendent of Elephants should provide for the following: the protection of the elephant-forests; stables, stalls, and places for lying down for male and female elephants and cubs that are under training or capable of work; the amount of work, rations, and green fodder assigned for them; allotting of work to them; their fastenings and equipment; their military trappings; and the retinue of attendants such as veterinarians and elephant trainers.
>
> He should have a stable constructed, a stable whose height, width, and length are twice the length of an elephant; which has additional stalls for female elephants, an entrance hall, and a "Princess" configuration;[41] and which faces the east or the north. He should have each stall constructed square in shape with each side the length of an elephant, a stall that is equipped with a smooth tying post and a floor made of smooth planks, and that has an outlet for urine and excrement. He should have

41. The meaning of this expression is unclear. Some think it is some sort of a structure built with beams. Why such a structure should be specified is unclear. Commentators take it to be a beam above the post to which the elephant is tied so as to make the tying of the elephant easier. These all seem like guesses.

a place for lying down that is the same in size as a stall but half as high prepared, within the fort for military and transport elephants, and outside the fort for elephants under training and for vicious elephants.

Within the eightfold division of a day, the first and the seventh are the times for bathing, and immediately thereafter for feeding. The time for exercise is the forenoon, and the time for the stimulating drink is the afternoon. Two parts of the night are for sleeping, while a third part is for lying down and getting up.

The time for capturing elephants is the summer. A twenty-year-old should be captured, while cubs, ones with small tusks, ones without tusks, the sick, and female elephants that are pregnant or suckling should not be captured.

The best is a forty-year-old elephant measuring seven Aratnis [1 Aratni = 48 cm] in height and nine in length, with a girth of ten; the middling is a thirty-year-old one; and the lowest is a twenty-five-year-old one. The rations for the latter two are successively one-quarter less. [2.31.1–12]

3.3 Revenue Streams

For purposes of generating revenue Kauṭilya analyzes the elements that comprise the kingdom as economic activities, including some of which the economic dimensions we might not immediately perceive, such as the "fort," the "province," and "forests."

In this way, the collector (§3.1), as the chief financial officer, oversees the state's economic enterprises divided into seven areas: fortified cities, rural hinterlands, mines, agricultural irrigation, forests, animal herds, and trade routes. Each of these represents a complex set of systems requiring investment from and oversight by the state and yielding various streams of revenue. They constitute the domestic "corpus of revenue": the body of income on which the state depended. In simpler terms, these seven categories divide the state according to the various spheres of economic activity.

The *Arthaśāstra* illustrates each area in detail. Their respective components are both obvious sources of income (such as duties and fines generated within the fortified city) as well as activities supporting the generation of income indirectly (such as standardization of weights and measures and the general office of the city manager). Collectively, the components of each area give us a bird's-eye view of directly and indirectly productive activities within the kingdom.

Having aggregated these activities and divided them according to where they occur, the collector also divides all revenue streams according to how income is generated through the transaction: price (direct sales by the state), share (taxation of goods in kind), surcharge (fixed charges applied to specific transactions), monetized taxes (of several kinds), fees for the right to mint coins, and fines. All of the revenue from directly productive activities could be theoretically placed also in one of these categories.

> The Collector should oversee the following: fort, province, pit-mine, irrigation works, forest, herd, and trade route.
>
> Duties, fines, standardization of weights and measures, City Manager, director of the mint, director of passports, liquor, abattoirs, yarn, oil, ghee, sweeteners, goldsmiths, commercial establishments, prostitutes, gambling, building compounds, unions of artisans and craftsmen, Temple Superintendent, and taxes at the gates and from outsiders—these constitute "fort."
>
> Agriculture, share, tribute, tax, trader, river warden, ferry, boat, port, pasture, road toll, land-survey, and capture of thieves—these constitute "province."
>
> Gold, silver, diamonds, gems, pearls, coral, conchs, metals, salt, and ores in the earth, rocks, and liquids—these constitute "pit-mine."
>
> Flower gardens, fruit orchards, vegetable plots, wet farm land, and root crops—these constitute "irrigation works."
>
> Forest preserves for game animals, deer, produce, and elephants—these constitute "forest."

> Cattle and buffaloes, goats and sheep, donkeys and camels, horses and mules—these constitute "herd."
>
> Land routes and water routes—these constitute "trade route."
>
> These constitute the corpus of revenue.
>
> Price, share, surcharge, monopoly tax, fixed levy, coining charge, and penalty—these are the categories of revenue. [2.6.1–10]

Taxation

Taxation in the *Arthaśāstra* is a complex issue. Given the variety of activities taxed and the manner of their taxation, a one-size-fits-all policy could hardly have been effective. The ascertainment and collection of these taxes are discussed as part of the duties of the collector (§3.1).

The *Arthaśāstra* spends a good amount of time discussing situations in which taxes should be decreased. Ideally, of course, the productivity of the people and land would be sufficient for them to pay at full rates. In fact, however, tax remediation was an important tool available to the royal administration to counteract the negative effects of famine, war, and other activities that damaged agricultural yields or manufacturing, mining, and trade in the kingdom.

Fees, Customs, and Levies

We have already seen (§3.2) that the king, as sovereign, regulated the flow of goods in and out of the kingdom, an activity that allowed for both the control of distribution as well as the generation of revenue through taxes on imports and exports. The assessment rates given in the *Arthaśāstra* are traditional guidelines that the king could manipulate to promote or inhibit the availability of different commodities. Because import and export duties heavily influenced the profitability of trade in a given item, the king and his officials could use the assessment of fees, customs, and levies to encourage or discourage it. The superintendent of customs, discussed before (§3.2), oversaw much of this activity.

The text of the *Arthaśāstra* is not explicit on this point, but it appears that exports were assessed a standard duty of one-fifth their value, payable to the state in kind, while the duty on imports was based on type. So, for instance, most agricultural imports required payment of duty equal to one-fifth their value, while more expensive items, such as precious stones, some foods, raw materials, and luxury items, were assessed a much lower duty. The reasons for these differences are not altogether clear, but such numbers were certainly calibrated to promote a balance between desired availability and maximum revenue. Value, durability, spoilage, and other factors probably explain some of the differences in duties assessed.

> What is external and what is internal constitute exchange. Export duty and import duty constitute customs duty.
>
> On imports the duty is one-fifth of the price.
>
> He should collect one-sixth portion of flowers, fruits, vegetables, roots, bulbous roots, fruits of creepers, seeds, and dried fish and meat.
>
> In the case of conches, diamonds, gems, pearls, corals, and necklaces he should get experts in each to make an estimate after he has come to an agreement with them as to the amount of work, the time for completion, the wages, and the final product.
>
> In the case of flax, Dukūla, silk, armor, yellow orpiment, red arsenic, antimony, vermilion, different kinds of metal, and ore; sandalwood, aloe, spices, ferment, and minor items; skins, ivory, bedspreads, coverlets, and silk cloth; and products of goats and sheep, he should collect one-tenth portion or one-fifteenth portion.
>
> In the case of clothes, four-footed and two-footed creatures, yarn, cotton, perfumes, medicines, wood, bamboo, bark, leather goods, and earthenware; as well as grain, fat, sugar, salt, liquor, cooked food, and the like, he should collect one-twentieth portion or one-twenty-fifth portion. [2.22.1–7]

Fines

In the *Arthaśāstra* the term *daṇḍa* is used to refer to any of the various instruments through which the king exercises coercive control over society: the army, punishment, and fines. Thus, fines are both a source of income for the state and an instrument for correcting and controlling the behavior of the king's employees and subjects.

Kauṭilya depicts a state in which the assessment of fines was a widespread and regular occurrence. Justices, most notably, could assess fines for malfeasance, but it also fell under the authority of various ministers and superintendents to levy fines, both against their own employees and against the subjects of the king whose regulation fell within their area of authority (such as merchants trading in the market). In some cases, we find that the payment of a fine could substitute for corporal punishment, a penalty usually reserved for egregious crimes. The overall appearance, then, is of a state equipped with a very broad and detailed set of rules and laws governing behavior in business, personal transactions, and public behavior that was predisposed toward the assessment of fines for punishing transgressions. It is for this reason that fines constitute one of the major streams of revenue.

3.4 Treasury

The treasury was the primary repository of the king's valuables not explicitly held in other, specialized storehouses (such as grains, armaments, or forest produce). Kauṭilya thinks of the treasury both in abstract terms, as the king's total wealth, and in concrete terms, as a physical structure within the capital (see the discussion of the treasurer at §3.1). Among the various constituents of the state (§2.1), only the king himself is considered more important than the treasury, as deficiencies elsewhere, such as among ministers, the army, forts, rural lands, and allies, could all be remedied by a generous outlay of money from the treasury.

As an abstraction of the king's wealth, the health of the treasury depends on successfully managing the various activities that bear on state expenses and income. Some of these activities—reducing tax remittances and keeping a close eye on state officials—as discussed in the following reading, increase the treasury, while others—lending money and making bad investments—reduce the treasury.

The treasury is constantly making disbursements to the ministers and superintendents tasked with managing different areas of state business. These officials are expected to return the principle invested plus some profit. Thus, when the text discusses things that decrease the treasury, it is referring not only to misallocations but also to incompetent or unethical behavior on the part of officials. Mismanagement and corruption resulted in stiff penalties, including potentially ruinous fines, for which the official was personally responsible, and even death.

As a physical structure, the treasury was managed by the superintendent of the treasury (*kośādhaykṣa*), who was expected to be a master of assessing the value of the many different kinds of items that might be deposited to the treasury, whether through taxes, duties, gifts, or other means of income. The duties of this official overlap with those ascribed elsewhere in the *Arthaśāstra* to the treasurer, indicating in this case some confusion within the extant text as to the relationship between these two officials. In all likelihood, the treasurer was understood to oversee all of the depositories of the kingdom, while the superintendent of the treasury manages the treasury building itself.

Although we can be certain that the superintendent of the treasury kept an exact record of what came into and left the treasury, his primary responsibility lay with the inspection of goods submitted for the purpose of determining their value. His office supported public confidence in the worth of the king's treasury. This position also meant that he was also the ultimate judge in the kingdom of the value of a given item. Because of the breadth of knowledge required by his position,

Kauṭilya gives detailed descriptions of the characteristics of various precious items from different parts of South Asia and the ancient world. The superintendent of the treasury needed to be able to determine, for example, whether a piece of coral deposited in the treasury matched the standard description of coral from a given region. He discharged this responsibility, assisted by teams of experts in different materials who could authenticate an item and assess its value.

> All undertakings presuppose the treasury. Before anything, therefore, he should attend to the treasury.
>
> The flourishing of procedures,[42] fostering customs, suppressing thieves, controlling the officials, success of crops, abundance of commodities, relief during misfortune, reducing exemptions, and gifts of money—these are the ways to increase the treasury.
>
> Obstruction, lending, trading, cover-up, causing loss, usufruct, substitution, and misappropriation—these are the ways to decrease the treasury.
>
> Obstruction consists of the failure to carry out projects, to harness their profits, or to hand over the profits; the fine for it is one-tenth of the amount. Lending consists of lending on interest articles belonging to the treasury, and trading consists of trading in merchandise; the fine for these is double the profit. When one records the established date as not the due date, or a non–due date as the due date, it is cover-up; the fine for it is one-fifth the amount. When one causes a reduction in the income or an increase in the expenditure that have been fixed, it is causing loss; the fine for it is four times the loss. Using himself or letting others use articles belonging to the king is usufruct; the punishment for it is execution if precious stones were utilized, the middle seizure-fine [200–500 Paṇas] if an article of high value was utilized, and if an article of low value or forest produce was utilized, its restitution and an

42. We think here this term has the meaning of ways of doing things prevalent in various regions. In this passage, the first four items deal with creating the climate within a region for economic activities to flourish. The last five directly contribute to the treasury.

equal amount as a fine. Taking articles belonging to the king and replacing them with other articles is substitution; and it is explained under usufruct. When one does not hand over accrued income, pay the expenses authorized in writing, or acknowledge a secured balance, it is a misappropriation; the fine for it is twelve times the amount. [2.8.1–19]

The Superintendent of the Treasury should accept articles to be received into the treasury—precious stones, articles of high and low value, or forest produce—guided by a bureau of experts in each commodity. Pearls come from Tāmraparṇi, Pāṇḍyakavāṭa, Pāśikā, Kulā, Cūrṇī, Mahendra, Kardamā, Srotasī, Hrāda, and Himavat,[43] and their sources are oysters, conches, and other diverse creatures. [2.11.1–2]

Gems come from Koṭi, Mālā, and Pārasamudra.[44] A ruby may

---

43. Tāmraparṇi often refers to Sri Lanka, but could also refer to a river in Tamil Nadu. Kālidāsa's (*Raghuvaṃśa* 4.50) reference to pearls from the area where the Tāmraparṇi flows into the sea also indicates a river. Some scholars identify the river as the modern Chittar, a river in Tinnevelly flowing into the Gulf of Mannar. Pāṇḍyakavāṭa is identified by commentators with Mount Malayakoṭi in the Pāṇḍya area of southern India. It is difficult to see how pearls could come from a mountain. A more likely identification is Negapatam or Ramnad, a port of embarkation in the Pāṇḍya country for Sri Lanka. Pāśikā is identified as a river by that name in the Pāṇḍya country. Commentators identify Kulā as a river in Sri Lanka, and Cūrṇī as a river in Kerala, identified as Muyirikkodu or Muyirikoṭṭa on the Malabar coast. Although the commentators locate Mahendra in the northeast, some scholars argue for locating it in the southernmost reaches of the Travancore hills, once again near the Gulf of Mannar. Thus, the first three kinds of pearls appear to come from the southern reaches of the subcontinent. Kardamā is also a river in the northwestern corner of the subcontinent, perhaps in Balkh in northern Afghanistan. Srotasī, according to the commentators, was located on the shore of Barbara or Parpara. If the connection made by a commentary of this word with Ālakanda is correct, then the place should be somewhere along the eastern North African coast, if not near Alexandria itself. Hrāda also is identified as a pool in the sea off the coast of Barbara by commentators. Himavat is probably the same as the Himalaya, and likely refers to some river or pool located in or near those mountains.

44. Koṭi has been variously identified as the region between the western Ghats (Malaya) of Malabar and the sea, as the mountain Koṭa, and as the modern Dhanuskoti at the tip of the subcontinent. Mālā, in all likelihood, refers to the Malaya or some areas of modern Kerala. Pārasamudra is Sri Lanka.

have the color of a red lotus, of a saffron flower, of a Pārijāta [Indian coral tree, *Erythrina indica*] flower, or of the morning sun. A beryl may have the color of a blue lotus, a Śirīṣa [*Albizia lebbeck*] flower, water, bamboo, a parrot's wing, turmeric root, cow's urine, or cow's fat. A sapphire may have blue streaks, the color of a Kalāya [*Diospyros tomentosa*] flower, a deep blue color, the radiance of a rose apple, or the luster of a dark cloud, or be a "delighter" or a "flowing-middle."[45] A clear crystal may have the color of a Mūlāṭī[46] flower, resemble a cool shower, or be a sun-stone. These are the gems. [2.11.28–32]

Diamonds come from Sabhārāṣṭra, Tajjamārāṣṭra, Kāstīrarāṣṭra, Śrīkaṭana, Maṇimanta, and Indravāna,[47] and their sources are pit-mines, streams, and other diverse sources. [2.11.37]

---

45. The meanings of these terms are totally obscure. Both may be simply gemological terms for certain kinds of stone. Perhaps the second, with something falling or springing from the middle, may refer to a star sapphire.

46. We have been unable to identify the plant *Mūlāṭī*.

47. We have been unable to identify these locations with any degree of certainty. The identifications offered by commentators appear to be mere guesswork.

Chapter Four

The Judiciary

We have seen in the previous chapter that most of the attention paid by the king to domestic affairs concerned the generation of revenue and the regulation of the various bureaucratic institutions and activities that supported a maximally productive society. At its heart, the enterprise of statecraft was about acquiring things: wealth, prestige, and other forms of power. We might, then, be tempted to think of the king's domestic rule as primarily extractive and exploitative. In fact, however, the monarch was also bound by the responsibilities traditionally assigned to kings, which tended to justify his preeminence by ascribing to him the responsibility of maintaining order, peace, and justice within society.

This meant that the king was not only responsible for the defense of his subjects from invasion and calamity, but also for the promulgation of order within society by lending his coercive authority to the enforcement of codes of conduct and the resolution of disputes. Here is the king in his paternal role of enforcer of law, chastiser of misdeeds, and resolver of disputes. This, the king as lawgiver and defender of social order, is the complement to the king as conquering hero.

Thus, the king was responsible for promoting justice and personally accountable—in theory—for the presence of injustice in his kingdoms. Discharging this duty meant using his coercive capacity to enforce the customs, traditions, and laws that, properly observed, were felt to produce a just, humane, and orderly society. The king could pursue this project in his own administration by investigating and levying punishments against corrupt and errant officials, but among the public at large this meant deterring crime, compensating for thefts he failed to prevent, and providing his subjects access to justice through courts of law. These courts were run by high-ranking justices (*dharmasthas*) and magistrates (*pradeṣṭṛs*). The latter of these, the magistrates, prosecuted primarily criminal offenses on behalf of the state and are discussed in Chapter 5 under the topic of "Internal Security and Suppression of Criminal Activities." Justices were responsible for the resolution of disputes between private parties.

Subjects that met specific requirements could bring their disputes to court and plead their case. The *Arthaśāstra* spends a good deal of time articulating the legal code by which justices tried and resolved private disputes. Legal thought in classical South Asia conceived such disputes as being based on disagreements about private transactions. Thus, the civil legal code discussed in the *Arthaśāstra* is organized into different headings, each of which represents a class of transactions out of which disputes might emerge: "marriage," "inheritance," "debts," and so forth (see §4.4). Civil cases could also be brought when one's reputation, dignity, or person had been attacked by another citizen. Such disputes were understood to arise out of transactions such as "verbal assault" and "physical assault."

Despite the detail with which this code is rendered in the *Arthaśāstra*, these rules did not constitute a body of "positive law" as understood in the modern West. This means that justices did not refer to the legal code of the *Arthaśāstra* as an inviolable set of rules created by the state and backed by its authority that the court was responsible for preserving and enacting. Justices in the *Arthaśāstra* do not engage in a careful examination of the wording and intent of a rule, nor do they rely on a body of precedent—historical examples of how the legal code had been applied to previous disputes—in deciding a case.

Rather, the legal code as found in the *Arthaśāstra* and other Sanskrit legal texts is an articulation of the rules customarily considered to be just within society. Justices themselves were experts in these timeless customs and traditions. When deciding a case, a justice would refer to and rule within his understanding of what was fair given the circumstances, an understanding strongly influenced by the legal codes and the traditional authority they sought to codify but not ultimately determined by them. Codes collecting these customs, such as that found in the *Arthaśāstra*, possessed some authority on their own, but justice did not result simply from the process of applying their rules to the dispute at hand.

4.1 Organization of Courts

Justices, as ministers, were appointed by the king and his advisers directly (see §3.1). Lawsuits were heard by a bench of three justices in courts within the capital as well as smaller cities. There, the plaintiff would register his plaint according to the type of transaction under dispute. After they had been summoned, the plaintiff and defendant would bring evidence and witnesses before the panel to make their cases. A court clerk would record the proceedings while the justices heard evidence, questioned the parties and witnesses, and ruled on the case.

The loser of the dispute would have to compensate the victor and pay a fine that went to the king himself. Victors were not awarded punitive damages. Courts, instead, only sought to enforce what they deemed should have been the appropriate outcome of the disputed transaction. In some cases, the guilty party's punishment could go beyond monetary fines to corporal punishment. There is no mention of an appeals process in the *Arthaśāstra*, although it is certain that the king, as the ultimate source of justice and law within the land, would have possessed the authority to overturn the rulings of his justices.

Cases involving criminal offenses, that is, cases involving the commission of offenses independently punished by the state, might also be tried in the courts of these justices as a kind of transaction (such as mugging, slander, etc.) if the identities of both parties were known and not in dispute. If, however, one party was dead (as in a murder) or unknown (as in a burglary), the matter would be referred to the magistrate, who was charged with investigating such cases (§5.2).

4.2 Valid Transactions and Transactors

All private disputes are understood, as already discussed, to arise out of transactions. Here, however, we must interpret the term "transaction" rather broadly to include not only marriage (the "giving" of a bride to a groom's family), but also verbal and physical assault (a transaction or exchange of words and blows, respectively). Before the court was willing to hear the grievance of a complainant, it had to determine whether the transaction in question was itself valid. This meant, above all, that it fit within one of the standard transactional types, or "grounds for litigation," and was carried out in a legitimate fashion. As such, the text describes in detail the circumstances that render transactions invalid (such as being conducted without witnesses) and, therefore, incapable of redress in a court of law.

These rules on valid and invalid transactions assume that transactions, if they are to be legal, must be carried out publicly and in accordance with tradition. The court would not help you if you were cheated in a transaction that was carried out in an unseemly or uncustomary fashion. In fact, you could be fined for carrying out a transaction in such a manner. The text does, however, recognize that there may on occasion be good reason to conduct a transaction out of keeping with traditional practices and specifies limited exemptions to the observance of customary rules (if the validity of such contracts is not contested by either party).

Finally, a transaction is only considered valid if the parties to the transaction are authorized to engage in them. Generally speaking, anyone who is dependent economically on another and not in control of their own financial resources (such as a minor or wife), who is barred from regular commerce (such as a convict or renunciate), or who is not of sound mind (such as someone who is drunk or enraged) are not valid transactors. The list of valid transactors in the *Arthaśāstra* is a fascinating document that gives a sense of how access to the public sphere was restricted to various individuals. Certainly such parameters indicate important dimensions of individuals' personal identities, public personas, and status in the classical period.

They should invalidate transactions carried out in absentia and those executed inside a house, at night, in the wilderness, by fraud, or in secret. Both the person executing it and the person who gets it executed receive the lowest seizure-fine [48–96 Paṇas]; each of the witnesses individually receives half that fine. Those taking part in good faith, however, forfeit the object.

Transactions carried out in absentia shall be valid when a debt is secured with an absent pledge or when they are viewed as not blameworthy. Transactions executed inside a house shall be valid when they are connected with inheritance, consignments, deposits, and marriage or contracted by secluded women and sick persons of sound mind. Transactions executed at night shall be valid when they are connected with forcible seizure, trespass, brawl, marriage, and royal command, and when they are contracted by individuals carrying out business in the early part of the night. Transactions executed in the wilderness shall be valid when they are done by people moving about in the wilderness amidst caravans, herds, hermitages, hunters, and bards. Transactions executed by fraud, moreover, shall be valid when they are among individuals with secret occupations; and transactions executed in secret shall be valid when they are done within a secret association.[48]

Transactions other than these shall not be valid, as also those executed by dependents, by a son living with his father, by a father living with his son, by a brother excluded from the family, by a younger son who is a coparcener, by a woman living with her husband or son, by a slave or a person given as a pledge,[49] by one who is below or beyond the legal age, and by a notorious criminal, renouncer, cripple, or someone who has fallen on hard times—except when they have been appointed to execute the transaction.

Even in such cases, transactions executed by a person who is enraged, deeply afflicted, intoxicated, insane, or under someone

48. The reference appears to be to associations that operate in secret, such as thieves. But these associations are never identified within the text.

49. This is someone given to a creditor as collateral. During the time the person is a pledge, he or she resembles a slave and cannot act independently.

else's control shall not be valid. These who execute such transactions, those who get them executed, and those who act as witness should be individually assessed the prescribed fine.

In each respective group, however, all transactions shall be valid when they are executed at the proper place and time, by someone with proof of ownership, observing all the formalities, with valid documentation, and noting down the appearance, distinctive marks, quantity, and quality. And among these, the last document should be trusted, except in the case of a directive or a pledge. [3.1.2–16]

4.3 Judicial Procedure

Although he does not give step-by-step instructions, Kauṭilya does provide guidelines for justices and court clerks on conducting a trial. These include requirements for the litigants, information to be recorded, advice on ascertaining guilt, standard fines, and penalties for failure of the parties to comply with the court's orders.

Filing of Lawsuits

The *Arthaśāstra* is silent on crucial information regarding courts that scholars would very much like to know, such as information on places in which trials were conducted, the permanence of courts, the issue of jurisdiction, frequency of hearings, the possibility of appeal, and information bearing on the role of the courts in social life. It does tell us that justices heard cases in all cities and towns larger than the village, which indicates a widespread judicial network. What is less clear is how often courts convened or how intensively they were used by the king's subjects, all of which bears on who actually had access to their services.

The following passage is concerned largely with ascertaining facts about a given dispute. Petitioners of the court were required to provide information to the court clerk on the nature of the case and provide guarantees to cover any fees and fines that might be assessed. After these formalities, the litigants were interrogated by the justices. The text does not give details of the procedure, if indeed there was a common procedure, by which this process was conducted.

What we do read of are certain kinds of behavior in the courtroom that would cause one of the litigants to lose the suit. For example, if a litigant were to promise one kind of evidence and present something different, the justices should rule for his opponent, as such behavior is indicative of dishonesty. This is a good example of how a text like the *Arthaśāstra* is not necessarily the origin of such rules, but an authoritative record of the sensibilities prevalent in the culture of the period.

> Justices of Ministerial rank in groups of three should conduct trials—in frontier posts, collection centers, district municipalities, and provincial capitals—of lawsuits arising from transactions. [3.1.1]
>
> [The court clerk] should first write down the year, the season, the month, the fortnight, the day, the Karaṇa,[50] the court, and the debt, as also the region, village, caste, lineage, name, and occupation of the plaintiff and the defendant, after they have provided competent sureties. Then he should record the interrogations of the plaintiff and the defendant according to the sequence of the topics; and he should review what he has recorded.
>
> The man casts aside the plaint as recorded and moves on to another plaint; does not make a point made subsequently accord with what was stated previously; after challenging an unchallengeable statement of the opponent, remains obstinate; promises to produce a document (*deśa*), but when told "Produce it," does not produce it, or produces a defective document (*hīnadeśa*) or something that does not constitute documentary evidence; puts forward a document different from the document specified; denies a significant statement in the document he has put forward, saying "It is not so"; does not accept what has been ascertained through witnesses; secretly carries on a

50. This is a division of a day. There are eleven such divisions, and they correspond roughly to half of a lunar day (*tithi*).

> discussion with witnesses with regard to a document which is prohibited from being discussed—these are the reasons for loss of suit.
>
> The fine for loss of suit is one-fifth of the amount. The fine for voluntary admission is one-tenth of the amount.
>
> Wages for the men is one-eighth. Provisions for travel are assessed according to the prevailing prices. The losing party has to pay both these.
>
> An accused shall not bring a countersuit, except in the case of a brawl, a forcible seizure, a caravan, and an association. An accused, furthermore, cannot be subjected to another lawsuit.
>
> If, after receiving a response, the plaintiff does not offer a reply on that very day, he loses the case; for it is the plaintiff who has made the decision with regard to the lawsuit, not the defendant. If the latter does not offer a reply, he may be allowed three or seven days. Thereafter, he should fine the man a minimum of three Paṇas and a maximum of twelve Paṇas. If he does not offer a reply after three fortnights, he should impose the fine for loss of suit, and pay the plaintiff's claim from whatever property the defendant may possess, with the exception of the tools of his trade. He should do the very same to a defendant who absconds. The plaintiff loses the case the moment he absconds. [3.1.17–33]

Evidence: Witnesses

As in all courts, justices relied on whatever evidence they could garner to decide cases. We have read already that valid transactions—that is, transactions liable to redress in the king's courts—required documentation by the parties involved. This documentary evidence was important to the resolution of transactional disputes, as seen in the previous passage, which deals with problems relating to documentary forms of evidence.

Documentation, however, frequently could not speak directly to the dispute at hand or might be absent or deficient for another reason. Courts, therefore, relied heavily on witnesses. After the validity of a given transaction had been established, the court still needed to ascertain the terms of the agreement and whether they had been met. Witnesses, when interrogated within certain guidelines, could provide this information. The text gives details as to the number of witnesses required, who makes a valid witness, how they are admonished to give accurate information, and how justices should rule in cases of conflicting testimony.

The following discussion of witnesses is of particular interest because, in discussing valid and invalid witnesses, the text gives a good sense of how society was seen through the eyes of the court. The list of individuals excluded from being witnesses, both absolutely and conditionally, tells us whom the court felt it could trust or who it felt could be compelled to testify in given situations. We note that the court was mistrustful of certain kinds of people for different reasons. Some are excluded because they bring vested interests to the case, such as certain relatives, anyone relying financially on the litigant, and enemies. Others are excluded based on apparently irredeemable defects of body or character: the physically disabled and convicts. Some seem to have been generally excluded from such transactions, such as ascetics, lepers, and outcastes, because of their marginality. Aside from those the court mistrusted, certain individuals could not be made to appear in court. Just as the king could not be a party to a civil lawsuit, neither could his officials testify in the cases of others. As always, the text makes specific exceptions for certain kinds of cases.

Although the *Arthaśāstra* makes no such provision, other Sanskrit legal texts indicate that Brāhmaṇas played a central role in the judiciary. Certain texts require all judges be Brāhmaṇas. While the office of the justice in the *Arthaśāstra* is not explicitly circumscribed by religious identity, a general connection between courts and Brāhmaṇas is evident in the custom of having a Brāhmaṇa serve as the focus for the swearing in of witnesses, providing a kind of divine authority compelling a witness's acquiescence and promise to be truthful. Interestingly, witnesses were sworn in differently based on their social class (*varṇa*). This is very much in keeping with the more orthodox perspective of the other Sanskrit legal sources that ascribed a greater degree of honesty to the upper classes. Provisions based on social class, such as these, are probably later additions to the legal code and represent the gradually increasing influence of orthodox Brāhmaṇas on the expert tradition of statecraft.

> It is the best if an admission is made. When there is no admission, however, witnesses provide the evidentiary proof, witnesses who are trustworthy, honest, or endorsed, and a minimum of three; or, if approved by the parties, even two; but never one with regard to a debt.
>
> The following are forbidden: a brother of the wife, an associate, a dependent, a lender, a borrower, an enemy, a cripple, and a man subjected to judicial punishment; as also those previously mentioned as ineligible to execute transactions; the king, a learned Brāhmaṇa, a village servant, a leper, and a man with sores; an outcaste, a Caṇḍāla, and one following a despicable profession; anyone who is blind, deaf, dumb, or self-appointed; and a woman or an official of the king—except within their own groups. In cases concerning assault, theft, and sexual offenses, however [all these are allowed], except an enemy, a wife's brother, and an associate. In the case of secret transactions, a single woman or man who has heard or seen it can be a witness, except the king and an ascetic.
>
> Masters may testify for their servants, priests and teachers for their pupils, and a father and mother for their sons—and vice versa—without being forced to do so. When they sue each other, moreover, the superiors who lose the case shall pay one-tenth of the amount under litigation, and the inferiors one-fifth.
>
> He should impanel the witnesses in the presence of Brāhmaṇas, a pot of water, and fire. In that context, to a Brāhmaṇa he should say: "Speak the truth!" To a Kṣatriya or a Vaiśya: "May you not receive the fruit of your sacrifices and good works! May you go, a potsherd in hand, to your enemy's house to beg for alms food!"—and to a Śūdra: "Any fruit of your meritorious deeds between your birth and death, all that will go to the king, and the sins of the king to you!—if an untruth is spoken. Punishment will also follow. Afterwards, furthermore, facts as seen and heard will become known. Single-mindedly present the truth." Those who fail to present it are fined twelve Paṇas after seven days; after three fortnights they should pay the claim.

> When the witnesses are divided, they should settle in favor of the party that has the support of the majority, or of those who are honest, or of those who have been endorsed; alternatively, they should adopt the middle course. Or else, the king should take that property.
>
> If the witnesses attest to an amount less than the claim, the plaintiff should pay the excess amount as a penalty. If they testify to an amount in excess of the claim, the king should take the excess.
>
> With respect to anything that has been poorly witnessed or badly written down through the folly of the plaintiff, or where the person providing the affidavit has died, the ascertainment, after a thorough examination, should be based solely on witnesses. [3.11.25–43]

4.4 Titles of Law

As mentioned before, civil disputes were heard in court based on the type of transaction from which the dispute arose. The legal code of the *Arthaśāstra* divides these transaction types into sixteen "grounds for litigation" or titles of law. The following selections are taken from among these sixteen titles and their subtopics, including family law, inheritance, debts, and employment. They give critical information as to how such transactions should be carried out, exceptions to these rules, and the fines and punishments appropriate to various breaches.

Family Law

"Transactions," says the *Arthaśāstra*, "presuppose marriage" (3.2.1). What Kauṭilya means here is that marriage is typically the first legal transaction in which an individual engages. As such, he begins his legal code with a discussion of marriage and other aspects of family law.

The *Arthaśāstra* comprehends family law as those transactions and disputes that relate in some way to marriage itself. The rights and obligations of wives and widows represent a particularly important dimension of marriage law, which is the primary context in which women are discussed in the text. We see that Kauṭilya seeks to protect to some extent a wife's control over her private property, albeit within limits. Notably, the *Arthaśāstra* requires a woman whose husband has died or has abandoned her to have sex with her husband's brother for the purpose of producing a male heir, a controversial practice known as levirate.

> A woman twelve years old has reached the age for legal transactions, as also a man sixteen years old. Thereafter, in the case of disobedience, for a woman the fine is twelve Paṇas; for a man, double that amount. [3.3.1–2]
>
> Woman's property consists of livelihood or ornaments. Livelihood is an endowment with a maximum of 2,000 Paṇas. There is no limit on ornaments.
>
> The wife incurs no fault if she uses it to support a son or a daughter-in-law and when the husband has gone away without providing for her support; nor does the husband if he uses it for countermeasures against bandits, sickness, famine, and dangers, or for obligations relating to Law; nor the couple if they use it jointly after they have produced a son and a daughter. [3.2.14–16]
>
> When the husband has died, if the wife desires to dedicate herself to the Law,[51] she should receive immediately the endowment and ornaments, as well as the remainder of the bride-price.[52] If, on the other hand, after receiving them she gets remarried, she should be forced to return both with interest. If she desires a family, however, at the time of her remarriage she should receive what was given to her by her father-in-law and husband. [3.2.19–21]
>
> If, on the other hand, she remarries against the wishes of her father-in-law, she loses what was given to her by her father-in-law and her husband. [3.2.23]

---

51. The meaning is that she refuses to remarry and dedicates her life to religious and meritorious activities, while remaining celibate. This is the alternative to remarriage.

52. The meaning appears to be that the bride-price often may have been paid in installments. The payment is normally made to the bride's parents. In the event of the husband's death, the remainder of the bride-price is paid to the widow probably from the husband's estate.

A man should wait for eight years if his wife does not produce offspring, does not have a son, or is barren; for ten years, if her offspring are stillborn; and for twelve years, if she gives birth only to girls. Thereafter, desiring a son, he may marry a second wife. If he violates this, he should give the bride-price, the woman's property, and half the compensation for supersession,[53] as well as a fine not to exceed twenty-four Paṇas. [3.2.38–40]

A wife who hates her husband should not be granted a divorce from him if he is unwilling, or a husband from his wife. Mutual hatred is grounds for divorce. Alternatively, if the man seeks a divorce because of an offense by the woman, she should give him what she has taken. If, on the other hand, the woman seeks a divorce because of an offense by the man, she should not give him what she has taken. There is no divorce in marriages contracted in keeping with the Law.[54] [3.3.15–19]

The wife of a man who is absent from home for a long time, who has become a renouncer, or who is dead, should wait for seven menstrual periods; for one year, if she has children. After that time she should go to a uterine brother of her husband; if there are several, to the one who is closest, the one who is righteous, the one capable of maintaining her, the youngest, or the one without a wife; and in their absence, even to one who is not a uterine brother: to a man of the same ancestry or a member of the same family who is close by. This is the strict order among them. [3.4.37–41]

Inheritance

Kauṭilya follows his treatment of marriage law with a discussion of inheritance, a transaction that undoubtedly gave rise to many disputes in classical South Asia, as it has in other regions and times. Inheritance was an important issue because both assets

53. The meaning appears to be that if the husband had already given his wife the bride-price and woman's property, then only half the standard amount of compensation for supersession is to be given. What the standard is appears to be hinted at in the next provision where the compensation is said to be equal to the total of the bride-price and the woman's property.

54. These are the first four of the traditional eight forms of marriage: Brāhma, Prājāpatya, Ārṣa, and Daiva. See *Arthaśāstra* 3.2.2–13.

and debts were, for the most part, understood to be held by a family jointly and handed down by the ancestors, even though the family's finances were under the control of the father. Thus, at the time of the father's death or retirement, the assets and debts of the family (aside from what had been earned by a member of the family on their own) were collected together, divided into shares, and then partitioned out among valid inheritors—usually sons, but also daughters, brothers, fathers, grandsons, and others under different circumstances.

Each inheriting son, as an actual or potential head of his own family, was (under normal circumstances) due an equal portion of his family's wealth. Moreover, unmarried children, both sons and daughters, received shares sufficient to cover their wedding expenses. One can, for these reasons, easily imagine the strain and tension felt by members of the family as well as the greater community during the partition of a family's wealth.

We should note here that the law of inheritance found in the *Arthaśāstra* grants an equal share of the father's estate to each son, although specific circumstances could alter this equation. As such, Kauṭilya promotes a system in which a family's wealth is continuously divided over the generations rather than a system that keeps whole the family property in the hands of the eldest son, who is then responsible for the well-being of his brothers and their families. Other legal texts of the period allow for latter, and it may have been that families with smaller and less secure holdings opted not to divide the family estate.

The inheritance model described in the following text is relatively generic, although certain factors could alter the inheritance distributed to each son. The *Arthaśāstra* goes into some detail on the kinds of circumstances that could reduce or increase a son's share of the family estate. One example of this is probably further evidence of the influence on the *Arthaśāstra* of the orthodox ideologies of the Brāhmaṇa class: near the end of its discussion on inheritance the text amends its earlier endorsement of equal shares for each son in favor of a model wherein a son's share of the family estate is based on the social class of his mother, with the sons of higher-class women receiving larger shares than their half-brothers born of women from lower social classes.

> Sons who have a father—whose father and mother are still there—are without power. After the father has passed on, there is a partitioning of the father's property among them.
>
> What has been earned by oneself is not subject to partition, except those things that have been generated using the father's property. [3.5.1–3]
>
> At a partition carried out when the father is still alive, the father should neither favor anyone, nor exclude anyone from partition without a reason. [3.5.16–17]
>
> Partition takes place among those who have reached the age for legal transactions. The shares of those who have not reached the age for legal transactions, after clearing any dues, should be deposited with their mother's relatives or village elders until they reach the age for legal transactions, as also the shares of someone who is away on a journey. They should give to those who are unmarried marriage expenses equal to expenses provided to those who are already married; and to unmarried girls, a sum to be presented at their wedding. [3.5.19–22]
>
> He should have the partition carried out in the presence of witnesses, saying with specific statements: "This is the extent of the common property. Of that, this is the extent of each share." [3.5.26]
>
> Among sons from wives belonging to the four social classes, the son of a Brāhmaṇa wife should take four shares; the son of a Kṣatriya wife, three shares; the son of a Vaiśya wife, two shares; and the son of a Śūdra wife, one share. [3.6.17]

Debts

The most common cases to come before justices in classical South Asia involved the issue of debt: when one party had lent something to another and charged interest for its use. Individuals and private parties might arrange the lending of such things as cash, land, and farm animals. Such transactions would have been common and were governed by strict rules pertaining to what could be lent, how long, the interest charged, fair use, and so forth. Like all transactions, such loans had to have been made in public, in front of witnesses, and conforming to specific standards before a court would hear a case regarding them (§4.2).

The rules concerning debts given in the *Arthaśāstra* make it clear that various disputes could arise out of lending transactions, from the failure of the debtor to repay on schedule to the failure of the lender to adhere to the guidelines governing the initiation, observance, and conclusion of a loan. Many of the rules found in the *Arthaśāstra* allow us to conclude that communities sought to protect borrowers somewhat from lenders. For example, the rate of interest on a loan charged by the lender was set and could not be increased. Likewise, a borrower could not be sued for unpaid debts simultaneously by two parties. If a borrower fell ill or into poverty or was engaged in rituals or seeking his own education, his debts ceased to accrue interest.

Loans typically required the borrower to produce a surety, a person or item that stood as collateral in guarantee of the loan. If the borrower failed to repay the loan, the amount owed would be taken from the surety. We know from elsewhere in the *Arthaśāstra* (3.1.35) that unpaid debts could be recovered through forced labor, presumably in situations wherein a surety was absent or insufficient. The text, however, makes exemptions for farmers and the king's servants, whose work was considered essential to the economic and political well-being of the kingdom.

Finally, the topic of debts intersects interestingly with the issue of family law. Like wealth, debts were inherited by an individual's heirs. We see also that the rules regarding debt given in the *Arthaśāstra* do not cover loans made within a family. This reflects a recognition that such arrangements within families did not fall under the jurisdiction of the state.

> For someone not accepting a debt that is being paid off, the fine is twelve Paṇas. If he gives a valid excuse, the debt, which ceases to bear interest, should be held by a third party.
>
> A debt that is ignored for ten years cannot be recovered, unless the creditor is a child, an old or sick person, or someone who has fallen on hard times, gone abroad, or emigrated, or when there is an upheaval in the kingdom.

> A money-lender's loan to a man who has died should be paid by his sons, or by the heirs who inherited his estate or the sureties who assumed co-responsibility—and not any other liability of a surety. A surety's liability, however, relating to a pauper or a child,[55] when its place and time have not been specified, should be paid by sons, grandsons, or heirs who take the estate. A surety's liability relating to life, marriage, and land, when its place and time have not been specified, on the other hand, should be borne by sons or grandsons.
>
> When several debts come due at the same time, two should not sue a single individual concurrently, except when he is about to go away. [3.11.11–19]
>
> Loans given to each other by husband and wife, by father and son, and by brothers who are coparceners, cannot be legally recovered.
>
> Farmers and king's officials shall not be detained during times when they must work; a wife, likewise, for a debt incurred by her husband to which she has not formally agreed, except in the case of herdsmen and sharecroppers. A husband, on the other hand, may be detained for a loan taken by his wife, if he has gone away without providing for her. [3.11.21–24]

Interest Rates

As previously mentioned, interest rates on loans were established by traditional standards rather than in response to fluctuating market forces. This indicates the extent to which society and the king's administration favored a stable lending market rather than a dynamic one that evolved over time in response to supply and demand. Such standardized rates somewhat constrained

55. The likely scenario is that a legitimate transaction, to which the deceased individual was a surety, at the current time involves a pauper or a child. That is, the money owed as a result of the transaction will go to such a person. We may assume that the original lender has now fallen on hard times and is in need of the money, or that the lender has died leaving the estate to his minor children, who are now the beneficiaries. In such cases, there is a stronger obligation on the part of the sons and heirs to pay back the loan of their dead kinsman.

the development of money lending as an important economic activity by limiting its profitability. They also, however, promoted the economic health of the society by seeking to prevent lending conditions pervasively ruinous to borrowers.

The rates given in the following passage tell us that "righteous" (*dhārmya*) rates of interest struck a balance between affordability for the borrower and risk for the lender: the state wanted to make sure that affordable loans were available to stimulate economic activity while recognizing that some loans, such as those for overseas trade, were far riskier for lenders and necessitated greater returns on investment. These conventions could be superseded if the king was unable to provide security sufficient to protect the undertaking for which the loan was taken.

> One and a quarter Paṇas per month on one hundred Paṇas is the righteous rate of interest; five Paṇas, the commercial rate; ten Paṇas for travelers through wild tracts; and twenty Paṇas for seafarers. For anyone charging or making someone charge more than that, the punishment is the lowest seizure-fine [48–96 Paṇas], and half that fine for each of the witnesses individually. When, however, the king is not providing security, he should take into account the customs among lenders and borrowers.
>
> Interest on grain is up to one-half if paid at the time when crops are harvested; after that, it is monetized and will continue to bear interest on that capital. Interest on investment capital is half of the profit; that interest is laid aside in a depository and paid annually. Someone who has gone away for a long time or who remains obstinate should pay twice the principal. [3.11.1–6]
>
> A debt shall cease to bear interest in the case of a person detained by a long sacrificial session, an illness, or in a teacher's house, and in the case of a child or a pauper. [3.11.10]

Employment

Legal employment began with a transaction during which a valid contract for labor was agreed to by employee and employer. The rules regarding these labor contracts in the *Arthaśāstra* seek to protect both parties.

The text recognizes standard wages for different kinds of work (while allowing that the parties may agree to more or less pay) and allows an employee to call on neighbors or observers to bear witness that the work was completed as assigned. An employee under contract could also be released from his obligation in the case that he proved unfit for the task or the work itself was unpalatable. Likewise, an employer could have an employee imprisoned if the latter accepted pay but failed to carry out the required work and also reserved the right to conclude that the work had been completed as agreed.

As elsewhere, we see in this section that Kauṭilya's perspective demonstrates a concern for the general health of the labor market, rather than disproportionately favoring exploitive practices.

> Those nearby should keep an eye on a laborer's application to his work. He should receive the wage agreed upon; one without a wage agreement, a wage proportionate to the work and the time. An agricultural worker, a cowherd, and a trader without a wage agreement should receive one-tenth of the crops, butter, and merchandise, respectively, in which each has had a hand; one with a wage agreement, however, the wage agreed upon.
>
> Groups who work with the expectation of remuneration, however, such as artisans, craftsmen, performers, physicians, bards, and attendants, should receive wages similar to others in their profession or as experts may determine. [3.13.26–30]
>
> For an employee who takes the wages but does not do the work, the fine is twelve Paṇas and detention until the work is done. If he lacks the strength, if the work is repulsive, or if he is sick or struck by a calamity, he should have the right either to rescind the contract or to get the work done by someone else. Alternatively, the employer should have the right to get the work done at the employee's expense. [3.14.1–3]
>
> When work has been carried out contrary to the right place and time or in a different manner, he may not, if he is unwilling, accept the work as done. If someone does a greater amount of work than agreed upon, he should not make that exertion fruitless. [3.14.10–11]

Sale without Ownership

Sale without ownership is one of the transactions in the *Arthaśāstra*'s legal code that could apparently be investigated whether or not the sale itself was a valid transaction. In essence, these rules protect the rights of a victim to recover stolen property and establish guidelines for punishing or absolving the party found in possession of the stolen items. Note that buyers of stolen property were not to be reimbursed: caveat emptor.

> With regard to sale by a nonowner, however—an owner, when he discovers a lost or stolen article, should get a Justice to impound it. Or else, if there is an urgency with regard to place and time, he may impound it himself and deliver it to him. The Justice, moreover, should interrogate the owner: "From where did you obtain this?" If he points out a customary method of acquisition but not the seller, he is freed by surrendering the article. If the seller is discovered, he should pay the price and the fine for theft. If he were to find someone who would exonerate him, he shall be exonerated—until persons providing exonerations are exhausted. When exhausted, that person should pay the price and the fine for theft. [3.16.10–16]

Verbal Assault

While the civil code found in the *Arthaśāstra* almost certainly had its origins in the kinds of material, economic transactions discussed in the preceding selections, it appears that the code was expanded at a certain point to include verbal and physical assault. The legal codes of ancient India include assault in the civil code because it is a transaction between private parties—an exchange of words or blows—in which the identity of both parties is known. The victim brought the attacker before the court to seek redress for his injuries.

The following passage on verbal assault distinguishes between "insults," which are verbal attacks involving real or supposed deficiencies, and "abuse," which is categorizing someone as a certain kind of person, such as a leper or being impotent. Fines for both depend on whether the deficiency is actual or fictional and whether the attacker used a facetious and mocking tone, which Kauṭilya particularly abhors.

In matters of verbal assault, as in other suits, social standing matters. Classical South Asian society, like many traditional societies, was acutely aware of the relative stature of the individuals in social exchange. We see that fines for abuse were doubled if an inferior insulted a superior and halved in the reverse case.

Note, finally, that this section makes explicit what is assumed throughout the text: men are the de facto subjects addressed by these codes. Penalties are ascribed for abusing "the wives of others," meaning that insults to married women were prosecuted as assaults on their husbands.

> Insult, abuse, and threat constitute verbal assault.
>
> Among insults relating to body, character, learning, occupation, and country, for an insult relating to the body with words such as "one-eyed" and "lame," the fine is three Paṇas if it is true, and six Paṇas if the insult is untrue. For disdain couched as praise of people who are one-eyed, lame, and the like, saying "What beautiful eyes you have!" the fine is twelve Paṇas.
>
> For abuse by referring to people as lepers, insane, impotent, and the like, depending on whether it is true, false, or disdain couched as praise the fines are twelve Paṇas increased progressively by twelve, if it is among equals. If it is directed at superiors, the fines are doubled; if it is directed at inferiors, the fines are cut in half; and if it is directed at the wives of others, the fines are doubled. The fines are cut in half if it is done through negligence, intoxication, folly, and the like. [3.18.1–5]
>
> A man who issues a threat to do something to another, saying "I will do this to you!" but who does not carry it out should pay half the fine prescribed for actually carrying it out. If he is incapable of carrying it out or if he offers the excuse of anger, intoxication, or folly, he should pay a fine of twelve Paṇas. If he harbors feelings of hostility and is capable of doing harm, he should provide a surety for as long as he lives. [3.18.9–11]

Physical Assault

With a few exceptions, unless a case of physical assault resulted in the death of the victim, it was addressed through a civil plaint brought by the victim. Cases of murder and certain other types of assault, such as sexual assault, were referred to a different branch of the king's judicial system, referred to euphemistically as the "Eradication of Thorns" (see Chapter 5). Such cases were overseen not by justices, but by magistrates who had the authority to investigate crimes and assess physical punishments, from imprisonment to death by torture.

The following passage, however, refers exclusively to private lawsuits brought in cases of physical assault. In assessing the punishment for a given instance of assault, the court took into consideration the relative status of the attacker and victim, the location on the person where the assault took place, the substances or items with which the assault was carried out, and the extent of the injuries.

The punishment for physical assault in these private cases was a monetary fine rather than any kind of corporal punishment, although some of the crimes also merit corporal punishment at the hands of a magistrate. The fines for particularly violent assaults—beating someone unconscious, breaking bones, harming organs, etc.—were very steep.

> Touching, menacing, and striking constitute physical assault.
>
> For someone touching someone's body below the navel with the hand, mud, ashes, or dust, the fine is three Paṇas; for doing so with the same that are impure or with the foot or spit, it is six Paṇas; and for doing so with vomit, urine, feces, and the like, it is twelve Paṇas. For doing so above the navel, the fines are doubled, and for doing so on the head, the fines are quadrupled—these apply among equals. When directed at superiors, the fines are doubled; when directed at inferiors, the fines are cut in half; and when directed at the wives of others, the fines are doubled. The fines are cut in half if these are done through negligence, intoxication, folly, and the like.
>
> For pulling the feet, garment, hands, or hair, the fine is six Paṇas increased progressively by six. For pressing, squashing,

> twisting, dragging, and pinning down, the punishment is the lowest seizure-fine [48–96 Paṇas]. For running away after throwing someone down, the fine is half that amount. [3.19.1–7]
>
> For someone causing pain without drawing blood using any of the following objects: stick, clod, stone, metal rod, or rope, the fine is twenty-four Paṇas; it is doubled if blood is drawn, except in the case of infected blood. For someone beating a man almost to the point of death without drawing blood, or for dislocating a hand or a foot, the punishment is the lowest seizure-fine [48–96 Paṇas]; as also for breaking a hand, foot, or tooth; for cutting an ear or the nose; and for opening up a wound, except in the case of infected wounds. For breaking the thigh or neck, for damaging an eye, or for causing an impediment to speech, movement, or eating, the punishment is the middle seizure-fine [200–500 Paṇas], and in addition the expenses for recovery. In the case of death, he should be brought before the agency for the Eradication of Thorns.
>
> For a group of people beating a single man, each is assessed double the fine. [3.19.12–16]

Gambling and Betting

Gambling, specifically, betting on throws of shells or dice, was a popular pastime in South Asia, particularly among the noble and warrior classes, for whom gambling held a special, sometimes ritual, importance. Attitudes about gambling in the classical period ranged widely. While some other classical South Asian jurists felt that gambling should be entirely outlawed in society, Kauṭilya supports gambling regulated under the office of the superintendent of gambling (*dyūtādhyakṣa*), making it a state-run industry.

The chief benefits of regulating the gambling industry are twofold: wealth and security. The state took a cut of all winnings, rented out gambling implements and spaces, and oversaw the pawning of personal items. Equally as important, however, was that oversight of gambling houses allowed state officials to ferret out those individuals in the kingdom who had money to gamble that was out of keeping with their public profession: these individuals were almost certainly receiving some kind of secret (i.e., illegal) income. It is interesting to note that the state's regulation of alcohol, also a controversial issue in the period, was also partly motivated by an interest in using the intoxicant to gain information about individuals.

Cheating is the primary offense arising out of gambling. Someone who felt they had been cheated could bring his opponent to court in an attempt to recoup his losses. In successfully prosecuted cases, the victim would receive his money back and both parties would pay a fine—a tactic meant to prevent frivolous lawsuits. Interestingly, the *Arthaśāstra* indicates that teachers of old favored fining the victim in these cases more than the cheater, presumably in an attempt to forestall spurious claims arising because the victim could not bear the gambling loss. Kauṭilya, however, disagrees with the traditional practice. He argues that such a policy will have the effect of discouraging cheated gamblers from seeking justice. This exchange is an example of the kinds of debates and inquiries into justice carried out by jurists in the classical period.

> The Superintendent of Gambling should have gambling carried out in one location—for anyone gambling elsewhere the fine is twelve Paṇas—so as to find out those who have secret occupations.
>
> "In a lawsuit relating to gambling, the winner receives the lowest seizure-fine [48–96 Paṇas], and the loser the middle fine [200–500 Paṇas]; for the latter, being foolish by nature, craves to win and cannot bear to lose": so state the Teachers. "No," says Kauṭilya. "If a loser is assessed a double fine, then no one will come to the king. For, by and large, gamblers cheat when they play."
>
> The Superintendents should provide for them genuine shells and dice. For substituting other shells or dice, the fine is twelve Paṇas; for cheating at play, the lowest seizure-fine [48–96 Paṇas] and the forfeiture of the winnings; if there is fraud, in addition the fine for theft.
>
> The Superintendent should take five percent of the winnings, as well as the rental charges for shells, dice, leather straps, and ivory cubes; and charges for water, ground, and play. He should

carry out the pledging and sale of articles. For not interdicting offenses with respect to dice, ground, and hands, the fine is doubled.

That also explains betting, with the exception of betting on learning and craftsmanship. [3.20.1–13]

Chapter Five

Internal Security and Suppression of Criminal Activities

Modern legal systems typically distinguish between civil law and criminal law. The former pertains to disputes between private parties, while the latter refers to offenses independently prosecuted by the state. The *Arthaśāstra* deals with civil law under the rubric of transactional disputes (see Chapter 4). The prosecution of criminal offenses by the state, however, is not treated in the text as an independent branch of law. Instead, Kauṭilya addresses what we might think of as criminal law as part of a larger group of practices meant to address various threats to the stability of the kingdom.

Collectively, the various threats to the kingdom are called "thorns," evoking the thorny brambles that threaten to overtake land and render it useless for human agriculture or settlement. Such "thorns" might include everything from unethical business practices among merchants or tradesmen to corrupt or treasonous officials, crimes, black-market activities, famine, fire, and plague. Some of these threats were neutralized by the king's internal secret service, while the elimination of others fell to a group of officials, agents, and practices known collectively as the "Eradication of Thorns."

Ultimately, the internal secret service and the Eradication of Thorns were meant to protect the security of the kingdom and, most specifically, the rule of the king. Because of the critical importance of this undertaking, we see that the state in the *Arthaśāstra* is generously provided with various security services, from spies to magistrates, who were constantly engaged in surveillance, investigation, spreading propaganda, and the neutralization of enemies to state, a practice known as "silent punishment."

5.1 Internal Secret Service

The chief means by which the king and his security agents were able to police society—both private citizens and governmental employees—was through a vast and robust network of spies and secret agents. These secret service officials represented a complex and diffuse network of informants, assassins, and *agents provocateur* under direct control of the king and his counselor-chaplain (see §3.1). The *Arthaśāstra* tells us that the king met secretly with these agents in the small hours of the night, receiving their reports and guiding their activities (§1.3).

Chief among the king's concerns was the loyalty and honesty of the officials in his government, and much of the work of his spies sought to identify trustworthy individuals and expose those who might work against his interests, either for purposes of self-enrichment or out of loyalty to one of the king's enemies. To this end, the king employed networks of informants and agents who operated by assuming inconspicuous roles in society, such as a wandering beggar or nun, student, musician, merchant, or farmer. These individuals, appearing to be regular people, gathered information on their targets and transmitted it through a network of agents back to the king and his counselor-chaplain. Agents might then be deployed for further information gathering, to frame a political opponent, or to carry out an assassination.

In this way, the king sought to discover and address security threats within his administration. Officials who proved trustworthy and loyal would be promoted to important positions, while antagonistic officials might be punished or silently neutralized. The king also sought to identify those officials who were at risk of turning against the king's interests. The text calls these at-risk officials "seducible," and advises the king to attempt to cultivate their loyalties or, failing that, to have them dealt with.

It is hard to overstate the importance of spies and secret agents to the administration portrayed in the *Arthaśāstra*. They are an irreplaceable means for the king to project his power and coercive capacity to both his officials and his subjects. All of the king's subjects and officials would have been, to a greater or lesser extent, continually aware that one of the king's informants might be observing them. We read very little in the *Arthaśāstra* of any formal or transparent procedure for prosecuting offenses against the king. Likely, the punishment for such activities (real or perceived) was simply the automatic levying of a fine, imprisonment, corporal punishment, or, simply, disappearing. The king had eyes and ears everywhere, and most of his subjects almost certainly endeavored to stay above the suspicion of his ubiquitous secret services.

Clandestine Operatives: Informants

The *Arthaśāstra* divides the king's spies into two groups: "clandestine establishments"—informants recruited from private society to pass on information to which their everyday social roles might give them access—and "mobile agents"—specialized, roving spies who could be sent on specific missions or act as go-betweens. The five kinds of informants and four kinds of mobile agents are given in the first sentence of the following passage.

The rest of the passage describes the five kinds of individuals recruited to the clandestine establishments. The king's agents would identify individuals that met a specific profile, and those persons would be recruited to the king's service by the counselor-chaplain. This involved approaching the potential recruits in secret with promises of financial rewards and other honors and giving instructions to report any suspicious activity to one of the king's other agents.

Potential recruits were drawn from among students, renunciates, merchants, and agriculturalists. Students with ambition and political prowess were attractive because, not yet householders, they lived relatively more mobile lives and had relatively greater access to homes and social institutions. Moreover, it was to the king's benefit to recruit talented and loyal agents from among the ranks of the kingdom's young, ambitious men. Other informants were drawn from the ranks of individuals in need of support, either because they had become disenchanted with the religious life or had been unable to support themselves at different kinds of economic activity.

> With the body of Ministers, whose integrity has been proven by secret tests, in place, he should commission clandestine operatives: crafty student, apostate recluse, and agent working undercover as householder, merchant, or ascetic, as well as secret agent, assassin, poisoner, and female mendicant-agent.
>
> The crafty student is a pupil who is bold and knows the vulnerabilities of others. After instigating him with money and honors, the Counselor should tell him: "Taking the king and me as your authority, report immediately anything untoward you may observe in anyone."
>
> An apostate recluse is someone who has reverted from renunciation and who is endowed with intellect and integrity. In a place assigned to him for some economic activity and supplied with plenty of money and apprentices, he should have the work carried out. From the profits of his work, moreover, he should provide food, clothing, and shelter to all renouncers. And he should instigate those who are looking for a livelihood: "Wearing this same outfit, you should work for the benefit of the king and come here at the time for rations and wages." All renouncers, furthermore, should similarly instigate their respective groups.
>
> An agent working undercover as a householder is an agriculturalist endowed with intellect and integrity whose means of livelihood has been depleted. In a place assigned to him for agriculture . . .—the rest is the same as above.
>
> An agent working undercover as a merchant is a trader endowed with intellect and integrity whose means of livelihood has been depleted. In a place assigned to him for his trade . . .—the rest is the same as above.

> An agent working undercover as an ascetic is a shaven-headed or a matted-haired ascetic looking for a livelihood. Living in the vicinity of a city with a lot of shaven-headed or matted-haired apprentices, he should eat a piece of vegetable or a handful of barley once a month or once in two months openly, while eating all the food he wants in secret. And apprentices of agents working undercover as merchants should eulogize him for performing secret rites for prosperity, while his own pupils should announce: "He is a thaumaturgic ascetic, able to secure prosperity." [1.11.1–16]

Clandestine Operatives: Mobile Agents

The "mobile agents" enumerated in the previous passage are specialists who can be sent on specific missions suited to the king's needs. While the female wandering ascetic is intended to maintain her persona, the other roving spies—the agent, the assassin, and the poisoner—can appear in a variety of guises, such as musicians, shampooers, and valets. The job of these agents is to gain access to difficult places, such as the homes of high governmental officials and other important persons, for the purpose of gathering information or assassinating a target.

In keeping with their more dangerous and difficult assignments, these spies were required to possess a specific set of skills and dispositions. We see, for example, that the spy called the "secret agent" needed expertise in many esoteric and magical arts, such as various forms of divination, illusion magic, the ascetical arts, and the art of associating with others from a variety of backgrounds and origins without creating suspicion. Some of these capacities helped with information gathering, while others provided an advantage in infiltrating different buildings and communities. The "assassin" and the "poisoner" were two kinds of killers, selected based on the requirements of the mission: was it to be an ambush in a remote region or an undetected poisoning in the official's home? Finally, the female ascetic played a critical role in gaining initial access to an official's home, exploiting the access granted to such trusted and revered figures.

Secret agents are those members of a corps who necessarily have to be maintained,[56] when they study the interpretation of signs, the interpretation of limbs, magical lore, creating illusions, Law of hermitages, interpretation of omens, and interpretation of the interstices of a circle, or when they study the science of association.[57]

Assassins are brave individuals from the countryside who, brushing aside personal safety, would do battle with an elephant or a vicious animal for the sake of money.

Poisoners are those who have no feelings toward their relatives, and who are cruel and lazy.

A female wanderer who is looking for a livelihood, who is poor, a widow, bold, and a Brāhmaṇa woman, and who is treated

---

56. These were probably bands of young warriors. These agents belonged to respectable families, and this explains their functions within the spy establishment, including employment to test the loyalty of princes and high officials.

57. *Interpretation of signs:* the meaning is unclear. It may refer to the interpretation of bodily marks. It is, however, unclear how this is different from the next. The signs here may have a broader meaning than simply bodily marks, such as natural phenomena, crying of birds, sight of various animals, and the like.

Interpretation of limbs: this expression may refer to a variety of prognostications using signs present on the body of a person. It appears that the astrologer puts a question to his client, and interprets the future by observing which part of the body the client touches, what sorts of persons or animals he sees, and the like.

Creating illusions: probably refers to various kinds of magical tricks.

Law of hermitages: some take *āśrama* in the original to mean the orders of life. This category is somewhat anomalous here. I take it to mean the duties relating to religious hermitages. Perhaps the reference is to spies who assume the guise of matted-haired ascetics.

Interpretation of the interstices of a circle: the circle has thirty-two sections (interstices). When the omen, the cry of a bird or animal, comes from the direction of a particular part of this circle, a particular interpretation is given. Thus, if it comes from the eastern division, it indicates the arrival of an officer of the king, the gaining of honor, or the acquisition of wealth.

Science of association: the meaning is unclear, and the commentators take it to mean the magical arts associated with love and sex. The term can also refer to certain planetary conjunctions.

respectfully in the royal residence, should visit the homes of high officials. Her case explains that of shaven-headed ascetics who are Śūdra women.

These are the mobile agents. [1.12.1–5]

Testing the Loyalty and Honesty of State Employees

One of the most important capabilities granted to the king by this network of informants and mobile agents was testing the loyalty and honesty of the individuals he had appointed to office. In particular, the ability of the mobile agents to infiltrate the homes of the wealthy made them an effective tool for these investigations. The text tells us that the king was to deploy his spies throughout the realm against all members of his administration.

The king should employ them—according to devotion and capabilities and with credible disguises in terms of region, attire, craft, language, and birth—to spy on these: Counselor-Chaplain, Army Commander, Crown Prince, Chief Gate-Guard, Head of the Palace Guard, Administrator, Collector, Treasurer, Magistrate, Commander, City Manager, Director of Factories, Council of Counselors, Superintendent, Commander, Commander of the Fort, Frontier Commander, and Tribal Chief.

Assassins, employed as keepers of umbrellas, pitchers, fans, shoes, seats, vehicles, and mounts, should find out their outdoor activities. Secret agents should report that to the clandestine establishments.

Poisoners employed as chefs, cooks, bath attendants, masseurs, preparers of beds, barbers, valets, and water servers, or disguised as hunchbacks, dwarfs, Kirātas (see note 7), dumb, deaf, mentally retarded, or blind or as actors, dancers, singers, musicians, bards, and performers—as also women—should find out their indoor activities. Mendicant women should report that to the clandestine establishments.

The apprentices of clandestine establishments should communicate the secret information gathered by spies through signs and written messages. Neither they nor the clandestine establishments should know each other. [1.12.6–12]

> When three report the same thing, it should be trusted. When they fail constantly, their removal is through silent punishment. [1.12.15–16]

These practices were meant to ferret out problematic officials, but before a minister could even be appointed he had to pass a series of secret tests administered by the king through his counselor-chaplain, army commander, and spies.

These tests were designed to determine whether a minister's loyalty to the king could be compromised by religious piety, greed, passion, or fear. Passing one of these tests made a minister eligible for specific appointments. For example, an official who had passed the test of relating to passion might be appointed to work in the palace, entrusted with duties that could bring him in proximity to the queen and the king's seraglio. Officials who passed all of the tests were appointed to the very highest offices, such as counselor.

In the test relating to righteousness, the king commands his counselor-chaplain to officiate at the sacrifice of someone forbidden by the sacred law of Brāhmaṇas: a severe infraction. To pass the test, the targeted minister must put his loyalty to the king above his respect for religious law. This test illustrates well Kauṭilya's fundamentally pragmatic attitude toward religion: he will endorse religious authority, but only insofar as it does not threaten the king's interests. It is easy to see why Kauṭilya was considered by certain religious traditions as a wicked teacher of "false" doctrines.

In the end, tests such as these can only have served to further empower the king: an official could never be entirely certain whether an opportunity to betray the king was genuine or engineered by the king himself.

> In cooperation with the Counselor-Chaplain, after installing the Ministers in regular departments, he should test their integrity with secret tests.
>
> The Counselor-Chaplain becomes indignant at being appointed to officiate at a sacrifice of a person at whose sacrifice one is forbidden to officiate or to teach such a person. The king should then dismiss him. He should send secret agents to instigate each Minister individually under oath: "This king is

> unrighteous. Come on! Let us install in his place some other righteous person—a pretender from his family, a prince in disfavor, a member of the royal household, the man who is the sole support of the kingdom,[58] a neighboring lord, a forest chieftain, or a man who has risen to power. Everyone likes this idea. What about you?" If he rebuffs it, he is a man of integrity. That is the secret test relating to righteousness.
>
> The Army Commander, dismissed because of the support he has given to bad people, should send secret agents to instigate each Minister individually with tempting monetary rewards to bring about the downfall of the king: "Everyone likes this idea. What about you?" If he rebuffs it, he is a man of integrity. That is the secret test relating to money.
>
> A female wandering ascetic who has won the confidence and is received with honor in the royal residence should instigate each high official individually: "The chief queen is in love with you and has made arrangements to meet with you. You will also receive a lot of money." If he rebuffs it, he is a man of integrity. That is the secret test relating to lust.
>
> On the occasion of a festivity, one Minister should invite all the Ministers. Alarmed at that, the king should imprison them. A crafty student who had already been imprisoned there should instigate each Minister individually who has been robbed of money and honor: "This king's conduct is evil. Come on! Let us kill him and install someone else. Everyone likes this idea. What about you?" If he rebuffs it, he is a man of integrity. This is the secret test relating to fear. [1.10.1–12]

Secret Punishments

The king's use of spies against his officers did not end after a minister had passed one or more of the tests and been appointed to a specific office. Ongoing efforts by the king's spy network sought to identify and root out traitorous or problematic officials. Ordinarily, the king might be able to move against the

58. The reference probably is to a minister, probably the chief minister, who comes right next to the king himself in importance for the kingdom.

offending officer in a public manner, with a fine, imprisonment, corporal punishment, or execution. In some cases, however, an official might be protected from public reproach, either because he is popular with the citizenry or supported by other powerful officials. If moving against an official publicly bore too high a cost, that official could be dealt with through what the text calls "secret punishment."

These secret punishments provide a pretext for arresting or killing a political enemy by using agents to frame him or to provide a reasonable pretext for his death. The lack of ethical concern demonstrated by such advice, which often involves the death of innocent individuals as a political expedient, has helped to promote Kauṭilya's nefarious reputation. These examples also show us, however, how Kauṭilya exploits existing social conventions and customs, even while disregarding them.

> Against those chief officers who live off the king by bringing him under their grip or who are equally partial to the enemy, success is achieved by employing clandestine operatives or by recruiting seducible factions, as described above; or else through instigation to sedition or espionage in the manner we will describe in the section on capturing an enemy settlement.
>
> Against those chief officers, however, who, being either favorites or banded together, impair the regime—traitors who cannot be subdued openly—he should employ secret punishment, finding delight in his duty.
>
> A secret agent should incite a brother of a traitorous high official, a brother who has not been treated with respect, and present him to the king. The king should urge him to attack the traitor by granting the use of the traitor's property. Once he has attacked him with a weapon or poison, he should have him executed on the spot, proclaiming "This man is a fratricide!" [5.1.3–7]
>
> Alternatively, the brother, incited by a secret agent, should request a traitorous high official for his inheritance. At night, as he is lying down in front of the door of the traitor's house[59]—or staying

59. This is a reference to a common practice in ancient India of a creditor remaining fasting until death outside the house of a debtor until he pays up.

> elsewhere—an assassin should kill him and announce: "This fellow has been killed as he was longing for his inheritance!" Then, taking the side of the dead man, he should arrest the other. [5.1.9–11]
>
> He should dispatch a traitorous high official with a weak army that includes assassins to destroy a forest tribe or an enemy town, or to install a Frontier Commander or a Commander of a province in a region separated by a wild tract, or to pacify a sector under the City Manager that is in revolt, or to take charge of a caravan escort along the frontier together with an area subject to recapture. As the battle is engaged during the night—or during the day—the assassins or agents in the guise of bandits should kill him, announcing: "He was killed during the offensive." [5.1.21–22]
>
> Alternatively, secret agents should get traitors in the fort or the provinces to invite each other as guests. On that occasion poisoners should give them poison. The others should be punished for this crime. [5.1.47–49]

Punishment of State Officials

Certain of the king's officials charged with carrying out the Eradication of Thorns also made extensive use of spies. While the king and his counselor-chaplain oversaw the investigation of high state officials, it fell to the collector (§3.1) to ascertain the integrity of lesser officials. Note the wide variety of individuals employed by the collector as spies. We see that, among the lower-level officials who held the posts of superintendent or village officer, Kauṭilya is most concerned about illegal forms of income (extortion, black market, etc.).

> The Collector should post in the countryside agents acting undercover as thaumaturgic ascetics, renouncers, traveling holy men, wandering troubadours, charlatans, entertainers, diviners, soothsayers, astrologers, physicians, madmen, mutes, deaf persons, idiots, blind persons, traders, artisans, craftsmen, performers, brothel-keepers, tavern-keepers, and venders of flat bread, cooked meat, and boiled rice. They should find out the honesty and dishonesty of village officials and Superintendents. And when he suspects any one of them of having a secret source of income, he should employ a secret agent to spy on him. [4.4.3–5]

Aided by magistrates—law enforcement officers with the power to both carry out investigations and hand down convictions (see §5.2)—the collector was responsible for policing the behavior of departmental superintendents, their underlings, and judicial officials.

When a magistrate had determined the guilt of an official or employee of the state, he could issue a punishment using the following code as a guideline. Note that the magistrates, unlike justices, had the power to execute offenders, such as those who stole valuable items from the state's mines or factories. In this case, the term "clean death" refers to simple execution. The other type of execution, "vivid death," refers to execution with or by torture.

> The Collector and Magistrates should first exercise control over the Superintendents and their assistants.
>
> For someone who steals an article of high value or a gem from pit-mines or factories for articles of high value the punishment is clean execution; for someone who steals an article of low value or a tool from factories for articles of low value, the lowest seizure-fine [48–96 Paṇas]. For someone who, from sites for merchandise, steals king's merchandise valued more than one Māṣa [a copper coin] up to a quarter Paṇa, the punishment is twelve Paṇas; valued up to two-quarters of a Paṇa, twenty-four Paṇas; valued up to three-quarters of a Paṇa, thirty-six Paṇas; valued up to one Paṇa, forty-eight Paṇas; valued up to two Paṇas, the lowest seizure-fine [48–96 Paṇas]; valued up to four Paṇas, the middle [200–500 Paṇas]; valued up to eight Paṇas, the highest [500–1,000 Paṇas]; and valued up to ten Paṇas, execution. [4.9.1–4]

Theft was not the only offense for which officials could be punished. The collector had the responsibility to punish justices, court clerks, and magistrates for mistreating litigants, failing to follow proper procedure, or punishing the undeserved. Corporally punishing an innocent person could bring the same punishment back on the justice or magistrate. Repeat offenders were removed from the bench. The severity of these rules indicates the importance of maintaining the integrity of the kingdom's courts.

> If a Justice threatens, reprimands, or drives out, or suppresses a man who has filed a lawsuit, he should impose on him the lowest seizure-fine [48–96 Paṇas]; if there is a verbal assault, the fine is doubled. If he questions someone who should not be questioned, does not question someone who should be questioned, or after questioning brushes it aside, or if he tutors, reminds, or prompts him, he should impose on him the middle seizure-fine [200–500 Paṇas]. If he does not request a document that needs to be produced, requests a document that need not be produced, lets the case proceed without documentary evidence, dismisses it under some pretext, drives away by delays someone who becomes tired, rejects a statement properly presented, assists witnesses with their memory, or takes up a case that has already been adjudicated and a verdict rendered, he should impose on him the highest seizure-fine [500–1,000 Paṇas]. In the case of a repeat offense, the fine is doubled and he is removed from office.
>
> If the court clerk does not write down what was said, writes down what was not said, writes correctly what was badly said, writes incorrectly what was correctly said, or alters a clear meaning, he should impose on him the lowest seizure-fine [48–96 Paṇas], or else a punishment corresponding to the crime.
>
> If a Justice or a Magistrate imposes a monetary punishment on a person who does not deserve punishment, he should impose on him a fine equivalent to double the amount he imposed; or eight times the amount by which it is less or more than (the prescribed fine). If he imposes corporal punishment, he should himself suffer corporal punishment; or double the standard reparation. Alternatively, when he dismisses a truthful lawsuit or sustains a bogus lawsuit, he should pay eight times that as a fine. [4.9.13–20]

The *Arthaśāstra* sets standards for the treatment of prisoners and makes jailers responsible for their observance. These rules give us one of the few glimpses inside the penal system of the text, which is not extensively described. There were several kinds of detention facilities run by the state (see also §5.3). The court lockup is probably a temporary holding place for use by justices in civil disputes. The jail may have held individuals who had lost civil disputes, but were unable to pay what was owed, as a way to demand payment from their families or for them to work off their debts. The role of the prison is obscure. As the *Arthaśāstra* tends to favor corporal punishment to incarceration, it is difficult to surmise who may have been housed there. Likely, it was used to hold serial offenders, political enemies, those convicted to die, and/or criminals whose circumstances (debt, popularity) made it unwise to execute them.

> For preventing someone from sleeping, sitting down, eating, answering calls of nature, or moving about, or for keeping someone bound up in a court lockup, a jail, or a prison, the fine on the perpetrator and on the person ordering it is three Paṇas for the first increased by three for each subsequent one.
>
> On anyone who releasing a man from a jail or letting him escape, the middle fine for forcible seizure [200–500 Paṇas] should be imposed and he should be made to pay the amount litigated; if from a prison, all his property is to be confiscated and he is to be executed. [4.9.21–22]
>
> For a Prison Superintendent who, without informing, allows freedom of movement to a prisoner, the fine is twenty-four Paṇas; who orders his torture, double that amount; who transfers him to a different station or deprives him of food and water, the fine is ninety-six; who inflicts excruciating pain or maiming, the middle seizure-fine [200–500 Paṇas]; who kills him, one thousand Paṇas; who violates a married female prisoner who is a slave or a pledge, the lowest seizure-fine [48–96 Paṇas]; a wife of a thief or rioter, the middle fine; an Ārya female prisoner, the highest fine [500–1,000 Paṇas]. For a prisoner doing that, execution on the spot. The same, he should know, applies in the case of an Ārya woman arrested during night curfew; when it is a slave, the lowest seizure-fine [48–96 Paṇas]. [4.9.23–26]

5.2 Magistrates and Police

The public officials most directly responsible for the Eradication of Thorns were the magistrates. As mentioned before, they operated under the authority of the collector and made use of the same spy networks. Like justices, the magistrates adjudicated cases in benches of three. Magistrates, however, had much broader powers than justices, powers that extend well beyond the courtroom, including, most importantly, the active suppression and disruption of suspected criminal elements.

As an adjudicator of legal cases, a magistrate acted not only as justice, but also as the investigator of the alleged crime and prosecutor of the state's case against the defendant. Although the procedure for these cases is not described, magistrates' courts would have lacked some of the disinterestedness of the justices' court. Ultimately, any given case would have rested on the ability of a magistrate to produce convincing evidence.

> Magistrates of Ministerial rank in groups of three should carry out the eradication of thorns. [4.1.1]

Investigations of Crimes and Murder

Much of the magistrate's expertise pertains to forensics and the interpretation of various forms of evidence. Rather than trying to ascertain what was just in a transaction between two private disputants like a justice, a magistrate was trying to ascertain who was responsible for the commission of criminal acts such as theft and murder. These requirements meant that the magistrate had to investigate crime scenes and develop expertise in identifying evidence as well as in interrogation.

In cases of theft, the magistrate begins by questioning the suspect, who may have been marked as such by physical evidence or witnesses. His alibi must check out completely, or the suspect is subjected to torture and interrogation. A magistrate needed to be circumspect, however. Failure to report a crime in a timely manner or a feud between accuser and accused might indicate that an accusation is spurious.

When the magistrate had himself begun to suspect someone, he then needed to produce material evidence and witnesses linking the suspect to the scene of the crime or the possession of the stolen goods. A magistrate presumably acquired these things through investigation and torture or, when torture is prohibited, through spies. Failure to find such evidence exonerated a suspect, even if there had been problems with his alibi. For, as the text notes, not everyone appearing or claiming to be a thief actually is.

> In the presence of the victim of the theft, as well as external and internal witnesses, he should interrogate the accused about his country, caste, lineage, name, occupation, wealth, associates, and residence. He should corroborate these by checking them against other depositions. Then he should interrogate him about what he did the previous day and where he spent the night until his arrest. If he is corroborated by the person providing his exoneration, he is to be considered innocent; otherwise, he is to undergo torture.
>
> A suspect may not be arrested after the lapse of three days, because questioning becomes infeasible[60]—except when the tools are found on him.
>
> For a man who calls someone a thief when he is not a thief, the fine is the same as that for a thief; so also for anyone who hides a thief.
>
> When a person accused of being a thief has been inculpated because of enmity or hatred, he is to be considered innocent. For someone who keeps an innocent man in custody, the punishment is the lowest seizure-fine [48–96 Paṇas].
>
> Against someone on whom suspicion has fallen, he should produce tools, advisers, accomplices, stolen goods, and agents; and he should corroborate his action by checking it against the entry, the receipt of the goods, and the partition of shares.
>
> When these kinds of evidence are lacking, he should consider him as just a blabbermouth and not the thief. For we see that even a person who is not a thief, when by chance he runs into thieves making their way and is arrested because his clothing, weapons, and goods are similar to those of the thieves or because he was lingering where the stolen goods of the thieves

60. The meaning is unclear. It appears that interrogations after a certain lapse of time are inadmissible as evidence in court. Questioning after three days may also be impossible because he may not remember what happened that far back. Indeed, both may be meant, because when memories fade their use as evidence becomes problematic.

> were found, may, just like Māṇḍavya-of-the-Stake,[61] confess "I am a thief" even though he is not a thief, because he fears the pain from torture. Therefore, he should punish only a man against whom there is convincing evidence.
>
> He should not subject to torture a person who has committed a small offense, a child, an old person, a sick person, an intoxicated person, an insane person, a person wearied by hunger, thirst, or travel, a person who has eaten too much or whose food is still undigested, or a weak person. He should have such people spied on by persons of the same character, prostitutes, attendants at water booths, or those who give them advice, accommodation, or food. He should outwit them in this way, or in the manner explained in the section on the theft of a consignment.
>
> When there is likelihood of someone's guilt, he should subject him to torture, but never a woman who is pregnant or within a month after giving birth. [4.8.1–17]

Cases of sudden death give the magistrate another kind of evidence on which to perform his forensic investigation: a corpse. The following passage outlines the indications left on a corpse by different causes of death. Some of these guidelines seem more or less valid, while others seem quite fanciful. Such information, however, allowed the magistrate to begin reconstructing the death of the individual and determining whether any wrongdoing was involved. Kauṭilya also indicates some of the standard suspects in murder cases: severely abused servants, malcontented wives, and greedy heirs. Note the patriarchal perspective implied

61. The story of the sage Māṇḍavya is narrated in *Mahābhārata* 1.101. Once, some thieves, with soldiers in hot pursuit, came to the sage's hermitage while he was observing a vow of silence and hid in his hermitage with their loot. When the sage would not reply to the soldiers' questions, and finding the thieves in his hermitage, they impaled him. Learning the truth, the king removed him from the stake, but he could not pull the stake out of him. A part of the stake (*aṇi*) remained embedded in his anus, and thus he came to be called Aṇi-Māṇḍavya. The *Arthaśāstra* version of the story is somewhat different in that here the sage does not remain silent but confesses to a crime he did not commit fearing torture.

by this list of suspects, which leads one to wonder about typical motives for murder and whether only certain sudden deaths received attention from the magistrates.

> He should examine a person who has died suddenly after he has been coated with oil.
>
> When urine and feces have spurted out, the abdominal skin is bloated with wind, the hands and feet are swollen, the eyes are open wide, and the throat has marks on it, he should know that the man was killed by suffocation through strangulation. When a man with those same marks has his arms and thighs drawn together, he should know that the man was killed by hanging.
>
> When the hands, feet, and stomach are swollen, the eyes are drawn in, and the navel is bulging out, he should know that the man was taken down (from a stake).
>
> When the anus and eyes are closed, the teeth have bitten into the tongue, and the stomach is distended, he should know that the man has drowned.
>
> When the body is smeared with blood, and the body is broken and cut, he should know that the man was killed by being battered with sticks or stones.
>
> When the limbs are broken up and blown apart, he should know that the man was thrown from on high.
>
> When the hands, feet, teeth, and nails have turned dark, the flesh, bodily hair, and skin droop, and the mouth is coated with foam, he should know that the man was killed with poison. When a man with those same marks has bloody fang marks, he should know that the man was killed by a snake or insect.
>
> When the clothes and limbs are contorted and excessive vomiting and purging have taken place, he should know that the man was killed by a coma-inducing mixture.
>
> He should find out whether a man was killed in one of the above ways, or whether, after killing him, his neck was lacerated by hanging because of the fear of punishment.
>
> He should examine the leftover food of a man killed by poison using birds. When material extracted from the heart

is thrown in fire, if it makes a crackling sound or becomes rainbow-colored, he should know that it contains poison; or when he sees that the heart remains unburned after he has been cremated. He should initiate a probe into any domestic servant of his who was subjected to severe verbal or physical abuse, or a wife of his who has been aggrieved or is enamored of another man, or a relative of his who covets his inheritance, livelihood, or wife. [4.7.1–14]

Suppression of Crimes

Magistrates were responsible not just for investigating crimes that had already occurred, but also for preventing future crimes and proactively disrupting criminal networks and bandits. This involved using secret agents to lure criminals into offenses that the magistrate could then use to their advantage in neutralizing the offenders. Note that the text sometimes defines criminals on the basis of a given crime (i.e., "bandits"; "adulterers") and other times effectively criminalizes entire groups such as "forest tribes," presumably based on the assumption that such tribes subsisted in part on robbery or other activities deemed illegal by the state. In fact, such forest tribes were often targeted simply as potential threats to the political power of the king.

The rules given in the following passage instruct the magistrate how to entrap certain kinds of criminals. Secret agents are crucial to this enterprise, as they not only provide the initial enticement in the form of helpful magical spells, but also stage events so as to make those spells and their creators seem efficacious. Once the secret agents have gained the confidence of the criminals, they can engineer their arrest in several different manners, such as having them mark their bodies in distinctive ways as requirements for using their bogus spells.

After the employment of secret agents—agents working undercover as thaumaturgic ascetics should entice criminals with magic skills for crime: bandits with a spell that induces sleep, makes one invisible, or opens doors; and adulterers with a love-inducing spell.

When they have been roused, they should take a large group of them at night and aim to go to one village. Going, however, to

> a different village where people posing as husbands and wives have been stationed, they should tell them: "Right here you will behold the might of our magic skills! It is difficult to go to that other village." Then, having opened the doors with the door-opening spell, they should tell them: "Enter!" With the spell that makes one invisible, they should make the criminals pass between guards while they remain awake. With the sleep-inducing spell, they should put the guards to sleep and get the criminals to move them around along with their beds. With the love-inducing spell, they should get women disguised as wives of others to have sexual pleasures with the criminals. Once they have become convinced of the might of their magical skills, they should instruct them to perform the preparatory rites and the like to provide a mark of identity.
>
> Or, they should get them to carry out their activities in houses containing marked articles. Or, once they have won their confidence, they should get them arrested in a single location. They should get them arrested while buying, selling, or pawning marked articles or when they are intoxicated with doped liquor.
>
> Once they have been arrested, he should question them about their previous offenses and their associates. [4.5.1–11]

Magistrates were also responsible for infiltrating and disrupting criminal bands and criminalized tribes that roved the wild places of the kingdom. This could be accomplished in several ways after their agents had won the trust of the targeted group. With these groups, however, it is permissible simply for the king's soldiers to slaughter the suspects. This is an indication of the extent to which these groups were wholly excluded from certain civil protections.

> Veteran thieves, cowherds, fowlers, and hunters, moreover, having won the confidence of forest thieves and forest tribes, should incite them to raid caravans, cattle camps, and villages abounding in fake money, forest produce, and wares. During the raid, they should get them killed by concealed soldiers or by means of provisions for the journey mixed with coma-inducing juice. They should have them arrested as they fall sound asleep, worn out by a long journey carrying heavy loads of stolen goods, or as they lie intoxicated with doped liquor at festive celebrations. [4.5.15–17]

5.3 Prisons and Jails

Precious little is known about the penal system in the *Arthaśāstra*. We know that the state constructed and ran a system of jails and prisons and that some of these were used by justices in civil disputes, while others were used for detaining high state officials. What is not clear is what the qualitative differences between the prisons were, what each was used for, or who comprised the prison population.

The *Arthaśāstra* does not tend to prescribe incarceration as punishment for crimes. As such, individuals must have ended up in prison for other reasons, such as an inability to pay their legal debts or through extrajudicial detention. Court lockups may have held individuals who had been arrested on charges and were waiting to see a justice or magistrate. The jails for detaining high state officials were places to hold them during tribunals and prisons may have been alternatives to corporal punishment for those too dangerous to release, but too popular or powerful to have killed. To account for the variety of inmates mentioned in the text, we have to assume that entire families could be incarcerated for different reasons (see also §5.1).

> The Treasurer should have a treasury, a depot for merchandise, a storehouse, a storage facility for forest produce, an armory, and a prison constructed. . . . He should have the following constructed . . . separately a lockup for the office of the Justices and a jail for tribunals of high officials with separate facilities for men and women, and a prison with well-guarded courtyards to prevent escape. [2.5.1, 5]

> For someone assisting an escape from a jail, the punishment is the middle seizure-fine [200–500 Paṇas] if done without breaching, and execution if it is breached; and if the escape is from a prison, both the confiscation of all his property and execution. [4.9.27]

> Children, old people, the sick, and the helpless, moreover, are released from prison on the day of the birth-constellation and on full-moon days. Pious men or individuals belonging to a group governed by conventions may pay a ransom for an offense. Every day or every fifth day he should discharge

the prisoners through bonded manual labor or monetary compensation. Release of prisoners is decreed when new territory is acquired, at the anointing of the Crown Prince, and at the birth of a son [2.36.44–47]

Even in the case of a serious crime, the Counselor-Chaplain is subdued by imprisonment or exile; the Crown Prince, by imprisonment or by execution if he has another virtuous son. [9.3.14]

Chapter Six

Foreign Affairs

While administration and internal security were critical issues for kings and their counselors to ponder, the kingdom's relationship with other states was considered to be the most important issue that faced a king. Economic distress, treason, and banditry could debilitate a king, but the fatal blow would almost certainly come from a foreign power. Conversely, kings weakened by internal or external conditions could buttress their position by means of beneficial treaties with allies. Ultimately, Kauṭilya saw the kingdom as surrounded by stronger and weaker states run by righteous and wicked kings, all interested in their own advancement. Skillful engagement in foreign affairs, was, therefore, crucial to the survival and success of the king's rule.

The threat from foreign kingdoms was not merely theoretical: the traditions of kingship and statecraft considered military campaigns to be frequent, if not annual, events. When the rains ended and the weather permitted, sufficiently powerful kings established massive military encampments and began campaigns into the surrounding regions. In general terms, the king sought to sign treaties with those states he could overpower as well as with those states that dramatically overpowered him. Such treaties involved the weaker state giving the stronger some form of advantage: wealth, land, aid, or fealty. The *Arthaśāstra* conceives of larger political formations as comprised in part by networks of such tributary relationships with subordinate states. In lieu of such treaties (and sometimes in spite of them), states would pursue war against one another in pitched battles and sieges. For the victor, these campaigns meant the seizure of great amounts of wealth; for the loser, they meant either destruction or subordination.

Contemplating and carrying out foreign affairs meant acting skillfully and strategically within this framework, cultivating advantageous alliances, addressing internal problems, weakening enemy states, finding glory in conquest, and enriching the kingdom. Navigating through these modes via counselors, envoys, spies, armies, and personal relationships was the stuff of foreign affairs. It is in these deliberations that the king spent much of his time and it was through their outcomes that he steered his kingdom through peace and war, through growth, stability, or decline.

6.1 Circle Doctrine of States: Allies and Enemies

As mentioned before, the political theorists of the classical period conceived of relations between kingdoms as playing out on a kind of chessboard. At the center was the realm of the home king—the *Arthaśāstra* calls him "the seeker after conquest." Surrounding the home kingdom in a circle on all sides were enemy states. Kauṭilya takes it as a given that any two states who share a border are "natural" enemies, hence the king is surrounded first by a circle of enemies. The menacing threat of this ring of hostile states is somewhat ameliorated, however, by a second circle, concentric with the circle of enemies, called the circle of allies. Because this circle of kingdoms (the second circle) also share borders with the king's enemies (the members of the first circle), they are "natural allies" to the home king. Such a map follows the well-known dictum that "my enemy's enemy is my ally."

This model of interstate relations is, for obvious reasons, called the "Circle Doctrine." It provides the basic foundation for assessing relationships with neighboring states and analyzing potential threats, possible alliances, and overall prospects for peace and war. It can be extrapolated to include a third circle (the circle of my enemies' allies), a fourth circle (the circle of my allies' allies), and so on.

Built upon the Circle Doctrine are specific refinements for theorizing relationships with neighboring states, such as distinguishing between different kinds of enemies based on their relative strength or weakness and allies based on the nature of one's relations. Another refinement to interstate political theory conceives of interstate relations not in concentric circles, but in linear terms. When the king sends troops out against a neighboring enemy, he must then consider the enemy who shares his opposite border as "the rear enemy," his ally beyond that enemy as "the rear ally," and so on. Once hostilities had begun with a specific state, the king would need to exploit this linear set of relationships to guard his vulnerable rear border.

All of this sounds very tidy if we consider only the relationships of the home state. When, however, we try to imagine how this would play out in reality, we come to understand that these doctrines and models are only conceptual apparatuses for trying to work out strategic relationships. In truth, things would always have been messier than this. This complexity is reflected in the theorizing of two other kinds of states, not included above: the "intermediate state" and the "neutral."

> The seeker after conquest is a king who is endowed with the exemplary qualities both of the self and of material constituents[62] [of the kingdom], and who is the abode of good policy. Forming a circle all around him and with immediately contiguous territories is the constituent comprising his enemies. In like manner, with territories once removed from his, is the constituent comprising his allies.
>
> A neighboring ruler possessing the exemplary qualities of an enemy is the "foe"; when he is facing a calamity, he is the "vulnerable"; when he is without support or with weak support, he is the "vanquishable"; and in the opposite case, he is the "oppressable" or the "enfeeblable." These are the different types of enemies.
>
> Beyond him in a series of contiguous territories toward the front are located the ally, the enemy's ally, the ally's ally, and the ally of the enemy's ally; and toward the back, the rear enemy, the rear ally, the rear enemy's backer, and the rear ally's backer.

62. They are given at *Arthaśāstra* 6.2.25: minister, countryside, fort, treasury, and army.

> One with an immediately contiguous territory is a natural enemy—one of equal birth is an innate enemy; and one who is hostile or acts with hostility is a contingent enemy.
>
> One with a territory once removed is the natural ally—one related to the mother or father is an innate ally; and one who has sought refuge for money or life is a contingent ally.
>
> One with a territory immediately contiguous to both the enemy and the seeker after conquest, and who is able to assist them both when they are united and when they are not and to overpower them when they are not united is the intermediate.
>
> One who is apart from the enemy, the seeker after conquest, and the intermediate, and more powerful than the constituents,[63] and who is able to assist the enemy, the seeker after conquest, and the intermediate both when they are united and when they are not and to overpower them when they are not united is the neutral. [6.2.13–22]

6.2 Six Measures of Foreign Policy

The Circle Doctrine is used as a theoretical device through which to contemplate different options for dealing with foreign kingdoms. Using the typology of the Circle Doctrine and its refinements, Kauṭilya identifies six different possible strategies, collectively called the "sixfold strategy."

Essentially, each of these six strategies represents actions or postures that a king might take depending on prevailing political conditions. The first two—peace pact and initiating hostilities—are the most basic activities. Short of choosing one of these, a king might decide rather to hunker down in his fortress or to march out threateningly. When the king has recourse to neither a successful pact nor a successful war, he might choose to flee and take refuge with another king. Finally, a king might combine a pact and hostilities, strengthening his position through an

63. The meaning of the term here appears to be the twelve constituents of the circle of kings listed in this very passage. The neutral king is, thus, the most powerful king among the kings that constitute the circle.

alliance on one side so that he might successfully prosecute an invasion on the other.

It was among these six options that the king and his counselors deliberated. While different conditions prompted different strategic decisions, we should keep in mind that the prosperity of the kingdom was not understood to result from finding peaceful relations with all neighboring states. The ultimate goal of a king was political domination, and all strategic decisions were made with this in mind. Whether subordinating enemies through intimidation and treaty or through invasion and siege, the king's identity was shaped by the promise of and duty to conquer and subordinate his neighbors.

> The basis of the sixfold strategy is the circle of constituents.
>
> "The sixfold strategy consists of peace pact, initiating hostilities, remaining stationary, marching into battle, seeking refuge, and double stratagem": so state the Teachers.
>
> "Strategy is twofold," says Vātavyādhi, "for by means of a peace pact and initiating hostilities the sixfold strategy is accomplished."
>
> "This is indeed a sixfold strategy, because there are different circumstances," says Kauṭilya.
>
> Of these, peace pact is a negotiated agreement; initiating hostilities is harmful action; remaining stationary is awaiting patiently; marching into battle is strength; seeking shelter is surrendering to another; and double stratagem is pursuing a peace pact and initiating hostilities at the same time. These are the six strategies.
>
> When he is getting weaker in comparison to the enemy, he should arrange a peace pact, and when he is getting stronger, he should initiate hostilities. When he realizes, "Neither is my enemy able to hurt me, nor am I able to hurt my enemy," he should remain stationary. When he possesses an abundance of the strategic advantages, he should march into battle. When he lacks power, he should seek refuge. With respect to a task achievable only with an accomplice, he should resort to the double stratagem. So are established the strategic measures. [7.1.1–19]

6.3 Envoys

The *Arthaśāstra* tells us that the king would sit and deliberate over foreign affairs regularly with his counselors (§1.2) and, once a decision had been reached, they would dispatch an envoy. This gives the impression that the groundwork for all interstate relations, whether they ultimately ended in peace or war, was laid by the diplomatic corps. Presumably, then, kings would usually signal an intention or negotiate through envoys before other actions were undertaken. The strategic exchange of envoys was at the heart of foreign affairs.

Kauṭilya assumes that individuals chosen for such activity will be drawn from the priestly Brāhmaṇa class, who, owing to their learning and high social regard, probably filled many of the upper governmental ranks. A Brāhmaṇa made a good choice for an envoy for several reasons. First, he would have been highly educated in both intellectual topics as well as cultural etiquette. Famous for their learning and strict self-control, a Brāhmaṇa would represent a formidable force in negotiating on behalf of the king's interests. Second, Brāhmaṇas, thought by many to be divine themselves, were held in high regard, and a king would have risked his own reputation by abusing, detaining, or harming a Brāhmaṇa envoy. Finally, the employment of a Brāhmaṇa would, for many, reflect well on the king and add a dimension of authority to his message. South Asia is not the only place in which elite religious specialists were the preferred messengers of kings.

According to custom, envoys were immune from harm at the hands of their hosts. It remained, nevertheless, a potentially dangerous job to deliver unpleasant messages to or negotiate with hostile kings. An envoy could expect not only very real threats to his life, but also that he would be spied upon and even seduced by his hosts. His position was a precarious one, and his office required many personal qualities from charisma and persuasiveness to cunning and insight.

Envoys possessed of great personal quality were entrusted with sensitive missions or the authority to negotiate on behalf of the king. The duties of an envoy, however, ranged beyond even this. As the king's agent in foreign territories, an envoy was responsible for communicating with outlying officers such as frontier commanders, collecting information about the enemy's kingdom, assessing military strengths and vulnerabilities, mapping out potential invasion routes, gathering intelligence about the foreign king, and making contact with the king's secret agents abroad. Important envoys might be carrying out multiple missions on a single trip, effectively acting on behalf of the king in many different spheres. The difference between peace and war often hinged on their reception and the success of their missions.

> Once the counsel has been taken, the employment of Envoys takes place.
>
> One who has the qualities of an exemplary Minister is an Envoy with a broad mission. One who lacks a quarter of those qualities is an Envoy with a limited mission. One who lacks half of those qualities is an Envoy who delivers royal decrees.
>
> He should set out after making proper arrangements for vehicles, mounts, and the retinue of assistants. He should travel rehearsing in this manner: "The royal decree should be communicated to the enemy in this manner. He will make this sort of a reply. This will be the response to that. In this manner he should be outwitted." As he travels, moreover, he should keep in close touch with Tribal Chiefs, Frontier Commanders, and the city and provincial chiefs. He should be on the lookout for areas suitable to station the army, to engage in combat, to locate reserve troops, and to make a retreat for both himself and the enemy. He should obtain information about the extent of the forts and the provinces, as well as the strength, sources of income, defenses, and the vulnerable points.
>
> When permission is granted, he should enter the enemy's dwelling and deliver the royal decree exactly as instructed, even if he perceives a danger to his life.
>
> He should interpret these as signs that the enemy is pleased: cordiality in his speech, face, and gaze; complimenting the Envoy's speech; asking what he would like; showing an interest in talking about his good qualities; offering a seat close by;

> treating him hospitably; recalling pleasant times; and placing confidence in him; and the inverse of these as signs that he is displeased.
>
> He should tell the enemy: "Kings—both you and others—speak through the mouths of Envoys. Therefore, even when weapons are raised, Envoys say exactly what they were instructed to say. Even the lowest born among them are exempt from being killed; how much more, then, the Brāhmaṇas. This is the statement of someone else. This is the Law with respect to an Envoy." [1.16.1–17]

6.4 Foreign Secret Service

We have already read about the precautions taken by kings against potentially treasonous elements in their own realms. Now we see that kings sought to exploit this vulnerability among their rivals. The *Arthaśāstra* refers to those individuals who might be turned to treason as "seducible," and, just as the king sought to neutralize them in his own territory, so he sought to win them over in his neighbor's territory.

To this end, Kauṭilya advises the king to dispatch secret agents to foreign lands to identify seducible elements and turn them to the king's interests. The *Arthaśāstra* outlines the kinds of conditions that produce disaffection in a subject, so that the agents might more easily identify seducible parties. Once these parties have been identified, the secret agents use elaborate ruses to turn the loyalties of the target. This typically includes gaining trust via agents in disguise, planting the seeds of sedition in the target's mind, and using various enticements to lure them away. Usually, this was a complex endeavor involving agents of different kinds acting out its many roles.

Thus, a king would complement his diplomatic and military assets with the activity of covert operatives. Foreign policy was a game of degrading the enemy's strengths, exacerbating his weaknesses, and utilizing his vulnerabilities. In the dynamic domain of interstate relations, conquest meant finding ways to outwit one's enemies and then continue to find effective ways to keep them under one's control.

> We have explained how seducible and nonseducible factions may be won over within one's own territory; we have yet to describe how it is carried out in an enemy's territory. [1.14.1]
>
> Among these, he should incite to sedition each individual belonging to a seducible faction through one of the agents working undercover as shaven-headed or matted-hair ascetics to whom he may be devoted. [1.14.6]
>
> Agents operating undercover as traders in his forts, agents operating undercover as householders in his villages, and agents operating undercover as cattle herders and ascetics in his frontier posts, should send a message to a neighboring ruler, a Tribal Chief, a pretender from his family, or a prince in disfavor accompanied by royal gifts, saying: "This region can be captured." When their clandestine operatives arrive at the fort, moreover, they should welcome them with money and honors and show them the vulnerable points in the constituent elements and attack those points along with those men. [12.4.1–3]
>
> Alternatively, having gained entry into the [enemy] king's quarters, they should kill the king during the commotion. Or, as he is fleeing, leaders of barbarian or tribal troops from all sides, taking cover in places of ambush or a fence of tree trunks, should kill him. Or, agents operating undercover as hunters should slay him during commotions created by a surprise attack with the means used in a fight by clandestine operatives.[64]
>
> Or, they should slay him either on a path that permits travel only single file or on a mountain, behind a fence of tree trunks, in a marshy land, or in water, using troops for whom that terrain is suitable. Or, they should engulf him with the strong current created by breaking dams in rivers, lakes, and reservoirs. If he is staying within a desert fort, forest fort, or

64. These forms of covert operations are described in *Arthaśāstra* 10.3.1–25.

water fort, they should destroy him with occult fire or smoke.[65] Assassins should dispose of him with fire if he is in tight quarters, with smoke if he is in a desert fort, with poison if he is in his residence, with ferocious crocodiles or people moving in water if he has plunged into water; or when he comes out of his residence that has been set on fire. [12.4.22–28]

65. Recipes for producing lethal kinds of fire and smoke are given in the *Arthaśāstra* 13.4 and 14.1.

Chapter Seven

War

Peace, argues Kauṭilya, is preferable to war. For, he explains, in war there are destruction, expense, travel far from home, and setbacks. All things being equal, the king is advised to pursue a pact when it accomplishes the same things as initiating hostilities. We should not, however, take from this that war was anathema to kings of the time. Quite the contrary. If, in war, there are destruction, expense, travel, and setbacks, then there are also glory, wealth, honor, and, most importantly, meaning. Kings were, first of all, warriors, and the military expedition was a tangible expression of kingship.

In classical South Asia, military expeditions and war were a regular part of the life of the kingdom. The king and his family usually came from warrior castes and were honor-bound to traditions and customs that governed when and how war was undertaken. For the nobles of the realm, then, war and the defense of their region provided the very reason for their existence. They lived by the profession of arms and hoped to accrue the honor that was provided by victory and noble engagement in armed conflict. War was the backdrop of some of the most beloved tales of the people, and great warriors gained a kind of immortality in the culture.

War, and the threat thereof, was not only an important political activity, forcing resolutions within a contested political order, but was also an important economic activity. Kings marched their armies on expeditions to gain prestige, wealth, and dominance: adversaries had to choose between buying them off with wealth or fighting them off through arms. Defeat meant not only the deposing of the current regime and their most powerful backers, but also the long-term material subordination of the conquered state, which would be required to surrender much of their wealth at the time of conquest and to continue to send regular tribute to the victor. Weaker states often depended on alliances with more powerful states for survival, alliances that inevitably required them to provide material and martial resources at the behest of their dominant allies.

The *Arthaśāstra* does not give instructions to the king on how to absorb conquered kingdoms into an ever-widening imperial structure. The king is not advised, for example, to develop an imperial bureaucracy to replace that of conquered states, nor is he advised to develop imperial infrastructure throughout conquered realms or impose a uniform code of laws. Kauṭilya intends that the conquering king install his own men or those disloyal to his vanquished enemy to govern the newly conquered territory. Various enticements, symbolic gestures, demands of tribute, and threats of further invasion may have been sufficient to keep such subordinated kingdoms in thrall. Moreover, treaties after conquest might require such concessions as to effectively grant hegemony over the conquered state to the conquering kingdom. Conversely, the administrative system of the kingdom, described in Chapter 3, is theoretically flexible enough to be extended into other regions. It is possible that the ambiguity in the text is not an oversight, but is either intentional or informed by a commonsense understanding to which we as modern readers do not have access.

Proceeding in this fashion, from pitched battle to fortress siege to political domination, the king is advised to spread his dominion across the land until he becomes sovereign to the "four corners of the earth" (6.1.17).

7.1 The Structure of the Army

The classical South Asian army, as described in the *Arthaśāstra* and other texts, is composed of four "limbs" or branches: elephant corps, cavalry, chariot corps, and infantry. Each of these branches of the military was overseen, it appears, by a superintendent. These superintendents seem to have reported to the army commander (*senāpati*), who was ultimately responsible for all dimensions of military activity in the kingdom from ensuring the readiness of the troops to guiding battle arrays in combat.

The *Arthaśāstra* does not tell us much about the king's standing army, but various cities and forts of the kingdom are constantly kept under the protection of soldiers. Presumably these are the "hereditary" troops mentioned in the following passage, individuals born to the king's own caste or to martial castes that have traditionally served the king. The king would have paid and garrisoned these soldiers on a permanent basis. The *Arthaśāstra* tells us that they are the best kinds of troops, because, in military matters, they "have the same sentiment as [the king] and always enjoy his respect."

Aside from permanent garrisons of infantry troops, we also know that the king maintained a standing cavalry, chariot corps, and elephant corps (§2.2). Such was the importance of these types of military units that the king could not hope to martial them on an as-needed basis, but would have had to keep himself well equipped at all times.

While such a standing army was sufficient for most needs, large-scale military campaigns and defensive undertakings required that the king augment his forces with other kinds of troops.

> These are the proper times for deploying hereditary troops, hired troops, corporate troops, troops supplied by the ally, troops supplied by the enemy, and tribal troops. [9.2.1]
>
> Further, it is better to equip for war each previous one among these. Hereditary troops, because they have the same sentiment as he and always enjoy his respect, are better than hired troops. Hired troops, being always nearby, quickly mobilized, and submissive, are better than corporate troops. Corporate troops, coming from the countryside, coalescing for the common goal, and having the same rivalries, animosities, successes, and gains, are better than troops supplied by an ally. Troops supplied by an ally, having no limitations as to place and time and because they coalesce for a common goal, are better than troops supplied by an enemy. Troops supplied by an enemy, commanded by Āryas, are better than tribal troops. Both the

> latter two have plunder as their aim, and in the absence of plunder, as also during a calamity, they pose the same danger as a snake. [9.2.13–20]

The army commander was one of the highest-ranking officers in the kingdom, and his was a position not infrequently held by a member of the king's family, such as a king's brother or son. Because the army was fundamental to the king's ability to project power and, thereby, to rule, the army needed to be in the hands of a trusted compatriot. A treasonous army commander could prove the king's fatal foe.

The duties and responsibilities of the army commander are vast. He was himself to be a master soldier with the charisma, intelligence, and authority to command all aspects of the military. His attention is turned constantly to keeping the armed forces in a state of readiness, to strategic assessments of time and place, and to the study of battlefield strategy.

> The Army Commander—trained in the science of every kind of warfare and weaponry and a renowned expert in riding elephants, horses, and chariots—should have a thorough knowledge of the very same things, as well as of the management of the activities carried out by the four divisions of the army. He should keep an eye out for the terrain suitable for his side, the proper time for war, configuring the right counterarray, breaking through unbroken ranks, closing up broken ranks, breaking through compact ranks, destroying broken ranks, destroying a fort, and the proper time to start a military expedition. [2.33.9–10]

Each branch of the army was overseen by a superintendent—of horses, elephants, chariots, or infantry. They were responsible for equipping and training their respective branches. The *Arthaśāstra* highlights the expertise required by the superintendents of horses and elephants in cultivating and maintaining a supply of beasts for the military and other endeavors (see §3.2), but it is not clear whether they were military or civilian officials.

Modeled after the superintendent of horses are the superintendents of chariots and infantry. In keeping with the nature of their constituencies, the duties of these superintendents are more explicitly militaristic.

The superintendent of chariots (*rathādhyakṣa*) was responsible for the manufacture and outfitting of various kinds of war chariots, the tanks of the ancient battlefield. The greatest warriors of South Asian history fought with a bow from the back of a chariot, which was guided by their trusted charioteer. Like elephants, chariots could shatter the enemy's lines of infantry. But, unlike elephants, chariots could be nimble and responsive, moving around the battlefield at great speed and applying tremendous firepower quickly as needed. The superintendent of chariots had to coordinate the activity of craftsmen, attendants, horses, charioteers, and warriors.

> The discussion of the Superintendent of Horses explains also what pertains to the Superintendent of Chariots. He should have factories for chariots constructed.
>
> Ten-man high with a twelve-man interior is a standard chariot. When the interior is reduced successively by one-man up to a six-man interior, we obtain seven kinds of chariot.[66] [2.33.1–4]
>
> He should have a thorough knowledge of the arrangements of bows, javelins, armor, and equipment, and the assignment of charioteers, chariot attendants, and chariot horses to various activities, as well as giving rations and wages to both servants and nonservants[67] until the completion of the tasks, providing exercise and protection to them, and regaling them with gifts and honor. [2.33.6]

The superintendent of infantry (*pattyadhyakṣa*) was a master of men, thoroughly versed in the strengths and weaknesses of the units he commanded. He also needed to be an expert in military

66. A chariot "ten-man high" would be approximately 2.3 meters, and "twelve-man" would be 2.8 meters, if "man" is taken to be about 23 centimeters. The term "interior" probably refers to the length of the chariot.

67. The technical term *bhṛtaka* (or *bhṛtya*) appears to indicate a long-term relationship between the servant and the master. Thus, an *abhṛtaka* (nonservant) may indicate a hired laborer who does not have such a lasting relationship.

operations of all kinds, from pitched battles to secret military operations that only human troops could undertake.

> The above explains also what pertains to the Superintendent of the Infantry. He should have a thorough knowledge of the following: the strengths and weaknesses of hereditary, hired, corporate, ally's, enemy's, and tribal troops; military operations carried out in water and on land, openly and in secret, in trenches and in the open, and during day and night; and the deployment and nondeployment in various tasks. [2.33.7–8]

As is to be expected, each of these four branches of the military had different roles on and off of the battlefield. A successful commander would use them in concert to greatest effect (§7.3). The following passage gives us a good sense of the capacities of each of the branches and the breadth of activities required for a successful military campaign. Skillful use of these resources meant using the right tool for the right job, and lists such as these were meant to indicate the kinds of familiarity with their units required of effective army officers.

We find mention at the end of this passage of the labor corps, a vital component of the military expedition tasked with supporting the massive undertaking. Their brief mention belies the critical importance of their efforts to the campaign.

> These are the tasks of the cavalry: scouting the terrain, places for camping, and forests; securing a route with unrugged land, water, fords, favorable winds, and sunshine; destroying or guarding supplies and reinforcements; clearing and stabilizing the army; undertaking expansive foraging raids; repelling attacks; undertaking first strikes; penetrating; piercing through; reassuring; gathering; dispatching; altering the course of a pursuit; carrying away the treasury and the Crown Prince; charging the hind and the tips; pursuing the weak; escorting; and rounding up.

> These are the tasks of the elephant corps: marching at the vanguard; making new roads, camping places, and fords; repelling attacks; crossing and descending into water; holding the ground, marching forward, and descending; entering rugged and crowded places; setting and putting out fires; scoring a victory with a single army unit; reuniting a broken formation;

> breaking an unbroken formation; providing protection in a calamity; charging forward; causing fear; terrorizing; demonstrating grandeur; gathering; dispatching; shattering parapets, doors, and turrets; and taking the treasury safely in and out.
>
> These are the tasks of the chariot corps: guarding one's own army; obstructing the army of four divisions during battle; gathering; dispatching; reuniting a broken formation; breaking an unbroken formation; terrorizing; demonstrating grandeur; and making terrifying noises.
>
> These are the tasks of the infantry: carrying weapons in all places and times, and engaging in military exercises.
>
> These are the tasks of the labor corps: activities relating to clearing military camps, roads, reservoirs, wells, and fords; transporting mechanical devices, weapons, armor, equipment and food; and carrying away from the battlefield weapons, armor, and the wounded. [10.4.13–17]

7.2 Military Expedition

Military expeditions, even if they did not lead to pitched battles, were an important means of negotiating relationships between states. An army on the march is an intimidating thing, and a military expedition might be organized simply to project the king's power and encourage foreign kingdoms to capitulate to the king's demands. This is true only, of course, because military expeditions meant that the king was threatening war, and this was precisely the outcome in many cases. We note, in this regard, that "marching into battle" is part of the sixfold strategy of foreign policy discussed before (§6.2).

A military expedition was a massive undertaking that required detailed planning and provisioning. The route would be laid by the king and his advisers with an eye to their ultimate goals, and encampments, either in existing villages or in the wilderness, would be planned based on the strategic advantages and resources they provided. Fortified encampments were not made at every stop, but only at planned intervals, to serve to resupply and refresh the army and as forward bases of operation.

While the prototypical combat scenario was a pitched battle waged from an encampment serving as a forward operating base, the army would not infrequently have to engage in battles while on the march, typically because of an attack by the enemy. Kauṭilya keeps these many requirements in mind in his advice for marching and for the construction of the military encampment.

Marching

A great deal of planning preceded the king's military expeditions. Kauṭilya's general advice for such marches emphasizes overpreparation and constant wariness. Ideally, the king could use the location of villages to his advantage while transporting food and fuel for the troops. In some cases, however, provisions might need to be sent out ahead of the troops. In the worst cases, soldiers would be required to glean their sustenance from the land.

The march itself was undertaken in an orderly fashion with the army typically moving in one of several defensive formations depending on where an attack was anticipated. The structure of some of these formations, such as the "wheel" and the "needle," are self-evident. Others, however, such as the "lightning bolt" and "propitious-on-all-sides," are rather more obscure.

The speed of the march was set by conditions. The next passage indicates when it was advantageous for the king to proceed slowly. The lowest speed for the army was one *yojana* per day, the standard distance traveled by draft animals between "yokings," something just over nine miles according to the *Arthaśāstra*. The fastest was twice this. Under normal circumstances, however, the army should move at one and half *yojanas* per day.

> He should undertake a military expedition after estimating the encampments in villages and wild tracts along the way contingent on the supply of green fodder, firewood, and water, as well as the time for sojourns, stopovers, and travel. He should arrange for the transport of double the quantity of rations and equipment needed to take care of those eventualities. Alternatively, if he is unable to do so, he should

either delegate it to the soldiers or stockpile them at intervals along the way.

The Commander in the front, the king and his family in the center, horses on the flanks to repel attacks, elephants or expansive foraging raids at the borders of the wheel formation, and the Army Commander in the rear—so should they march and encamp.

Obtaining subsistence from forests on all sides constitutes a foraging raid. Influx from one's own country constitutes supplies. Troops supplied by an ally constitute reinforcements. The location of the family is the hideaway.

If an attack is expected from the front, he should march in the crocodile formation; if from the rear, in the cart formation; if from the two flanks, in the harpoon formation; if from all sides, in the "propitious-on-all-sides" formation; and in a terrain where only marching single file is possible, in the needle formation.

When there are two alternate routes, he should march on terrain best suited for him; for in a battle those who operate on terrain best suited for them get the better of those operating in terrain least suitable for them.

Traveling one Yojana [1 Yojana = 14.5 km] is the lowest speed; one and a half Yojanas, the middle speed; and two Yojanas, the highest speed; or else the speed should be determined according to what is achievable.

When he has to take countermeasures against a rear enemy, his backer, the intermediate king, or the neutral king who is providing shelter or destroying quality land; when he has to clear a dangerous route; when he has to wait for the treasury, the army, the troops supplied by an ally or an enemy, tribal troops, laborers, or the proper season; or when he thinks: "A degradation of the fortification, stockpiles, and defensive measures undertaken by him, despondency on the part of the troops he has purchased, and despondency on the part of troops supplied by his ally will come about"; or, "Those who have been dispatched to instigate sedition are not acting very swiftly"; or, "My foe will accede to my demands";—under these conditions he should march slowly, and under opposite conditions, quickly.

> He should arrange the crossing of bodies of water using elephants, bridges of tree trunks, dikes, boats, and pontoons of wood and bamboo, as well as gourds, leather baskets, skin bags, rafts, tree trunks, and ropes. If the ford is in enemy hands, he should cross at another point during the night with the help of elephants and horses and get to a secure location.
>
> In a waterless region, he should have wagons and draft animals transport according to their capacity the amount of water needed for the journey. [10.2.1–16]

Military Camp

At certain points on the march, the army would stop and build a more permanent and robust encampment. These camps were really more on the order of temporary cities, furnished with moats, earthen ramparts topped by walls, turrets, gates, and settlement zoning. Like in the capital, the king's quarters lay just north of center (§2.2). It was protected by successive, concentric, fortified enclosures that housed his soldiers and culminated in the camp's main ramparts and defenses. The king was surrounded immediately by many of the same individuals and institutions as in his capital: his counselor-chaplain, members of his court, his assembly hall, his treasury, and his stables. While a regent oversaw affairs back in the capital, the military encampment became the center of government, with the king issuing orders and overseeing his business from its precincts. The directive to "keep the seal guarded" at the end of the passage refers to the king's signet ring, with the impression of which he sealed all of his official decrees.

The construction of the military camp was a vast undertaking. Everything needed to support an army of thousands of men and animals as well as the functions of the government was required. In addition to the governmental institutions already mentioned, the encampment was furnished with accommodation for thousands of soldiers as well as storehouses, armories, and facilities for repairing and manufacturing military equipment. An army of laborers was needed to clear the terrain and construct the camp itself. Like a city, the encampment had a main highway running in front of it on which merchants and prostitutes plied their wares and saw to the needs and appetites of the multitude of troops. A camp administrator, much like the city manager, was responsible for managing the encampment, in which activities that might adversely affect the troops, such as drinking and gambling, were strictly prohibited.

> On a site recommended as a building site, the Commander, carpenters, and astrologers should have a military camp constructed during a time of danger and when it is time to halt, a military camp that is circular, rectangular, or square, or in accordance with the terrain, that has four gates, six paths, and nine zones, and is outfitted with a moat, a rampart, a parapet, gates, and turrets.
>
> The royal compound should be located in the one-ninth sector to the north of the middlemost. It should be one hundred Dhanuṣes [1 Dhanuṣ = 1.82 m] long and half as much wide. The royal residence should be located in its western half. At its perimeter, moreover, he should station the palace guard. At the front he should set up the assembly hall; to the right, the treasury and the offices for issuing royal commands and for assigning tasks; to the left, the yard for elephants, horses, and carriages for the use of the king.
>
> Beyond that are to be located four enclosures, each separated from the next by one hundred Dhanuṣes, constructed with posts in a cart formation, columns in a creeper formation, or a parapet.[68]
>
> Within the first, the Counselor and Chaplain are housed in the front; the storehouse and kitchen on the right; the depot for forest produce and the armory on the left. Within the second are the quarters for hereditary and hired troops, for horses and chariots, and for the Army Commander. Within the third are housed the elephants, corporate troops, and the camp administrator. Within the fourth are housed the laborers and the Commander, as well as troops supplied by the ally and the enemy and tribal troops, all under the command of his own officers.

68. This statement must refer to defensive fortifications around the royal compound. We take cart and creeper to be particular arrangements of the fortifications. The term "cart," for example, is used for a particular battle formation.

> Traders and prostitutes should be located along the main highway. Fowlers and those who hunt with dogs should be located outside the camp carrying drums and fire, as also undercover sentries. Along the path through which an enemy may attack he should have pits, hidden traps, and barbed strips positioned. He should have the guards of the eighteen groups[69] rotated, and daytime watches also maintained in order to spot spies.
>
> He should stamp out disputes, drinking, fairs, and gambling, and keep the seal guarded.
>
> The Regent should arrest any soldier who returns from the army without a written permit. [10.1.1–16]

7.3 Battle Tactics

As mentioned, the prototypical combat scenario in the *Arthaśāstra* is the pitched battle. Planning for these battles began by scouting the terrain and assessing its suitability to one's different military units. Not only would a king and his commanders try to find the terrain upon which their troops would be maximally effective, but they would also try to determine how to make best use of their units based on the terrain with which they might be faced.

Once the site of the battle had been determined and its strategic dimensions assessed, it was time to rouse the troops to heroic action. To this end the king and his high officials used a variety of tactics from encouragement to cash incentives. Troops were then arrayed in one of a number of different battle arrays, depending on the terrain and the battle array of the enemy. The selection of these arrays and the distribution of troops within them was of critical importance, and Kauṭilya spends a great deal

69. The reference is unclear but it is probably to the groups mentioned in sentences 6–9, taking horses and chariots as a single group: counselor, chaplain, storehouse, kitchen, depot, armory, hereditary troops, hired troops, horses and chariots, chief of armed forces, elephants, corporate troops, camp administrator, laborers, commander, ally's troops, enemy's troops, and tribal troops.

of time discussing the merits and demerits of different arrangements. Often, accounting for terrain and adapting to the enemy's battle formations were the decisive factors in determining the outcome of a battle.

Accounting for Terrain

The *Arthaśāstra* distinguishes between "suitable" and "most excellent" terrain. The former outlines the conditions sufficient to allow military units to operate effectively, while the latter indicates terrain that grants given units the greatest advantages. Surveying the land around them, the king and his commanders could decide where to deploy their units, how they could maneuver, what pieces of land they wanted to control, and where they wanted to force their enemies.

What was true of the battlefield terrain was also true of the encampment terrain. The same elements that presented obstacles on the battlefield could also make an encampment uncomfortable, inconvenient, or hazardous.

> For both fighting and setting up camp in the case of infantry, horses, chariots, and elephants, it is advantageous to find a terrain suitable for each. For men fighting in deserts and forests and on water and dry land; for men fighting in trenches and open spaces and during day and night; and for elephants operating in rivers, mountains, marsh land, and lakes; as well as for horses—the desirable terrains and times for fighting are to be determined according to the needs of each.
>
> A terrain suitable for the chariots is one that is flat, hard, clear, and without holes; in which wheels, hooves, or axles will not get stuck; that does not contain hazards caused by trees, shrubs, creepers, tree trunks, swampland, craters, anthills, sand, or mud; and that is free of clefts. Such a terrain is also suitable for elephants and horses, as well as for men, in fighting and in setting up camp, in both an even and an uneven battle formation.[70]

70. The two terms refer to the two basic kinds of battle formations recorded in 10.5.14–17 (see "Battle Arrays and Combat").

> A terrain suitable for horses is one in which there are small stones and trees, shallow and traversable craters, and whose only drawback is minor clefts. A terrain suitable for infantry is one that has large tree trunks, rocks, trees, creepers, anthills, and shrubs. A terrain suitable for elephants is one that contains traversable hills, water, or rugged land, trees that can be ripped up, creepers that can be lopped off, and mud hazards, and that is free of clefts.
>
> The most excellent for foot soldiers is a terrain that is without thorns and not overly rugged, and provides room for retreat. The most excellent for horses is a terrain that provides double the room for retreat, is free of mud, water, and marshes, and contains no gravel. The most excellent for elephants is a terrain that has places containing dust, mud, water, reeds, and rushes, is devoid of "dog's teeth,"[71] and free of obstructions created by large tree branches. The most excellent for chariots is a terrain that contains water reservoirs and havens, has no holes, is devoid of swampland, and permits turning around.
>
> For all, the suitable terrain has been described. Through that explanations have been given regarding encampment and fighting by all elements of the military. [10.4.1–12]

Much of the strategy of combat involved controlling the best terrain and forcing the enemy to use the worst. In the end, however, the army had to adapt its formations to whatever terrain it was faced with, although certain types were considered fatal to any army.

> He should organize his battle formations in a terrain best suited for him and in such a way that they do not face the south, and do have the sun at the back and the wind blowing from a favorable direction.[72] And in the event that his battle formations are in a terrain more suitable for his enemy, he should make his horses move about there.

71. At *Arthaśāstra* 2.3.15 there is a long list of defensive obstacles placed in the path of advancing soldiers. The exact meaning of these devices is unclear.

72. The meaning is that they should not face the sun, so that the blinding glare would affect the enemy soldiers. Likewise, the wind should be at their back, so that it would blow at the faces of the enemy and make their arrows and missiles less effective (10.3.23). South is an inauspicious direction.

> Where the terrain is unsuitable both for standing firm and for swift movement of a battle formation, he will be defeated either way, whether he stands firm or moves swiftly. In the opposite case, he will win either way, whether he stands firm or moves swiftly.
>
> He should find out whether the terrain to the front, on the flanks, and in the rear is flat, rugged, or mixed. If it is flat, he should employ the staff and the circle formations; if it is rugged, the snake and the noncompact formations; and if it is mixed, the uneven formations.[73] [10.3.48–53]

Encouraging the Troops

For a variety of reasons, kings preferred to fight pitched battles rather than impromptu engagements. Fixed battles were felt to represent the most honorable form of conflict. Moreover, they were potentially decisive events that allowed the king to put the strategic talents of his commanders to best use. They also provided him with the opportunity to rouse his troops.

Immediately before the battle was to be joined, the king personally addressed his troops. He tried to motivate them by invoking their commonalities and delivering a formal request that they attack the enemy. While the language might seem dry in textual form, powerful kings were certainly adept at inspiring their troops by invoking their sense of honor, tradition, and history. Also before the battle, the army commander addressed the troops and outlined the bounty that would be paid for the killing of officers in the enemy's army.

Various agents of the king carried out a diffuse campaign to encourage the troops. They were to circulate among the troops telling convincing stories of past successes, using astrology to predict victory, talking about the use of magic and spells, and praising the might of the troops themselves. Medical officers and suppliers of food and drink were stationed to the rear of the battle array, to provide support and encouragement to the men in combat.

73. These formations are described in *Arthaśāstra* 10.6.

War at a preannounced time and place, however, is the most righteous.

Having gathered the army together, he should proclaim: "I receive the same remuneration as you. It is imperative that I enjoy this kingdom along with you. It is my request to you that you should attack the enemy." [10.3.26–27]

He should get the Counselor and the Chaplain to rouse the soldiers, pointing out the eminence of their military formations. His astrologers and similar groups, moreover, should embolden his own faction and terrify his enemy's faction by proclaiming his omniscience and his intimacy with gods. [10.3.32–33]

Bards and panegyrists should proclaim heaven for the brave and exclusion from heaven for the timid, and extol the castes, associations, families, deeds, and conduct of the soldiers. Assistants of the Chaplain should speak about the employment of black magic and sorcery, and mechanics, carpenters, and astrologers about the success of their own activities and the failure of those of the enemies.

The Army Commander should address the army in battle array after it has been gratified with money and honors: "100,000 Paṇas for killing the king; 50,000 Paṇas for killing the chief of armed forces or the Crown Prince; 10,000 Paṇas for killing a leader of eminent warriors; 5,000 Paṇas for killing an elephant- or chariot-fighter; 1,000 Paṇas for killing a cavalryman; 100 Paṇas for killing a leader of infantry; and 20 per head; and, in addition, double the pay and individual plunder." The leaders of groups of ten should determine that with regard to them.

Physicians carrying surgical instruments, medical devices, medicines, oils, and bandages, and women in charge of food and drink with the duty of emboldening the men should be stationed at the rear. [10.3.43–47]

Battle Arrays and Combat

A little over half a mile in front of the king's fortified encampment, the battle would be joined. The army was first collected outside the camp and officers were assigned their units. They formed ranks in such a way as to give each room to fight. Units of the same type were set together closely, while more space was required between different kinds of units. Finally, each formation within a battle array was spaced from the others a slightly greater distance. When fully arrayed, they would march out to meet the enemy.

Kauṭilya describes troop formations in increasing levels of complexity. He begins by describing the smallest unit. Each of these elementary units is comprised of a horse, chariot, or elephant, and accompanying troops. The prototypical unit is the chariot unit, which contains a chariot, fifteen infantry and five horses in front, and fifteen ground troops guarding the chariot on foot. Three rows of three chariot units make a chariot formation. These formations can be enlarged by adding two rows of three chariot units at a time, up to twenty-one rows of three chariots. Each is under the command of a chief.

Each of these formations constitutes one of the five sections of a battle array: center, two wings, and two flanks. Any enlargement of one of the sections of the battle array required an equal enlargement of the other sections. For some reason, Kauṭilya prefers odd numbers of rows in each section, possibly because that provides each formation with a discrete center and flanks. The battle arrays are themselves under the command of the army commander and the commander.

The cavalry battle array and the elephant corps battle array are built in a similar manner, differing only in the number of foot soldiers that accompany each horse or elephant.

Once the battle arrays are drawn, the remaining troops are apportioned into "insertion units" and added to the arrays. The manner in which this is done bolsters the strength of the center section of the array more than the wings and flanks.

> He should initiate a battle after setting up a fortified stronghold at a distance of five hundred Dhanuṣes [1 Dhanuṣ = 1.82 m], or as dictated by the terrain.
>
> Having dispatched the army out of sight with its various units apportioned to chief officers, the Army Commander and the Commander should organize the battle formations.

He should space foot soldiers one Śama [1 Śama = 28 cm] apart, horses three Śamas apart, and chariots or elephants five Śamas apart. He should position the battle formations separated by two or three times those distances. In this way one can fight comfortably without being crammed.

A Dhanuṣ is five Aratnis [1 Aratni = 48 cm] long. He should place an archer at that distance, a horse at a distance of three Dhanuṣes, and a chariot or an elephant at a distance of five Dhanuṣes.

At five Dhanuṣes is the link point of wings, flanks, and breast of a battle formation.

There should be three men fighting in front of a horse; fifteen in front of a chariot or an elephant, as also five horses. The same number of foot guards should be employed for a horse, a chariot, and an elephant.

He should deploy a chariot formation consisting of three rows of three chariots each at the breast, and the same on the flank and wing on both sides. Thus, in a chariot formation there are 45 chariots, 225 horses, 675 men fighting in the front, and an equal number of foot guards.

This is the even formation. It may be increased beginning with two chariot rows up to twenty-one rows. In this way, odd numbers become the ten basic constituents of an even formation.

When there is an uneven number in the wings, flanks, and breast with respect to each other, it is an uneven formation. It also may be increased beginning with two chariot rows up to twenty-one rows. In this way, odd numbers become the ten basic constituents of an uneven formation.

Then, he should create an insertion unit with the troops left over after constituting the military formations. He should insert two-thirds of the chariots in the limbs and keep the rest at the breast. In this manner, one should make an insertion unit of chariots consisting of one-third less.

This also explains the insertion units of elephants and horses. He should make an insertion in such a manner that it will not cramp the fighting of horses, chariots, and elephants.

> A surplus of troops constitutes an insertion unit. A surplus of infantry constitutes a counterinsertion unit. A surplus of one outer section is a side-insertion unit. A surplus of traitorous troops is an overinsertion unit.
>
> Insertions should be made, according to his troop strength, up to four or eight times the insertion and the counterinsertion made by the enemy.
>
> The chariot formation also explains the elephant formation. [10.5.1–30]

Kauṭilya has, probably for ease of explanation, begun his discussion with battle arrays built around one type of unit formation: chariots, horses, or elephants. He continues, however, by giving instructions on mixed battle arrays. The terrain and the enemy's forces would dictate which battle arrays the king and his commanders chose, but it is likely that mixed arrays like those described next were the norm.

In mixed arrays the various types of units and formations can be deployed in a number of different configurations. The standard mixed array put the chariots at the center and the cavalry on the flanks, with the elephant corps arrayed around them. When the commanders wanted to break through the enemy lines, however, they would concentrate the elephants at the center or sides, depending on which part of the enemy formation they were targeting.

> Alternatively, a mixed formation consists of elephants, chariots, and horses—elephants at the borders of the army, horses in the two flanks, and chariots in the breast. When elephants are in the breast, chariots in the two flanks, and horses in the two wings, it is a formation where the breakthrough is done with the center. When the formation is reverse of this, the breakthrough is done with the edges. [10.5.31–32]

Another variation available to the commanders of the army were what Kauṭilya calls the "pure" formations—specialized formations containing only specific kinds of troops rather than the units previously described that mixed foot soldiers with different kinds of mounted troops. These formations called for restructuring of the battle arrays. Note that the pure elephant formations feature a "breast," "hind," and "tips," and use the trained war elephants as the heart of the formation, followed by riding elephants and ringed by the most savage and difficult elephants, the "vicious."

> A pure formation, however, consists only of elephants—with war elephants forming the breast, riding elephants the hind, and vicious elephants the two tips; a horse formation—with armored horses forming the breast and unarmored horses, the flanks and the wings; an infantry formation—with men in protective armor at the front and archers in the rear. These are the pure formation. [10.5.34–37]

Mixed arrays could be also be constituted out of these "pure" formations.

> Infantrymen in the two wings, horses in the two flanks, elephants in the back, and chariots in the front—or the reverse depending on the formations employed by the enemy—that is the troop arrangement containing two limbs. This also explains the troop arrangement with three limbs. [10.5.38–40]

Finally, Kauṭilya advises the king to make wise use of his troops based on their individual skill. Having assessed and ranked his troops into four groups from best to worst, the king is to place a higher proportion of his best troops in the central formation of the battle array: he assigns a third of his best men to only one-fifth of his array. Interestingly, Kauṭilya favors leading with the weakest troops: best to let them absorb the crushing initial blows of the enemy's advance and allow the superior troops to engage after the first onslaught. Alternately, when desiring to resist an enemy's advance, he might choose to put his best troops up front and his weakest in the middle.

> With respect to men, the best troops are endowed with the exemplary qualities of the army. With respect to elephants and horses, the special distinction comes from pedigree, breed, spirit, youth, stamina, height, speed, vigor, skill, steadfastness, stateliness, obedience, auspicious marks, and good conduct.

> He should position one-third of the best infantrymen, horses, chariots, and elephants as the breast; two-thirds as the flank and wing on either side; the next best directly behind; the third best directly in front; and the weakest directly in front. In this way he would put everyone to good use.
>
> By deploying the weakest troops at the edges he will be able to resist an onslaught.
>
> Having deployed the best troops at the front, he should deploy the next best at the tips, the third best in the hind, and the weakest in the middle. In this way it will become capable of resistance. [10.5.41–48]

The king had a special formation of troops assigned to defend him during combat and tried to hide his identity during combat. With a faux-king acting in his stead at the front of the formation, it is unclear how much combat he was actually expected to engage in. Severe injury or death would have grave implications for the stability of the kingdom.

> He should make the central core of his military formation consist of soldiers who are brave, skilled, of high birth, and loyal, and who have not been slighted with respect to money and honors. A plain formation without flags and consisting of soldiers related to each other as fathers, sons, and brothers is the location for the king. The conveyance for the king is either an elephant or chariot with a cavalry escort. He should mount the one most used by the troops or on which he was trained. A man disguised as the king should be placed at the front of the military formation. [10.3.38–42]

Battle was not, however, exclusively a question of offense. Commanders needed to deploy defensive arrays periodically as well. When faced with the oncoming charge of elephants or chariots, the soldiers of the army needed to be well trained enough to reconfigure themselves in specific defensive patterns. Those listed below are standard responses to an enemy's attack. Note how each defensive array is equipped with specific troops to absorb the attack as well as specific devices, such as "hair-grabbers"—long hooked instruments—for counterattack.

> A force with elephants, mechanical devices, and carts at its center, and equipped with lances, javelins, spears, bamboos, and darts, is the counterforce for an elephant force. The same, but with a large quantity of stones, clubs, armor, hooks, and "hair-grabbers," is the counterforce for a chariot force. The counterforce for a cavalry force is the very same, or else elephants with armor or horses with armor. Chariots with defensive coverings and infantrymen with protective armor are the counterforce for an army with the four divisions. [9.2.26–29]

7.4 Taking a Fort

A military expedition might achieve its task if the enemy were to surrender on the battlefield. More likely, however, a king facing defeat in battle would retreat to one of his fortified cities or defensive fortifications. The task of the expedition then turned from engaging in pitched battles to the besieging of the fortress.

As the endgame of violent conflict between two states and a course of action with potential for a tremendously destructive outcome, besieging a fort was an exercise in military skill, covert operations, and public relations. Thus, the king and his commanders ordinarily sought to find a strategy that would leave their prize as intact as possible.

The first order of business, therefore, was to attempt to prevent the populous around the fortress from fleeing. In classical South Asia land was always more plentiful than the people to work it, so a king needed to do his best to preserve this valuable resource in his targeted kingdom. Moreover, these subjects might eventually owe him allegiance, and it was best to restrict one's fury to the current regime. To this end, the besieging army was supposed to provide safety for the inhabitants around the fortress. This is a far cry from the pillaging and marauding typical of invading armies, and one wonders how well it translated into actual practice. Only when he is unable to gain access to the fortress itself is the king advised to pursue a scorched-earth policy.

The work of taking a fortress begins with the use of secret agents. They attempt to dispirit the enemy's people and lure them into sedition. Alternatively, the king might take a more direct approach and use his agents to attempt an assassination of the enemy. Once the king and his advisors determine that conditions are favorable, meaning that his own army is fully supplied and established in a secure military encampment and the enemy has begun to suffer from a shortage of supplies, disease, or failing morale, the siege proper begins. Preliminary work begins with the encircling of the fortress and steps to poison its water supply and surmount its defenses.

When the time has come for the actual assault, the king resorts to the tools of his engineers and the strength of his elephants. Collectively, they attempt to undermine and sunder the walls of the fortress. If these assaults are ineffective, the king will seek to use fire to force his enemy out. Birds and animals are smeared with flammable mixtures and released into the besieged fortress. More effectively, a variety of incendiary weapons are lobbed over the city walls in hopes of starting a conflagration. Kauṭilya cautions against this route, however, owing to its indiscriminate destructiveness.

> The work of laying siege is preceded by weakening.
>
> He should keep the countryside, to the extent that it is settled, out of danger. He should get anyone who is setting out to remain by providing favors and exemptions. He should settle those fleeing elsewhere on land away from the fighting or make them live in one location. "For, there is no countryside without people and no kingdom without a countryside," says Kauṭilya.
>
> He should destroy the sowings or crops of someone ensconced in an inaccessible place, as also his supplies and foraging raids.
>
> By demolishing foraging raids and supplies, by also destroying sowings and crops, by depopulating, and by secret killings one brings about the weakening of the constituents.
>
> He should lay siege when he thinks: "My army is fully supplied with grain, forest produce, mechanical devices, weapons, armor, laborers, and ropes in large quantities and of the finest

quality. A good season is ahead, but it is a bad season for my enemy. His stores and defenses are weakening because of disease and famine. The troops he has bought, as well as the troops supplied by his ally, are despondent."

He should first make arrangements for the protection of the military camp, supplies, foraging raids, and the road; encircle the fort around the moat and ramparts; poison the water; and drain the moats or fill them up. Then he should have the rampart and palisade taken by means of an underground tunnel or a cave room, and the gate with an armored elephant. He should have the wetlands covered with a mantle of dirt. He should destroy a massive fortification with mechanical devices. Drawing them out from the egress door,[74] they should attack them with horses. During pauses between attacks, moreover, he should seek to achieve success by employing the strategies restrictively, optionally, or in combination.

After getting hawks, crows, nightjars, vultures, parrots, mynahs, owls, and pigeons living within the fort captured, he should attach an incendiary mixture to their tails and release them into the enemy's fort. From his military camp that has been moved back a distance or being protected by raised flags and bows, he should set fire to the enemy's fort with "human fire."[75] Clandestine operatives, moreover, working as guards within the fort should attach an incendiary mixture to the tails of mongooses, monkeys, cats, and dogs and release among reeds, stocks, defenses, and houses. They should place fire in the abdomens of dried fish or in dried meat and get birds to carry it away by offering it to crows.

Balls of Sarala-pine [*Pinus roxburghii*], Devadāru-pine [*Cedrus deodara*], stink-grass, bdellium, pine resin, Sal resin [*Shorea*

---

74. As its name suggests, it was a door through which people could exit. The purpose of the exit is unclear, whether it was to flee or to confront an enemy at the rampart. The term as used again implies a door or gate through which the attackers drag out (perhaps soldiers) and attack with horses. This door is listed in the construction of a fort (2.3.14). If this door was connected to the clandestine way, then it may have been an escape route from the fort in the case of a successful siege by an enemy.

75. This appears to be a fire produced by using human bones. Such a fire is described in *Arthaśāstra* 14.2.38.

robusta], and lac, as well as the dung of donkeys, camels, goats, and sheep—these retain fire well.

Powder of Priyāla [*Buchanania lanzan*], soot of Avalguja [*Psoralea corylifolia*], beeswax, and the dung of horses, donkeys, camels, and cattle—these form an incendiary mixture that is to be hurled. Either the powder of all metals with a fiery color or the powder of Kumbhī,[76] lead, and tin, along with the flowers of Pāribhadraka [*Erythrina indica*] and Palāśa [*Butea frondosa*], the soot of Keśa,[77] oil, beeswax, and pine resin form an incendiary mixture that is attached or is a Viśvāsaghātin, that is, an arrow coated with it and wrapped with hemp or the bark of Trapusa [*Cucumis sativus*]. Such is an incendiary mixture.

He should, however, never hurl fire when there is an opportunity for an assault; for fire is treacherous and is a divine affliction, causing the destruction of innumerable creatures, grains, farm animals, money, forest produce, and goods. Even if acquired, a kingdom with all its stocks lost leads only to further losses.

That concludes the work of laying siege. [13.4.1–24]

At certain times during the siege, action on the part of the king will become advisable, whether through the king's own strength, the enemy's weakness, or the threat of reinforcements or unfavorable alliances. At these times the king is advised to strike.

When he thinks: "I have all the equipment and laborers needed for the task. My enemy is ill, his constituents have turned against him because of secret tests, or the construction of his fort and the procurement of stocks have not been carried out. Whether he is without reinforcements or has reinforcements, he will soon conclude a peace pact with his allies"—that is the time for taking by storm.

When a fire has erupted spontaneously or has been deliberately set; during a festivity; when people are engrossed in seeing a

---

76. The meaning is unclear. A commentator takes it to be the plant *Gmelina arborea,* while some scholars take it to be a kind a metal.

77. The identity is unclear. If it is the same as *keœara*, it would be *Mimusops Elengi*, the Spanish cherry.

show or military formation; during a drunken brawl; when his troops are exhausted by constant battles; when his men have been injured and killed in numerous battles; when people have fallen asleep, being wearied by keeping watch; on a rainy day; when the river is flooded; or when there is a thick fog—on these occasions he should take by storm. [13.4.25–26]

Having launched a surprise attack against the enemy's fort or military camp, they should grant safety to those who have fallen down, turned back, surrendered, loosened their hair,[78] or put down their weapons, or are contorted through fright, as well as to noncombatants.

Having captured the enemy's fort, he should enter it after he has cleared it of people belonging to his foe's faction and taken precautions inside and out against secret punishment. [13.4.52–53]

7.5 Conduct in Victory

It was critical for a conquering king to pacify the conquered territory quickly, lest it lose its productive capacity and descend into chaos. The king began by acting in a magnanimous manner toward the citizens in an attempt to win their loyalty. These exertions were targeted at both the populous in general as well as important individuals. The king also richly rewarded those individuals who had turned on their former king and aided his conquest. Most interestingly, rather than advising the king to force his own customs and laws on the newly conquered territory, he is instead advised to adopt their dress and habits.

Once again, the king's secret agents swing into action, secretly spreading his propaganda to various chiefs and leaders in the region, whose status and privilege he also protects. In general, the king displays a very pious demeanor, patronizing festivals of the gods of the realm, hermitages, local religious figures, and eminent intellectuals. He prohibits killing on a regular basis to demonstrate his adherence to conservative religious customs.

78. This is traditionally a sign of surrender.

> After acquiring a new territory, he should eclipse the enemy's faults with his own virtues, and the enemy's virtues with twice as many virtues of his. He should, moreover, promote what is cherished by and beneficial to the subjects by carrying out his own duties and by granting favors, exemptions, gifts, and honors. And he should have favors granted to the seducible party according to agreements; more, if they have made extraordinary efforts. For a man who does not keep to an agreement is not to be trusted either by his own people or by his enemies, as also a man whose conduct is contrary to that of the subjects. Therefore, he should adopt the habits, dress, language, and conduct similar to theirs, and demonstrate his devotion to them during festivals in honor of the gods of the region, festivities, and recreational activities.
>
> Secret agents, moreover, should constantly point out to the chiefs of districts, settlements, castes, and associations the misdeeds of the enemy, as also the king's extraordinary fortune and devotion to them, and the king's palpable respect for them. And he should exploit them by preserving their customary privileges, exemptions, and protection.
>
> He should arrange for the veneration of all gods and hermitages and for the donation of land, wealth, and exemptions to men preeminent in knowledge, eloquence, and righteousness, as also for the release of all prisoners and for assistance to the wretched, the helpless, and the sick. There is to be a suspension of slaughter for a fortnight at the beginning of each forth-month season; for four nights at each full moon; and for one night at the constellations of the king and the region. He should prohibit the killing of breeding females and the young, as well as castration.
>
> Whatever custom he may consider to be detrimental to the treasury and army or to be very unrighteous, he should set it aside and establish a righteous convention. [13.5.3–14]

7.6 Conquering the Earth

The substantive discussion of statecraft in the *Arthaśāstra* concludes with the topic of the king's conquest. We are meant to understand, however, that this is only the beginning for "the seeker after conquest." Enriched, strengthened, and emboldened by the conquest of his enemy, the king turns his attention to the rest of the kings in the "circle" (see §6.1) until he has "conquered the earth." Kauṭilya envisions several paths to such ultimate victory. These depend on the political map that he faces and whether he chooses to use invasion or strategic coercion.

> In this way, after gaining the enemy's territory, the seeker after conquest should seek to seize the intermediate king, and, when he has been subdued, the neutral king. This is the first path to conquering the earth.
>
> If there is no intermediate or neutral king, he should subdue the enemy constituents through strategic preeminence, and then the constituents beyond that. This is the second path.
>
> If there is no circle, he should subdue the ally by means of the enemy, and the enemy by means of the ally, using a pincer movement from both sides. This is the third path.
>
> He should first subdue a weak or a solitary neighbor. Becoming by means of him twice as powerful, he should subdue a second; and becoming thrice as powerful, a third. This is the fourth path to conquering the earth. [13.4.54–61]

Index of Passages

Word Index